Sunflower

Helianthus strumosus

FLOWER COOKERY

The Art of Cooking with Flowers

FLOWER COOKERY

THE ART OF COOKING WITH FLOWERS

by

Mary MacNicol

New York

FLEET PRESS CORPORATION

1967

Original endleaf drawings by Roy MacNicol

TO ROY

"I wish unto you by dayly Prayer and fruition
of the Heavenly Paradise cravying of the Omnipotent
and provident God, the guider of that gorgeous
Garden that hee would vouchsafe to graunte unto
you the sweete savour of his chiefe fragrante
floures, that is his comfort to cleave fast unto
you, his mercy to keepe you and his grace to guyde
you nowe and evermore."

> (Epistle dedicatory addressed to William
> Cecil, Lord Burghley; Lord High Treasurer
> of England.—The Gardeners Labyrinth, 1577)

TO THE READER

All these things heer collected, are not mine
But diverse grapes make but one sort of wine;
So I, from many learned authors took
The various matters printed in this book—
What's not mine own by me shall not be father'd
The most part I in fifty years have gathered,
Some things are very good, pick out the best,
Good wits compiled them, and I wrote the rest.
If thou dost buy it, it will quit thy cost,
Read it, and all thy labour is not lost.

John Taylor, the Water Poet–1652

Preface

In early 1950 my husband and I moved to Mexico. We first owned a national monument built in Coyoacan by one of Cortez' captains. We later purchased D. H. Lawrence's house at Lake Chapala and were surrounded by flowers of the area.

While living there I read W. H. Prescott's CONQUEST OF MEXICO and was fascinated by the fact that when Cortez arrived in Tenochtitlan (Mexico City) he found Montezuma and his subjects using flowers extensively in their cuisine. From that moment, I was "sparked" and for the next twelve years engaged in research on the use of flowers in food and the extensive historical link of gardening and cooking. The Mexican Department of Agriculture in a pamphlet urged a return to the use of flowers in cooking as their ancestors did. I found that once my attention was focused on this subject, information began to come to me from many sources.

After returning to New York, I found much material in the New York Public Library, New York Horticultural Society Library, New York Botanical Library, New York Medical Society Library (this library has over 6,000 cookbooks), and the Morgan Library.

Flowers have been used in cookery not only for their actual substance, but also for their beauty, flavoring and aroma. It is a fact that their vital forces are of supreme energy derived straight from the source.

The study of cookery of other nations became an enchanting literary hobby for me and it had many directions: history, geology, bio-chemistry, botany, folklore, legend, philology, but most of all, the experimentation in my own kitchen.

The Chinese were too practical to live in a flower kingdom and not utilize their flowers. When they saw a new substance that was also a delight to the eye, their first thought was, "What will it taste like and has it therapeutic value?" They have a proverb, *"If you have two loaves of bread, sell one and buy a lily."* The Scriptures tell us that the leaves of the trees are for the healing of the nations.

It was in the Tertiary Age, just before the creation of man, that flowering plants appeared, providing food and medicine for man. Legend says that the lotus was the first flower to appear on earth.

The by-products of the tropical palms (coconut, sago, date) are as important as the oil from the olive tree. The banana tree produces more nourishment than wheat or potatoes. The apricot with its copper and iron is beneficial to anemics. Ginseng and rue are good for the infirmities of old age. There are restraining plants for almost every appetite, aberration or mood, including fear, eroticism, grief and terror. Orchids were considered such a powerful aphrodisiac that salop was sold in the coffee houses in England.

The bypaths of this study were endless and intriguing—its legends, use in art, customs and fashions, history, heraldry, symbolism, miracles, religion (especially associated with saints and martyrs), charms, medicine, cookery and cosmetics.

Have a curious and inquiring mind in the kitchen . . . the discoveries can be joyous. We all have a desire to experiment with unfamiliar foods. To project ourselves into the past is easier than to project ourselves into the future. We are all concerned about the food supply of future generations, and it is well to assemble what is known of neglected food sources. They may be of real economic importance. In our civilized and sophisticated communities today, we need to lift our sights beyond the conventional dishes. Experiment—you will find some surprisingly attractive foods which will enhance your experience.

M. MacN.

New York
August, 1967

Acknowledgments

My grateful thanks to the publishers, authors and others for permission to use extracts from the following works:

A Mine of Serpents by Jocelyn Brooke, A. M. Heath & Co. Ltd.; *Flowering Judas and Other Stories* by Katherine Anne Porter, Harcourt, Brace & World; *Remembrance of Things Past* by Marcel Proust, Random House; *A Bouquet From Fellowman Roseman from Five Pens in Hand* by Robert Graves, International Authors N.V.; *The Finest Indian Muslim Cooking* by S.N.M. Khan, Routledge & Kegan Paul, Ltd.; *Forest of Fear* by Ernst Lohndorff, Souvenir Press; Thomas Merton Poetry, Harcourt, Brace & World; *Mimosa* by Padraic Colum; General Dwight D. Eisenhower for his nasturtium vegetable soup recipe; *Finegans Wake* by James Joyce, Viking Press; *Edible Wild Plants of Eastern North America* by Merritt Lyndon Fernald and Alfred Charles Kinsey, Harper & Row; "Rosemary in Snow," *The Herb Grower Magazine*, Vol. 1, 1947; Walter de la Mare, Excerpts, Literary Trustees of de la Mare estate and Society of Authors; "Red Roses" from *Tender Buttons, A Rose is a Rose is a Rose* by Gertrude Stein, Gertrude Stein estate and Donald Gallup; *Names of Flowers* by Gertrude Stein, Yale University Press; Dr. Roberta Ma's recipe for lily soup, *Herbarist Magazine;* "Calendula Officinialis" by Majorie Gibbon, The *Herbarist Magazine;* "Some Notes Upon the Use of Herbs in Norwegian Households" by Sigrid Undset, *The Herbarist; Pot Luck at a Fifth Avenue Florist* by Margaret Fishback, E. P. Dutton & Co.; *Please Don't Eat the Daisies* by Jean Kerr; *Acacias* by Sir John Squire, Macmillan & Co. Ltd. and St. Martin's Press; *Bouquet de France* by Samuel Chamberlain; *Fit for a King* by Merle Armitage, Duell Sloan & Pearce; *A Spring Song and Rose* by Witter Bynner; *Boccaccio* by Francis MacManus, Sheed & Ward; *Green Fingers* by Reginald Arkell, Herbert Jenkins Limited; *How to Cook and Eat in Chinese* by Burei Yang Chao, John Day Company; *Real French Cooking* by Savarin, Faber and Faber Ltd.; Gladioli salad recipe by Ford Frick; *The Epicure in Imperial Russia* by Marie Alexandre Markevitch, Colt Press; *Collected Poems of Edna St. Vincent Millay,* Harper & Row; *Time Remembered* by Jean Anouilh, Putnam, Coward McCann; Article by Leonard Schecter, *New York*

Contents

FLOWER COOKERY

The Art of Cooking with Flowers

ACACIA BLOSSOMS

The acacia tree is foreign; it grows in Egypt. We have from it two drugs; the Acacia juice, like liquorice juice, hard and black. Also the Gum arabic; both astringent, useful in stranguries, and in coughs, hoarseness, etc. Given in solution. An ounce boiled in a quart of barley water, or in powder as an electuary.... Gum Arabic powdered, or in thick solution, is a good application for burns and excoriations...combined with powdered resin, it is a good styptic. As diet it is nutritious. The wandering Arabs sometimes subsist wholly upon it.

M. Robinson — M.D., The New Family Herbal and Botanic Physician

The Acacia symbolizes friendship.

ACACIA FLOWER FRITTERS. Make a thin batter using half a cup of beer, and just before dipping the flowers in mix with the whites of two well beaten eggs. Select the flowers, dip in powdered sugar and sprinkle with kirsch or brandy, let stand for thirty minutes, dip in the batter, and fry in hot fat. Sprinkle with sugar before serving.

(Maitre Escoffier, in his Guide to Modern Cookery advises the same process for Elderflowers, Lily, and Vegetable Marrow-flower fritters, though in the latter two, the quartered corollas alone are used.)

Jean Conil in Haute Cuisine adds sureau, violets and roses to the above list, to be done in the same manner.

In Auvergne they make fritters of acacia blossoms, but do a whole spray at a time.

ACACIA HONEY. Bourbon bees produce a greenish honey, which retains the perfume of their Acacia blossom diet.

TO CANDY FLOWERS OR GREENS IN BRANCHES WITH GUM ARABIC. Steep your gum arabic in water, wet the flowers with it and shake them in a cloth that they may be dry; then dip them in fine sifted sugar, and hang them on a string tied across a chimney that has fire in it; they must hang two or three days till the flowers are quite dry.

> Mrs. Mary Eales, Receipt Book, 1719
> Confectioner to Queen Anne

Acacia Blossoms

ACACIA SYRUP. To every two ounces of flowers allow three-quarters of a pound of sugar. Select a bowl and arrange flowers and sugar in alternate layers. Set aside for a few hours and then pour over it a pint of boiling water, then set aside again for a day and a night. Prepare a light sugar syrup using a pint of water and a half cup of sugar, while boiling strain, gently, the flower mixture into the hot syrup and bottle it.

ACACIA BLOSSOM LIQUEUR. Pick a sufficient quantity of acacia blossoms to obtain ½ lb. of petals, and put them to steep for four days in 2 quarts of spirit of wine registering 50 degrees by Gay Lussac's alcoholometer. Boil 1½ lbs. of loaf sugar with 1½ pints of water, clarify the syrup with some whites of egg and boil until it registers 30 degrees on the saccharimeter. Strain the acacia spirit, and mix it with the cold syrup. Filter the liquer, with some paper, through a filtering bag, and continue pouring it through until it is quite clear and bright. Put the liquer into bottles previously rinsed out with spirit of wine, cork and seal them carefully.

> Jules Gouffe, Book of Preserves (Chef of the Paris Jockey Club; translated by Alphonse Gouffe, Head Pastrycook to Her Majesty Queen Victoria, 1871)

And over all his rough and writhing boughs and tiniest twigs
Will spread a pale green mist of feathery leaf,
More delicate, more touching than all the verdure
Of the younger, slenderer, gracefuller plants around.
And then when the leaves have grown
Till the boughs can scarcely be seen through their crowded plumes,
There will softly glimmer, scattered upon him blooms,
Ivory white in the green, weightlessly hanging.
  J. C. Squire, Collected Poems, London. 1948

AGRIMONY

A herb of princely authoritie.
          Pliny

It symbolizes gratitude.

AGRIMONY TEA. Put a handful of the plant-stems, flowers and leaves into a pot and pour over it a pint of boiling water. Let it get cold and then strain. French peasants are very fond of this drink when agrimony is in flower.

The plant belongs to the rose order, and in some places is called Church Steeples because of its long flower spikes.

For flavoring beer, take about six ounces, put into a bag and hang in a barrel of beer for a week or so.

ALEXANDER BUDS

For every green herb, from the lotus to the darnel,
Is rich with delicate aids to help incurious man.
          M. F. Tupper 1810–1899

TO MAKE A GRAND SALLET FOR THE SPRING. Your Gardener, or those that serve you with herbs, must supply you with all manner of Spring-Sallets, as buds of Cowslips, Violets, Strawberries, Primrose, Watercresses, young Lettuce, Spinnage, Alexander-buds, or what other things may be got, either backward or forward in the Spring; having all these things severally and apart, then take of themselves Sampier, Olives, Capers, Broom-buds, Cowcumbers, Raisons and Currans parboyled, blanched Almonds, Barberries, or what other pickles you can obtain; then prepare your standard for the middle of your dish; it may be a waxed tree, or a standard of Paste (like a Castle), being washed in the yolks of eggs, and all made green with herbs; as also, a tree within that, in the like manner may be made, with Paste, made green, and stuck with Flowers, so that you may not perceive it, but to be a tree, with about twelve supporters round, stooping to, and fastened in holes in your Castle, and the other end bending out

Alexander Buds

to the middle of your dish; they may be formed with Paste; then having four rings of Paste, the one bigger than another (like unto hoops), your biggest must come over your Castle, and reach within three inches of the foot of your supporter, the second to be within two inches of that and so place as many as you please gradually, that they may be like as many steps going up to a Cross; you may have likewise four Belconies in your Castle with four Statues of the four Seasons; this done, place your Sallet, around of one sort on the upper-most ring, or step, so round all the other till you come to the dish, with every one a several sort; then place all your pickles from that to the brims of your dish severally, one answering another. As for example, if you have two of white, and two of green, let them be opposite, the white against the white, and the green against the green, and so all the other; so your dishes bottom being wholly covered below your Mount, garnish your dish with all kinds of things suitable, or afforded by the Spring; your Statues ought to have every one a Cruitt placed in their hands, two with Vinegar and two with Oyl; when this Sallet is made, let it be carried to the Table, and set in its place; and when the guests are all placed, unstop the Cruitts, that the Oyl and Vinegar may run on the Sallet; these Cruitts must be glasses not a quarter of a pint apiece, sized over on the outside, and strowed with flowers: After the same manner may you make your Sallet in Summer, Autumn, or Winter; only take those Sallets that are then in season, and changing your standard; for in the Summer, you ought to resemble a green tree; and in the Autumn, a Castle carved out of Carrots and Turnips; in the Winter a Tree hanged with Snow: This only is for great Feasts, and may inform the Practitioner in such Feasts, for the honour of his Master, and benefit of himself. The Paste that you make your Castle or Standard with, must be made of Rye.

᪐ There is nothing of more constant use in our sallets than *good* Vinegar so we think it not amiss to give the following (much approv'd Receipt).

VINEGAR. To every gallon of Spring water, let there be allowed 3 lbs. of Malaga-Raisins. Put them in an earthern Jarr and place them where they may have the hottest sun from May till Michaelmas. Then pressing them well Tun the liquor up in a very strong iron-hoop'd Vessel to prevent its bursting. It will appear very thick and muddy when newly pressed but will refine in the Vessel and be as clear as wine. Thus let it remain untouch'd for three months before it be drawn off and it will prove excellent Vinegar.

John Evelyn, Acetaria, 1699

A Grand Sallet of Alexander Buds. Take large Alexander-buds, and boil them in fair water after they be cleaned and washed, but first let the water boil, then put them in, and being boiled, drain them on a dish bottom or in a cullender; then have boiled capers and currans, and lay them in the midst of a clean scoured dish, the buds parted in two with a sharp knife, and laid about upright, or one half on one side, and the other against it on the other side, so also carved lemon, scrape on sugar, and serve it with good oyl and wine vinegar.

Alexander Buds

> Robert May, The Accomplisht Cook, or the Art and Mystery of Cookery. London, Printed for *Obadiah Blagrave* at the *Bear* and *Star* in St. Paul's Church-yard, 1685

BANANA BLOSSOM

Where the banana grows man is sensual and cruel.
Ralph Waldo Emerson — Society and Solitude, 1870

Banana Blossom Kilawain

2 banana blossoms
1 cup shelled shrimps
4 cloves chopped garlic
1 onion—cut in slices
4 tablespoons lard
2 cups shrimp juice
Vinegar, salt, and pepper to taste

Remove the tough covering of the blossom. Slice thin—crosswise. Squeeze it with salt and rinse. Set aside. Mix the shrimps, sliced onion, and vinegar. Saute the garlic and add the shrimp mixture. Add shrimp juice and continue cooking. Then add the blossom. Turn over constantly until tender. Season with salt and pepper. Serve hot.

Banana Blossom, Paella Style

Banana Blossom

 2 cups banana blossom, cut in pieces, worked in salt and rinsed
 ½ cup clams—boiled meat
 ½ cup pork, cut in strips
 14 small shrimps, blanched and peeled
 ½ of a small onion, sliced fine
 1 section garlic pounded
Achuete—red annato seeds used for food coloring
 1 tablespoon salt
2½ cups clam stock
 1 bay leaf
Dash of pepper
 1 cup rice
 1 tablespoon lard

❧ Saute garlic, onion, pork, and shrimps. Add stock and boil. Add banana blossom and continue cooking. Season with salt and pepper.

❧ Add rice, achuete water, bay leaf, and cook until done, stirring from time to time, to avoid burning. Serve garnished with shrimps, clams and a few pieces of the tender part of banana blossom.

Both recipes from "Recipes of the Philippines" by Enriqueta David-Perez Printed by Capitol Publishing House — 1953

Common name for the banana is "Adam's Apple."

❧ Also well-liked in the Philippines is Kari-Kari. Cubes of beef are boiled until tender and then sauteed in garlic, then add sliced banana buds.

Young banana flower heads are commonly used as a vegetable in Ceylon.

The Chinese like them pickled.

BETONY ⌇⌇⌇⌇⌇⌇⌇⌇⌇⌇⌇⌇⌇⌇⌇⌇⌇⌇⌇⌇⌇⌇

"Sell your coat and buy betony."

"May you have more virutes than betony."
Old Italian Proverbs

Betony symbolizes emotion and surprise.

CONSERVE OF BETONY. (The Italian Way.) Betony new and tender one pound, the best sugar three pound, beat them very small in a stone mortar, let the sugar be boyled with two quarts of betony water to the consistency of a syrup, then mix them together by little and little over a small Fire, and so make it into a Conserve and keep it in Glasses.
W. M., The Queen's Closet Opened,
Cook to Queen Henrietta Maria, 1655

BETONY TEA. Put two ounces of the herb, flowers and leaves, into two quarts of water, and let it simmer to three half-pints.

Antonio Musa, physician to Emperor Augustus Caesar, wrote a book about the virtues of Betony, and they are many. Culpeper's comment after reading it was that it was not the practice of Caesar to keep fools about him.

DOCTRINE OF SIGNATURES
"Stinking weeds and poysonous plants. They would not be without their use, if they were good for nothing else but exercise the Industry of Man to weed them out . . . Why may not poysonous plants draw to them all the maligne juice and nourishment that the others may be more pure and refined, as well as Toads and other poysonous Serpents licke the venome from the Earth, or that the Gall of Man should draine his body of superfluous Choler . . . Helle-bore is dangerous given to delicate bodies, yet it may be safely given to Countrey people, which have tough bodies, so that the constitution of the party receiving, as well as the quality of the thing to be received, is to be considered, for that which is one man's Meat, is another man's Poysen."
William Coles, 1656

BLACK CURRANT BUDS

Now will the Corinths, now the rasps supply Delicious draughts.
  Phillips

Symbolical significance: Thy frown will kill me.

BLACK CURRANT BUDS ICE CREAM. Make two cups of sugar syrup in which two handsful of black currant buds are cooked. To this add the juice of half a lemon, then strain, chill, and put in an ice pail. This is a deliciously flavored dessert, and it is regrettable that it can only be made two or three weeks, at the most during the year.
  Marie Alexandre Markevitch, The Epicure in Imperial Russia,
  Colt Press-San Francisco, 1941

BLACK CURRANT-BUD LIQUEUR. Take 1 lb of the budding shoots of some black currant trees, and put them into a jar with 3 quarts of spirit of wine registering 50 degrees by Gay Lussac's alcoholometer, and let them remain therein for a fortnight, keeping the jar closed. Strain the spirit through a hair sieve: mix it with 2½ quarts of syrup registering 30 degrees on the saccharo-meter, and some filtering paper, and pour the whole into a filtering-bag. Bottle the liqueur and keep it in a cool place.
  Jules Gouffe, Book of Preserves

The French make a liqueur from the fruit of the black currant called Cassis. A good punch can be made by mixing tea, Cassis and ginger ale, added just before serving.

Corinth, Greece, gave black currants to the world, hence the name.

BORAGE ⚘⚘⚘⚘⚘⚘⚘⚘⚘⚘⚘⚘⚘⚘⚘⚘⚘⚘

Borage, forage for bees
And for those who love blue. . . .

      Edna St. Vincent Millay, Mine the Harvest

"The leaf of the borage hath an excellent spirit to repress the
fuliginous vapours of dusky melancholy and so cure madness. . . .
It will make a sovereign drink for melancholy passions."

     Francis, Lord Bacon

BORAGE IN CLARET CUP. Borage with its gallant blue flower is freely grown in the kitchen garden for claret cup and the bees.

   'To enliven the sad with the joy of a joke
   Give them wine with some borage put in it to soak.'

The fresh herb has a cucumber-like fragrance, and when compounded with lemon, and sugar, in wine, with water, it makes a delicious "cool tankard" which is refreshing, and restorative, as a summer drink. Chemically the plant contains potassium, and calcium, combined with mineral acids.

     Dr. Fernie, Meals Medicinal, 1905

John Swan in his *Speculum Mundi*, 1643, advised his gentle readers "to be discreet in their generation, and to gather to themselves great armsful of *never-dying Borage* (so called because of its fair blew flowers, ripe seeds, and buds, which may all be seen on it at once), and bravely plunge it into wine, where it cannot but be good . . . it increaseth wit, and memoire, engendereth good blood, maketh a man merrie, and joyfull, and putteth away all melancholie, and madness."

A TARTE OF BORAGE FLOWERS. Take borage flowers and parboyle them tender, then strayne them with the yolckes of three or foure eggs, and sweet curdes, or else take three or four apples and parboyle wythal and strayne them with sweete butter and a lyttel mace and so bake it.

A Proper Newe Book of Cookerie, 1575

Borage

CONSERVE OF BORAGE. Take of fresh borage flowers four ounces, of fine sugar twelve ounces, beat them well together in a stone mortar, and keep them in a vessel well glazed.

The Queen's Closet Opened, 1655

BORAGE IN WINE. The sprigs, in wine, are of known virtue to receive the hypochondriac and cheer the hard student.

John Evelyn, Acetaria, 1699

A perfect accompaniment for Pimm's Cup.

Borage adds distinction to various salads, potato salad, tossed salads, cream or cottage cheese.

CANDIED BORAGE FLOWERS. Gather and candy as violets or mint leaves. Brush with egg white, sprinkle with sugar, and let them dry slowly in a warm place. Use to decorate cakes or cookies.

BORAGE TEA. Dry the flowers, and use a heaping teaspoonful to a pint of boiling water.

Decorate your lemonade with sprigs of borage flowers.

The Herbal of Renodaeus advises, 'Its flowers put into broth give a special taste.'

BORAGE FLOWER SYRUP. Infuse the flowers in water for a period of eight to ten hours, heat the water, strain and add fresh flowers, let it set again, add a cup of sugar to a cup of the flower water and boil to a syrup.

Columbus sowed borage on Isabella Island.

Borage is one of the four cardinal flowers of the ancients. (Others are rose, violet, alkanet or bugloss.)

Ego Borago   *I, Borage*
Gaudia semper ago.   *Bring alwaies courage.*

There is a famous syrup of Borage, highly commended by Laurentius . . . in his tract of melancholy.

Burton, *The Anatomy of Melancholy, 1621*

Borage   *Dioscorides and Pliny claim that borage is the famous nepenthe of Homer, drunk in wine it brought absolute forgetfulness.*

To CANDY BORAGE. Boil sugar and rose-water a little then put the flowers, thoroughly dry, with the sugar, and boile them a little; then strew the powder of double-refined sugar upon them, and turne them, and let them boile a little longer, taking the dish from the fire; then strew more powdered sugar on the contrary side of the flowers. These will dry of themselves in two or three hours in a hot sunny day, though they lie not in the sunne.

The Queen's Closet Opened, 1655

BORAGE OF BALM IN A COOL TANKARD OR BEER CUP. A quart of mild ale, a glass of white wine, one of brandy, one of Capillaire, the juice of a lemon, a roll of the peel pared thin, nutmeg grated at the top, a sprig of borage or balm, and a bit of toasted bread. (A few of the blue flowers can be floated on top.)

Dr. Kitchener, The Cook's Oracle, 1823

Capillaire is often mentioned as an ingredient, the recipe is as follows:

CAPILLAIRE SYRUP:
  3 qts. water
  3 lbs. brown sugar
10 lbs. white sugar
  6 egg whites
  1 pt. orange-flower water

Beat egg whites with water; add sugar; boil & skim 2 or 3 times; lastly add orange-flower water, strain and bottle.

BROOM

The Scots often chant its praise:

> *"O, the broom, the bonny, bonny broom,*
> *The broom of the Cowden Knowes;*
> *For sure so soft, so sweet a bloom*
> *Elsewhere there never grows."*

Some florigraphists claim that the broom is emblematic of ardor, others that it signifies neatness and humility.

With a great sprig of broom which he bore as a badge in it
He was named from the circumstance Henry Plantagenet.
> *Ingoldsby Legends*

PICKLED BROOM BUDS: Take as many broom buds as desired and put into a pickle of vinegar, salt and mustard. Let stand overnight. Strain and boil the vinegar, place buds in jars and cover with pickling juice. Stir, strain and seal.

"To be eaten all the yeare after as a sallet of much delight, and are called Broome capers, which doe helpe to stirre up an appetite to meate, that is weak and dejected."   Parkinson, Theatrum Botanicum

Pickled broom buds were served at the coronation feast of James II.

Another recipe includes white wine and tarragon vinegar in the pickle mixture.

PICKEL BROUM BUDS. Ly your buds in salt and water all night yn make a pickel of salt and venegar boile it and poure it hot upon the buds; cover ym close; boile it 3 or 4 times & put it hot & cover it close.
> Elizabeth Wainwright, The Receipt Book of a
> Lady of the Reign of Queen Anne, 1711

How charming the tables of our ancestors with their dishes of candied and pickled flowers and jugs of flower syrups.

BRAVE SALLET. The ingredients must be gathered and mixed so, "not only so as to agree with the Humours of those who eat them but so that nothing should be suffered to domineer, so should none of them lose their Gust, Savour, or Vertue. These must be in correct proportions, the cool and refreshing to extinguish thirst, attemper the Blood, repress Vapours, the Hot, Dry, Aromatic Cordial and friendly to the Brain, the bitter and mordaunt, the mild and insipid, animated with the piquant and brisk. In the composure every Plant must bear

its part and they must fall into their places like the Notes in Music, and there
must be nothing harsh nor grating. And tho' admitting some discords (to
distinguish and illustrate the rest), striking in the more sprightly and sometimes gentler Notes, reconcile all Dissonancies and melt them into an agreeable
composition." John Evelyn, Acetaria, 1699

Broom

SALLET-ALL-SORTS. The Almonds blanch'd in cold water, cut them round and
thin and so leave them in cold water. Then have pickled Cucumbers, Olives,
Capers, Berberries, Red-Beet. Buds of Nasturtium, Broom, etc., Purslan stalk,
Sampier, Ash-keys, Walnuts, Mushrooms, with raisins of the Sun ston'd, citron
and orange peel. Strew them over with any candy'd flowers and so dispose
of them in the same Dish both mixt and by themselves. To these add Marrows,
Pine kernels and of Almonds four times as much of the rest with some Rose-
water. Here also come in the Pickled Flowers and Vinegar in little china Dishes.
And thus have you an universal winter Sallet or an All sort in compendium
fitted for a City Feast and distinguished from the Grand Sallet which should
consist of the green blanched and unpickled under a stately Pennash of Sellery
adorn'd with Buds and Flowers. John Evelyn, Acetaria

*In 1234 St. Louis of France founded a special order, its Colle de Genet was com-
posed of the fleur-de-lys and the broomflower.*

Tell me, being in the broom,
Teach me what to do
That my husband
Love me true.
When your tongue is still,
You'll have your will.

Wife in the 13th Century seeking aid from
a being in the broom.

Broom buds have an almond flavor.

BROOM WINE: Take a gallon of broom flowers and a gallon of water; add 3
pounds of sugar, the juice and rind of two lemons and 2 oranges, also 2
packages of yeast.
Boil the sugar, water, orange and lemon rinds for a half hour. Cool to lukewarm
and pour over the flowers. Add the lemon and orange juice, then stir in the
yeast. Ferment for three days. Then pour into a dry cask and let it work for
about 10 days. Close it and let it set for about six months . . . open and you
have a very wonderful drink.

BURDOCK ༄ལལལལལལལལལལལལལལལལལལལ

❧ Nature seems partial to the burdock. What extra pains she seems to have taken to perpetuate this worse than useless plant! So far as I know, nothing wants it or profits by it, though I have heard that the petioles when cooked suggest salsify. It is an Ishmaelite among plants. Every man's hand is against it, and nearly every animal has reason to detest it.
—John Burroughs, Field and Study

BURDOCK ALE:

  5 ozs. burdock root
  2 ozs. camomile herb
  4 ozs. ginger
2½ pounds sugar
 35 grns. saccharine 550
  2 ozs. (or a sufficiency) foam essence
  2 ozs. burnt sugar
10 gallons water

❧ Directions: Boil the burdock, camomile, and ginger in half the water for 15 minutes; add the burnt sugar and pour through a strainer on to the sugar and saccharine. Stir until it is all dissolved, and then add the remainder of the water and foam essence. Add a sufficient quantity of yeast, allow to work for 12 hours at a temperature of 65 to 75 degrees Fahrenheit. Skim off the yeast and bottle.

❧ Mrs. Grieve gives substantially the same recipe for burdock and dandelion ale, but using the leaves of both plants, and omitting the camomile and the ginger.

❧ In Japan it has been developed and according to some authors it is as important as the potato is here . . . in Europe the young roots, leaves and stems are popular. The roots are boiled in two waters, the first one should include soda to break the tough fibers. The stems are peeled and what remains is a tender and succulent pith—it, too, should be cooked in two waters. The pith can also be eaten raw as a salad with oil and vinegar dressing. It can also be candied.

❧ Yes, I know it is not a flower, but I tried this and found it very good.

Mother went rambling, and came in with a burdock on her shawl, so we know that the snow has perished from the earth. Noah would have liked mother.
—Emily Dickinson, Letter to Louisa and Frances Norcross, 1870
(Mabel Loomis Todd — Letters of Emily Dickinson)

BURNET ∾∾∾∾∾∾∾∾∾∾∾∾∾∾∾∾∾∾∾∾

The burnet shall bear up with this,
Whose leaf I greatly fancy.
            Draytor

BURNET WINE:
½ gallon burnets
 1 gallon water
 3 lbs. sugar to every gallon
 1 oz. bruised ginger

Boil for ¾ hour. Strain on to 3 oranges, 1 lemon, and 1 pound of raisins and the sugar, let it stand for 2 days, and then bottle; but do not cork until finished working.

BURNET VINEGAR. Take a quart of vinegar and pour it over half an ounce of well-dried and pounded Burnet seed. Pour it into a bottle and cork tightly. Shake the bottle well once a day for 10 days; strain and cork tightly—it will then be ready for use.

Bruised burnet smells and tastes like cucumber.

BURNET TEA. Make as you would any other tea and add lemon and sugar.

Burnet enhances many dishes, try it in cottage cheese or asparagus soup.

SPRING SALAD. Take the young and tender shoots and flowers of burnet, primroses, violets, mint, sorrel, borage, bugloss and roses, mix and serve with a good French dressing.

The French and Italians call Burnet "Pimpinella," and in Italy there is a saying that,
            "The salad is neither good nor fair,
            If Pimpinella is not there."

CALAMINT ᕫᕦᕫᕦᕫᕦᕫᕦᕫᕦᕫᕦᕫᕦᕫᕦᕫᕦᕫᕦᕫᕦᕫᕦᕫᕦᕫ

Aromatic plants bestow
No spring fragrance while they grow.
But crush'd or trodden to the ground
Diffuse their balmy sweets around.
                    —*Oliver Goldsmith*

Also known as mountain mint.

Calamint has blue flowers and a hot scent similar to peppermint.

CONSERVE OF CALAMINT. Gather the flowers on a dry day. Strip the flowers from the stems, weigh them and to every pound of flowers add 1½ pounds of sugar. Beat them together well and add sugar gradually. When well mixed put in jars and cover. Do not keep more than a year as there is not enough sugar.

CAPERS ᕫᕦᕫᕦᕫᕦᕫᕦᕫᕦᕫᕦᕫᕦᕫᕦᕫᕦᕫᕦᕫᕦᕫᕦᕫᕦᕫ

"I have noticed a curious fact in connection with the Caper, namely, that the common cabbage white butterfly (Pieris Brassicae) will sometimes lay her eggs upon it. Now the Crucifers or Cross flowers are the proper food plants of these white butterflies (Pieridae). But how does this insect know that the Caper is allied to the Crucifers? By what hidden faculty is the little creature made aware of a fact which the most accomplished botanist could never suspect?"
                    —*B. Quaritch, Riviera Nature Notes*

Dioscorides used the caper for an enlarged spleen.

The Romans called it Persian Mustard.

Capers are the flower-buds of the caper-bush (Capparis Spinosa): they are collected before expansion and preserved in wine vinegar.

CAPER CANAPE: Chop capers with anchovies and spice, then spread as a paste on rusks or toast.
                    Dr. Fernie, Meals Medicinal

It is also good on eggplant baked and then a sprinkling of capers and grated Parmesan cheese.

Capers

"Dr. Royle has proved that the caper-plant is the hyssop of Scripture, 'which sorubgeth out of the wall?' It has long trailing branches like the bramble, and it was on one of these that the sponge filled with vinegar was offered to our Savior on the cross. 'They filled a sponge with vinegar and put it upon hyssop.'
Kettner, Book of the Table

CARNATIONS

The curious choice clove July flower,
Whose kinds hight the Carnation,
For sweetness of most sovereign power
Shall help my wreath to fashion,
Whose sundry colours, of one kind,
First from one root derived
Then in their several suits I'll bind,
My garland so contrived.
Michael Drayton

GILLIFLOWERS TO PICKLE. Take Clove-Gilliflowers, when just blown, clip the white Bottoms from them, when taken out of the Husks, lay them to steep a little in fair Water, boil up some White wine Vinegar till the scum will come no more on it: squeeze the Water out of your Gilliflowers, and the Vinegar being cool, put them into it; then melt as much Sugar as convenient in Rose-water; put it to them with a little broken Cinnamon, and a few Blades of Mace; stop them up close, and when you use them, mince them small, and putting a little fresh Vinegar to them, strew a little white Sugar finely beaten and they are excellent Sauce for Mutton or Lamb.

William Salmon, the Family Dictionary, London. Printed for D. Rhodes, at the Star, the Corner of Bride-Lane in Fleet-street, 1705

GILLYFLOWER WINE. To ten gallons and half of pure Spring-water, add twenty pound of Sugar, boil it till the half gallon be consumed, scum it well; then take six Bushels of Clove Gilliflowers, the White and Green parts being cut away, put them in a Tub, and pour them on your Liquor boiling hot, stir it well; and cover it with Blankets, so close that it may keep warm as long as you can; let it stand twenty-four hours, then run the Liquor through a Jelly-bag; let it stand close covered till it settle, which will be about 24 hours; then turn it up in a close Vessel having first warmed it a little, if the weather be cold; then take a little Crust of Brown Bread, whereon put a little Ale Yeast; put the same into the Vessel, stop it up close till it begin to ferment, which will be about a Week, then Bottle it up with a little Sugar and Limon-peel.

Ibidem

Carnations

Our ancestors made a rich syrup as a sauce for puddings.

TO MAKE SYRUP OF CLOVE-GILYFLOWERS. Take a quart of water, half a bushel of flowers, cut off the whites, and with a sieve sift away the seeds, bruise them a little; let your water be boiled and a little cold again, then put in your flowers and let them stand close covered twenty-four hours; you may put in but half the flowers at a time, the strength will come out the better; to that liquor put in four pounds of sugar, let it lye in all night, next day boil in a gallipot, set it in a pot of water, and then let it boil till all the sugar be melted and syrup be pretty thick, then take it out and let it stand till it be thoroughly cold, then glass it.

The Queen's Delight, 1671

A SALLET OF ROSE-BUDS AND CLOVE-GILLYFLOWERS. Pick Rose-buds, and put them in an earthen pipkin, with White Wine Vinegar and Sugar; so may you use Cowslips, Violets or Rosemary-flowers.

J. Murrel, Two Bookes of Cookerie and Carving, 1650

PINKS. How to Dry Flowers. Take single pinks and take ye leaves out of ye husks and cut ym somewhat Long, leaving some of ye white to ye leaves; then put them in a flat glass wherein you have mingled half a spoonfull of Aquafortis with 12 spoonfulls of water, and when the leaves have layne in the water halfe an hour or more, take them out one by one and lay them on a paper ye right side down, not to touch one another; and after an hour or 2 when the water is well dryed up (as it will if the paper be laide on a woollen cloth), then strew them over with fine dry sand till they be all cover'd. So let them lye a fortnight in a place where the sun comes in, in which time they will be dry and stiff. Then take them off one by one, shaking off the sand, and wipe them between your fingers. Lay them in boxes till the winter, each colour by themselves, and then bind them up together by the white part of the leafe that remains, till they be of what bigness you please; and so put them into the green husk which must be kept for them; pickt early in the year they will keep the better, takeing the natural flowers out of them; rowle a little piece of paper up and fill the husk with it; lay them also in sand till they be dry. Use no water to them; when you put your flowers into the husk fasten them with a privet stick by ye green silk you bind them up withall, with a fine needle at the bottom of the husks. So many severall colours as you have must be put in severall glasses of water or the colours will not be perfect. Rose buds are only laid in water 2 or 3 hours and laid out on a woollen cloth to dry without sand, for marygolds, primroses, or larke heels or the like are only in sand without water. Experience must be ye best Mrs. to teach this art.

Carnations

> H. W. Lewer, A Book of Simples, Compiled and Edited by him from a MS book of the early eighteenth century. Published in 1906

Count de Mauduit suggests using gillyflowers in salads.

THE MAKING OF STRANGE SALLETS. Now for the compounding of Sallets, of these pickled and preserved things, though they may be served up simply of themselves; yet for better curiosity and the fine adorning of the Table, you shall thus use them.

❧ First, if you set forth any Red-flower, that you know or have seen, you shall take your pots of preserved Gillyflowers and suiting the colours answerable to the Flower, you shall proportionate forth, and lay the shape of the Flower in a Fruit dish.

❧ Then with your Purslan leaves, make the green Coffin of the Flower, and with the Purslan stalks make the stalk of the Flower, and the division of the leaves and branches.

❧ Then with the thinn slices of Cowcumbers make their leaves in true proportion, jagged or otherwise.

❧ Thus you may set forth some full blown, some half blown and some in the bud, which will be pretty and curious.

❧ And if you will set forth yellow Flowers, take the pots of Primroses and Cowslips: if blue Flowers then pots of Violets or Bugloss Flowers.

❧ And these Sallets are both for show and use, for they are more excellent to taste, than for to look on.

Gervase Markham, The English Housewife, 1615.

Carnations

"But what shall I say to the Queene of delight and of flowers, Carnations and Gilloflowers, whose bravery, variety, and sweete smell joyned together, tyeth every one's affection with great earnestness, both to like and to have them . . . The names of them do differ very variably, in that names are imposed and altered as every one's fancy will have them."
The Garden of Pleasant Flowers, 1629

Carnation, symbolizes pride and beauty.

Gillyflower: She is fair.

VINEGAR OF CLOVE-PINK. Take of flowers . . . one ounce; The best wine vinegar . . . sixteen ounces; Let them stand for fifteen days, strain and filter. Very good for sick-headache.

Richard Brooks, A New Family Herbal, 1871

A COMFORTABLE CORDIAL TO CHEER THE HEART. Take an ounce of Conserve of Gilliflowers, four grains of the best musk, bruised as fine as flour, then put it into a little tin pot and keep it till you have need to make this cordiall following. Viz: Take the quantity of one Nutmeg out of your tin pot, put to it one spoonful of cinnamon water, and one spoonful of the stirrup of gilliflowers, ambergreece, mix all these together, and drink them in the morning, fasting three or four hours. This is most comfortable.

Elizabeth Grey. A Choice Manuall of Rare and Select
Secrets in Physick and Chirurgery, 1653

TO MAKE A CORDIAL WATER OF CLOVE GILLY-FLOWERS. Put spirit of wine or sack upon Clove gilly-flowers. Digest it 2 or 3 days, put all in a glass-bottle, laying other Clove Gilliflowers at the mouth of it, upon a Cambrick or Butter-cloth: that the spirit rising and passing through the Flowers may tinge it self of a beautiful Colour: Add a head with a Limbecke and Receiver: then distil the spirit as strong as you like it, which sweeten with syrup of Gilly-flowers, or fine sugar.

Mrs. Mary Eales, The Accomplish'd Lady's Delight in
Preserving, etc., 1719

To Candy Gillyflowers. Take the weight of your Flowers in refin'd sugar, or Sugar Candy, sift it, put to it some rose water, and set it over a gentle Charcoal fire, put in your Flowers, and stir them till the Sugar be of a candied height; then keep them in a dryplace for use.

John Nott, The Receipt Book, 1723

Carnations

Gillyflowers Preserved Or Pickled. Clove Gilliflowers . . . *stratum super stratum*, a lay of flowers, and then strawed over with fine, dry, and powdered Sugar, and so lay after lay strawed over untill the pot be full you meane to keepe them in, and after filled up or covered over with vinegar, make a Sallet now adayes in the highest esteeme with Gentlemen and Ladies of the greatest note.

The Garden of Pleasant Flowers, 1629

The Countess Of Dorset Her Sweet Water. Take Rose-Leaves, Bay-Leaves, Lavender, sweet Marjoram, Eglantine, and Pinks, of each two handful; Cloves and Cinnamon, of each an ounce; bruise all these, and pour upon them two quarts of strong Ale (that is near the Grounds); let them infuse twenty-four hours, then distil it, and draw it till the Ingredients remain almost dry.

The Closet of Sir Kenelm Digby Opened, 1669

Sir Kenelm was beguiled by the story of Quercetanus, the famous physician of King Henry IV, who tells a story of a Polonian doctor who could raise flowers from ashes. Though he received the directions and tried many times he says, "but no industry of mine could effect it."

Mrs. Leyel recommends an infusion of Clove July Flowers in Mountain Wine. Drink a wineglassful three times a day as a nerve tonic.

Pliny says the clove carnation was discovered in Spain in the days of Augustus Caesar. The Spaniards like its spicy flavor.

In his letter to Cromwell, on the dissolution of the monastery of St. Andrew at Northampton, Robert Southwell wrote: 'There have growne no decay by this priour that we can lerne, but surely his predecessors pleasured moche in odoryferous savours, as it shulde seme by their converting the rentes of their monastery, that were wonte to be paide in coyne and grayne, into Gelofer flowers and Roses.'

PICKLED CARNATION PETALS. Very good with lamb and a welcome change. Prepare the required quantity of red Carnation petals by cutting off the white heels. Cover them with boiling white vinegar to which Cinnamon, Mace and sugar has been added. When cold, bottle. When required for use, the petals are minced small and made into a sauce with the vinegar and sugar.

Carnations

MARMALADE OF CARNATIONS. Half a pound of sugar, a cup of water, and half a pound of fresh red carnations. Crush in a mortar the tops of the carnations, using only the red part. Put the sugar and water in a saucepan and boil to a syrup, add the crushed carnations, and boil very slowly till they are in a pulp. Stir well and pour into small jars.

RATAFIA OF PINKS:
  1 lb. striped pinks, no stamens
  2 pts. brandy
  ½ lb. sugar
  2 cups strawberry juice
  ½ teaspoon saffron
  2 sticks cinnamon
Mix and bottle.

CARNATION JELLY. Pour into the mold about a half inch of gelatine, orange with carnation would make a good combination of taste and color, let it set firmly, then place the flowers, and pour in more jelly carefully so as not to disturb the petals, building this up layer upon layer until the mold is full.

William Coles in "Adam and Eden", (1657) says, "being pickled (gillyflowers) with Vinegar and Sugar, are a pleasant and dainty Sawce, stir up the Appetite and are also of a Cordiall faculty."

The pink was a favorite flower of Henry the Fourth of France.

The derivation of the word "carnation" comes from "coronation" because the flower was a festival flower.

TO MAKE PASTE OF FLOWERS OF THE COLOUR OF MARBLE TASTING OF NATURAL FLOWERS. Take every sort of pleasing flowers, as Violets, Cowslips, Gillyflowers, Roses, or Marygolds, and beat them in a Mortar, each flower by itself with Sugar, till the Sugar becomes the Colour of the flower, then put a little Gum Dragon steept in Water into it, and beat it into a perfect paste; so when you have half a dozen colours, every flower will take of his nature, then rowl the Paste therein, and lay one peece upon another, in mingling, so rowl your paste in small rowls as bigge and as long as your finger, then cut it off the bigness of a small nut, overthwart, and so rowl them thin, that you may see a knife through them, so dry them before the fire, till they be dry.

The Queen's Closet Opened, by W. M., Cook to
Queen Henrietta Maria, 1655

Carnations

To CANDY CLOVE JULYFLOWERS. Gather a Quantity of Clove Julyflowers when they are full open, but before they begin to fade, pull them out of the cups singly, one whole Flower at a Time, and cut off the white Ends with a Pair of Scissors. As they are cut put them into an earthen Pan, and see that no white Part be left, only the pure Purple is to be used. Cover the Pan with a Pewter Plate, and they will keep fresh till you are ready for them.

Break some small treble-refined Sugar into small Lumps, dip them one by one into clear Water, and throw them wet into a Silver Saucepan: The Water they thus take up will be enough to melt the Sugar, and it must be kept on the Fire till it is thick, and will draw in Hairs.

When the Sugar is in this Condition put in the Julyflowers, and stir them round that they may be well mixed, then pour the whole into Cups and Glasses; when it is of a hard Candy break it in Lumps, and lay it high, then dry it in a Stove, and it will look like the finest Sugar-candy, with the Flowers in the Pieces.

Any other Flowers may be candied in the same Manner, but none does so well.

Martha Bradley, The British Housewife.

The most famous grower of carnations in Queen Elizabeth's reign was 'Master Tuggie' of Westminster. Just from reading the list you know that they were "Gems richer than in Karkanet".

Pinks and clove gillyflowers were ingredients of hippocras, canary wine, mead and metheglin. These flowers staid in the kitchen garden about four hundred years, from the fourteenth to the eighteenth century.

TO MAKE A CONSERVE OF CLOVE JILLY FLOWERS AS AN EXCELLENT CORDIALL. Take to every ounce of flowers all the white cut off 3 ounces of sugar beat them very small so keep them to a pound which put into an earthen or silver bason set it over the fire. Stir it till the Sugar dissolve and to a pound put an ounce and half of powder of cloves and half a grain of beaszer half a grain of unicorns horn the juice of half a lemon mingle all well together and keep it for your use.

H. W. Lewer, A Book of Simples, 1908

Carnations

CARNATION BUTTER. Use the heavily scented carnations, mix with butter. Toast bread, cut into desired shapes, spread butter and garnish with a fresh carnation petal.

GILLYFLOWER—Ratifia d'Oeillets. For twenty-four pints of brandy, take a pound of carnation flowers, called ratifia pinks; take nothing but the red of the flowers, which is put into the brandy, with a drachm of bruised cloves; observe that it is a pound of the red leaves of the flowers; leave them a month in infusion; drain, and press the flowers well; dissolve two pounds of sugar in eight pints of water; mix it well with it; strain and bottle.

Beauvilliers, The Art of French Cookery

CATMINT ᘓᘓᘓᘓᘓᘓᘓᘓᘓᘓᘓᘓᘓᘓᘓᘓᘓᘓᘓᘓᘓᘓ

If you set it the cats will eat it;
If you sow it the cats won't know it.
—Old Proverb

Catmint tea is similar to mint tea, and in France the young shoots are used in salads and in the flavoring of dishes.

CONSERVE OF CATMINT. Strip the flowers from their stems and weigh them. Add 2 pounds of sugar to every pound of flowers. Beat them together gradually. A mortar is recommended. When thoroughly mixed, put it in little pots and cover well.

CHAMOMILE ⟨⟨⟨⟨⟨⟨⟨⟨⟨⟨⟨⟨⟨⟨⟨⟨⟨⟨⟨⟨⟨⟨⟨

*"Like the meek chamomile it grew
Luxuriant from the bruise anew."*
                                        J. W. Eastburne

The symbolical meaning is energy in adversity.

❧ He found savour in listing details, as in L'Ameto. There was interlaced syringa, healthy sage with abundant heads of pale leaves, sweet rosemary, betony that is full of many virtues, fragrant marjoram, cold rue, tall mustard that is enemy to the nose, wild thyme gripping the earth with the slenderest of arms, curly basil that imitates cloves with its scent at certain seasons, chamomile, mallow, dill, savory, fennel, parsley, meadowsweet, traveller's joy, wild rose and pheasants eye narcissus, hyacinths, and daisies. There were palms, too, laurels, cypresses "seeking the sky with their summits," firs, orange trees, figs that the crows watch, chestnuts, oaks, pale olives, walnuts, tall elms festooned with vines, plums, hazelnuts and pines; and there were beans, peas, chick-peas, cabbages such as Cato worshipped, lettuces. Beets, onions covered with many coats, leek, garlic, long melons, yellow pumpkins and rotund cucumbers. The names as well as the things themselves, enchanted him: the scents and odours, the colours and shapes—and the uses. His gardens were places of provisionment as well as repose.

Boccaccio by Francis MacManus

CHAMOMILE TEA. Francatelli directs to "put about thirty dried Chamomile flowers into a jug, and to pour over them a pint of boiling water, covering up the infusion; when it has stood for a quarter of an hour, pour it off from the flowers into another jug, and sweeten with sugar, or honey."

Chamomile smells like a ripe apple causing the Greeks to call it the apple of the earth.

Talleyrand was partial to chamomile tea; it was also a favorite of Queen Adelaide.

CHAMOMILE BEER. 12 ozs. chamomile, 4 ozs. ground ginger, 4 ozs. cream of tartar, 35 grns. saccharine (550), 2½ lbs. sugar, 2 ozs. burnt sugar, 10 galls. water. Infuse the chamomile and ginger in 5 gallons of boiling water for 15 minutes in a covered vessel. Strain and pour on to the sugar and saccharine, and stir until dissolved. Then add the burnt sugar, cream of tartar, and 5 gallons of cold water. Mix well, add the yeast, and ferment in the usual way.

Chamomile

CHAMOMILE SYRUP. Take 4 ozs. of the dried flowers, put in a covered jar, add 3 pints of boiling water, and let it steep for six hours, keeping the jar closed. Strain and filter, add 3½ lbs. of sugar and boil for ten minutes. This is one of the recommended syrups in the Paris Pharmacopoeia, 1866.

GOOD NEWS FROM SCOTLAND. 2 ounces of gentian root, one-half ounce each of cloves, cinnamon stick, camomile flowers and orange peel (Seville orange is better). Mix with some coriander seed and two quarts of whiskey. More flavor will be released if they are pounded in a mortar first. Put into air-tight bottles or crock and let stand for two weeks. Strain and bottle.

The Spanish sherry which is called Manzanilla is flavored with chamomile flowers.

CHICORY (OR SUCCORY)

There is a beautiful piece of fancy in the page representing the common blue chicory. Its current Latin name in the fifteenth century from its rayed form was 'Sponsor Solis'. But its blue colour caused it to be thought of as the favourite not of the sun only but of the sky. And the sun is drawn above it with a face, very beautiful in the orb, surrounded by vermillion and golden rays which descend to the flower through undulating lines of blue, representing the air. I have never seen the united power of Apollo and Athene more prettily symbolized.
—John Ruskin

It symbolizes frugality.

The flower opens so regularly at 7 a. m. and closes so precisely at noon that Linnaeus placed it in his floral clock.

It is used in France to adulterate coffee, but the flowers were used in the days of the merry monarch Charles II to make tablets, one of his favorite confections.

CHICORY TABLETS: 1 cup chicory (or succory flowers), 1 cup powdered sugar, 1 cup granulated sugar and ¾ cup water.

Chicory

🌀 Soak in cold water for five minutes. Drain. Place on a soft towel and pat dry. Put the powdered sugar and water in a saucepan, cook for 10 minutes over slow heat, then boil for five minutes. Remove from heat and stir in flowers. Cover well with syrup and leave for three minutes. Take out one at a time and place on cold platter for crystallizing or powder with confectioner's sugar or place in an oblong pan to make the tablets. I prefer the crystallized ones.

🌀 In Elizabethan days the flowers were pickled and Syrup of Succory was sold in the shops in the 18th century. Conserve of chicory was also very popular.

CHRYSANTHEMUM 〰〰〰〰〰〰〰〰〰〰〰〰〰

They are there, under the immense transparent dome, the noble flowers of the month of fogs; they are there, at the royal meeting-place, all the grave little autumn fairies, whose dances and attitudes seem to have been struck motionless with a single word. The eye that recognizes them and has learned to love them perceives, at the first pleased glance, that they have actively and dutifully continued to evolve towards their uncertain ideal. Go back for a moment to their modest origin: look at the poor buttercup of yore, the humble little crimson or demask rose that still smiles sadly, along the roads full of dead leaves, in the scanty garden-patches of our villages; compare with them these enormous masses and fleeces of snow, these disks and globes of red copper, these spheres of old silver, these trophies of alabaster and amethyst, this delirious prodigy of petals which seems to be trying to exhaust to its last riddle the world of autumnal shapes and shades which the winter entrusts to the bosom of the sleeping woods; let the unwonted and unexpected varieties pass before your eyes; admire and appraise them.

Maurice Maeterlinck, Chrysanthemums, 1904

CHRYSANTHEMUM SALAD. Toss together: 1 jar (8½ ozs.) artichoke hearts, drained, 1 pound cooked shrimp, 3 cubed cooked potatoes, 6 sliced hard-cooked eggs, 2 tablespoons capers, 4 washed, chopped chrysanthemums. Season with ⅓ cup saffron-flavored French dressing. Garnish with chrysanthemums. Serves 4.

PRESERVING CHRYSANTHEMUM FLOWERS FOR FLAVORING TEA. Fill an earthenware jar with the flowers of the Sweet Chrysanthemum, picked when covered with dew. Add one or two fruit of the white-flowering Plum, then fill the jar to the brim with salt water. Press with a heavy stone and cover tightly. Keep this until the sixth or seventh moon of the following year. After removing the salt water, place one flower with the tea leaves in a cup and pour the boiling water over them. You will find this tea delicious and fragrant, and very refreshing in the heat of summer.

Wang Tzu-ch'iao in the Hsien Ching

Chrysanthemum

CHRYSANTHEMUM WINE. Supposed to insure long life. It is made by picking the flowers with the stems and leaves, fermenting them with millet. A year later, on the 9th day of the 9th moon it is ready for use.

Hsi Ching Tsa Chi

The Chinese call the fragrance of the chrysanthemum—cool.

The chrysanthemum symbolizes a life of ease and retirement.

In China it is believed that eating chrysanthemums increases longevity, that it will turn white hair black again, make the body light and vigorous, and that after two years of taking pills made of chrysanthemum (stems, roots and flowers) the teeth will grow again.

The Wild Chrysanthemum
Late, its enchanting colour springs out from the
wild hedge,
Its cool fragrance clings to the autumn water.
Wang Chien, T'ang Dynasty

CHINESE CHAFING DISH. During the fall when the chrysanthemums are in season, this fragrant dish is very popular, either as a midnight snack or as refreshment when people gather for an evening of friendly conversation. The Chinese Chafing Dish is similar to those used in the West except that charcoal is burned at the base to supply the necessary heat, and a chimney goes up through the center. The ingredients given below are those used in China, but substitutions may easily be made to suit the fancy of the hostess.

1 chicken	3 cups sliced celery cabbage
7 cups water	8 chicken livers, sliced
3 tablespoons soy sauce	2 cups sliced fish
Salt to taste	4 cups hot cooked rice
1 bundle long rice	6 eggs
2 cups oil	
3 cups spinach, cut in 1-inch lengths	Petals of 4 large white chrysanthemums

Chrysanthemum

Skin chicken and remove all the meat from the bones. Slice breast meat very thin. Cover chicken bones and dark meat with 7 cups of water and add soy sauce. Bring to a boil and simmer 20 minutes. Add salt to taste. Put half of the bundle of long rice to soak in cold water. Heat oil and deep fry the other half.

Arrange ingredients on separate plates around the chafing dish in the following order: vegetables, meats, rice, raw eggs, and chrysanthemum petals. Heat chafing dish and add half of the hot stock. Invite each guest to take his chopsticks and place portions of the ingredients in that section of the chafing dish directly in front of him, in the following order: (1) Add a portion of each vegetable and let simmer 2 minutes. (2) Add a portion of chicken and fish and let simmer 3 minutes. (3) Add some of the long rice. (4) Break an egg into the chafing dish to poach. (5) Add chrysanthemum petals. When the eggs are poached let each guest fill his bowl ¼ full of cooked rice and then add ingredients from the chafing dish.

If a second serving of the fragrant food is desired, pour the remaining stock into the chafing dish and repeat process. Serves 6.

Mary Sia, Chinese Cookbook, University of Hawaii Press, 1956

CHRYSANTHEMUM SOUP. Pour 1 pint of milk in a pan, heat, and when it is just coming to the boil, stir in 2 tablespoons of flour and continue to stir until thick. Add the chopped petals of 1 large or several small chrysanthemums which have been previously soaked in boiling water for 2 minutes and stir for 10 minutes. Add sugar or salt to taste and serve hot.

CHRYSANTHEMUM *SALAD.* The French first scald the petals, then cool and mix with various salad greens and French dressing. It is also good as a garnish for fruit salad.

Another way: Take a mixture of white and yellow petals, but do not wash, mix with salad dressing containing a little sugar.

Still another way: Tear off the petals of some twenty flowers and wash them in several waters. Blanch them in slightly salted and acidulated water. Drain them and dry them in a linen cloth. Mix them with a salad made of potatoes, bottoms of artichokes, shrimps, and capers. Pour a little vinegar over all. Arrange the salad in a bowl and ornament it with cut beetroot and hard-boiled egg. You may add to the exotic character of this salad by seasoning it with a pinch of saffron. (Prosper Montagne'.)

The chrysanthemum has a history of cultivation in the orient for more than 2000 years.

It is the personal emblem of the Mikado.

The flag of Japan is not the rising sun, but a chrysanthemum with sixteen petals arranged around a disc.

Chrysanthemum

The Chinese cultivate them for food as well as beauty.

CHRYSANTHEMUM CHAFING POT.

First ingredients to go into the pot:
6-8 cups water
  2 tsp. salt
  1 tbsp. lard
Main ingredients for the pot and their preparation:
  1 big head of white chrysanthemum flower—Take off the petals and wash them clean.
  1 lb. celery cabbage—Wash and cut into shreds.
1/6 lb. peastarch noodles—Fry in deep oil for 1 min.
  (If you cannot get peastarch noodles in Chinatown you can substitute with
  ½ lb. very fine egg noodles. Prepare the noodles in the same way.)
  ¼ lb. spinach—Wash clean and leave whole.
  ½ lb. pork tenderloin—Cut into flying-thin slices.
      (Because the cooking time is short.)
White meat of 1 spring chicken of about 2-3 lbs.—Cut into flying-thin slices also. (Save the other parts of the chicken for other chicken dishes.)
  ½ lb. fresh shrimps—Take off the shells, peel off the dark gritty line along the back, and slice into two slices along the back. If the shrimps are big, slice again into thinner slices.
  ½ lb. chicken's, duck's, or pig's liver—Also cut into 3 flying-thin slices.
  4 pig's kidneys—Wash the kidneys and take off the outer thin skin. Cut off as many flying-thin slices as you can until you reach the central dark and white part, which should be thrown away.
  ½ lb. raw oysters without shell—Wash clean.
  2 tbsp. sherry
  1 tbsp. cornstarch
  2 tbsp. water

✐ Divide each ingredient into two parts and place each part in a small plate. In the case of the meat, the chicken, the liver, the shrimps, etc. arrange the slices in symmetrical designs.

Chrysanthemum

✎ Mix the sherry, cornstarch, and water together and put a little of the mixture on each of all the non-vegetables.

✎ Ingredients for sauce to be used during the eating:
½ cup soy sauce or shrimp sauce

✎ Sometimes a beaten raw egg with 1 tsp. soy sauce for the bowl of each person.

✎ The cooking and the eating: Place the 20 small dishes on the dining table. After the guests have been seated, bring on the electric stove (since the other cannot be had in America) and the pot which already has boiling water, lard and salt. These are placed in the center of the table. Everyone then uses his chopsticks and helps put all the vegetables and noodles in (but not the chrysanthemum). When the soup boils again, each person helps himself from the big pot into his own plate or bowl. Now the hostess puts in the chrysanthemum. She may then add salt, for soy sauce is never put into the big pot. Some times we break a whole raw egg into our bowl and then pour hot soup over it; sometimes we beat the egg in the bowl before pouring hot soup over it; and sometimes we like to place a couple of raw eggs in the big pot itself. This last process is now popularly known as "depth-charging."

✎ Chafing pots are usually served from November to March.

Buwei Yang Chao, How to Cook and Eat in Chinese
John Day Company, 1945

From the pavilion on the west side of the farm the chrysanthemum beds could be seen in full bloom. To the east and west were two lofty summer-houses, of which the eastern was surrounded with young peach trees . . . while the western . . . was provided with large collections of the chrysanthemum. It was now autumn and the abundant richness and beauty of the flowers spread around the base of the building like a variegated carpet of gold.

✎ *Their slender shadows fill the enclosure, and a scattered scent pervades the flower-beds . . . the deeper and lighter tints reflect a yellow light, and the leaves shine beneath the drops of dew. . . . The gazer sympathises with the languishing blossoms, bending their heads all faint and delicate.*

Sir J. F. Davis, Chrysanthemum Garden,
excerpt from The Fortunate Union, 1829

Chrysanthemum

GOOK FAR YU JOOK. (Fish chowder with Chrysanthemum Flower)

5 ozs. Soft Rice
4 Pints Water
½ oz. Ginger (fresh)
1 oz. Chung Choy (Preserved Parsnips in Bundles)
1 oz. Mai Fun (Rice Noodles)
1 lb. Dover Sole filleted
1 Egg, well beaten
1 Teaspoonful Cornflour
2 ozs. Yoon Boy (Dried Escallops)
1 Extra Large White Chrysanthemum Flower

(a) Place the Rice Noodles in a saucepan of boiling oil and cook for 2 seconds, then take out.
(b) Place the Rice, Water and Dried Escallops in a saucepan and boil for 2½ hours. First bring to a boil and then simmer.
(c) Remove all the petals from the flower, then wash them thoroughly.
(d) Cut the Dover Sole into very fine pieces. Mix the Cornflour with ½ cup of water to a smooth paste, then immerse the Fish into the Cornflour water.
(e) Cut the Preserved Parsnips and Ginger into very fine slices.
(f) Add the Preserved Parsnips, Ginger and Dover Sole to the Rice Chowder and cook for 2 minutes.
(g) Share out the prepared Chowder into four bowls, then place in each one, a few drops of Sesame Oil, a few drops of Soya Sauce, a little Pepper and Salt and a few drops of the oil in which the Rice Noodles were cooked. Stir well.
(h) Garnish each bowl with the Rice Noodles, the beaten Egg and a few fine slices of Spring Onions and Lettuce. Place on top the Chrysanthemum Petals.
(i) The Chowder must be served hot. When the Chowder is ready to be eaten, stir well so that the Chrysanthemum is well mixed with the Chowder.

Sao-ching Cheng, Chinese Cookery Book

"The ceremonial dish is a fish, usually sweet and sour. The Chinese in the Yantze area have a shad-like fish, the Samlai, which is probably the most delicious fish in its first runs, that can be found anywhere. When Samlai is done into a kind of salad with chrysanthemum blossoms, it is almost worth the labor of a trip around the world."

George Sokolsky, Sunday, November 25, 1962, New York Journal American

CLARY ᖷᖷᖷᖷᖷᖷᖷᖷᖷᖷᖷᖷᖷᖷᖷᖷᖷᖷᖷ

"It restores natural heat, and comforts the vital spirits, and helps the memory, and quickens the senses.

William Turner

CLARY WINE: Boil 5 gallons of water with 15 pounds of sugar. Skim it. When cool, stir in 2 ounces of compressed yeast; and pour the liquid on the clary flowers. The flowers must be gathered dry, and if you don't have enough, they may be added as you get them until you have put in four quarts of flowers. When it ceases to hiss and all the flowers are in, stop it up for four months. Rack it off and empty the barrel to the dregs. Add a quart of brandy and let it stand for another 6 to 8 weeks. Bottle it and keep for six months before drinking.

(Another recipe for clary wine suggests Malaga raisins as an ingredient.)

Clary is reminiscent of the Middle Ages when it was very popular in the use of wine, food and medicine.

TO MAKE A CLARY AMULET. Beat eight or ten Eggs, with a little Pepper, Salt and Nutmeg; then put into it two Gills of cream, and a Handful of Clary chopped very fine; Mix them well together, put some Butter or Beef-drippings in your Frying-pan, and when it is boiling hot, pour in your Amulet; fry it on both sides, and send it up hot. You may make one of Parsley and Chives the same way.

Elizabeth Cleland, Easy Method of Cookery, 1755

CLARY FRITTERS. Make a good stiff batter with half a pint of new milk, four eggs, and flour; grate in a little lemon-peel and some nutmeg, put in two ounces of powder sugar, and a small glass of brandy; then take a dozen Clary leaves, cut away the stalks, put them into batter, taking care that they have plenty of it on both sides; have a pan of boiling hog's-lard, put them in one by one, and fry them quick on both sides to a light brown; then take them out, lay them on a sieve to drain a moment, put them in a dish, strew powder sugar over them, and glaze them with a hot iron. Note—You may dress Comfrey or Mulberry leaves the same way.

> Richard Briggs, Receipt Book, 1788
> Many years Cook at the Globe Tavern, Fleet Street, the White Hart Tavern, Holborn, and at the Temple Coffee House.

Clary

(For a delightful luncheon dish serve the fritters with hollandaise sauce.)

TO MAKE A LIQUOR WHICH WILL GIVE A WINE TASTE TO ALL SORTS OF LIQUOR. Take some pounds of Clary-flowers, and as much Lees of Wine as will wet the Flowers, which must be grossly pounded; suffer them to macerate for some days; then distil and rectify them thrice on other flowers, and so putting some drops of it into water, or some other liquor, it will make it taste like Muscadine.

> Dictionnaire Oeconomique, M. Chomel,
> Translated by R. Bradley, 1725

CLOVER

The pedigree of honey
Does not concern the bee;
A clover, any time, to him
Is aristocracy.
> *Emily Dickinson*

Clover symbolizes the Holy Trinity.

RED CLOVER WINE
4 quarts red clover flowers
4 lb. white sugar
1 oz. yeast
2 oranges
3 lemons
4 qts. water
1 cup warm water

Gather the clover on a dry day. If it is at all dewy, leave it to dry in the sun. Remove the flowers from the stalks, keeping only mature ones at their prime.

Measure them, put them into a crock, and pour over them the boiling water. While the liquor is cooling, slice the oranges and lemons, and when it is lukewarm put them in, together with the sugar. Dissolve yeast in 1 cup warm water and leave for five days, stirring twice daily; strain, and leave for another five days; strain again, and leave for three days longer. Bottle, leaving the corks loose for ten days; then cork up, and leave for a month.

Clover   In the early days of San Francisco wild clover cordial was very popular.

FLOWER HONEY. Pick 6 red clovers, 30 white clovers, and 4 full blown roses. Boil 5 cups sugar with 1¼ cups water and 1 level teaspoon alum for a minute or until it is clear. Pour over the flowers, let stand 10 minutes and bottle.

CLOVER SANDWICHES. Spread a round of white bread with clover butter. Lay on it a circle of clover flowerets with the petals curling out over the edge of the bread. Place another buttered bread round on top.

TO MAKE AQUAMIRABILIS THE LADY ATKINSES WAY. Take Cardimum, cubibs, mellilot (a form of clover) flowers, gallingall nutmegs; ginger mace and Cloves of each a dram all these must be bruised and infused one night in 3 pints of white wine one pint of aquavite one pint of the juice of salendine the next day distil them in a close Still twill run a pottle keep the first quart of it by it Selfe you must put to the whole three quarters of a pound of white Sugar candy beaten very finely. Divide it between 2 glasses and let the mirabilis drop into the Sugar candy and it will dissolve when you put all these things into your close Still put in a little bag of Saffron put to ye infusion a handfull of ye tops of rosemary flowers which will give it a delicious taste.

H. W. Lewer, A Book of Simples, 1908

Melilot water improves other flavors.

Bread made from the seeds and dried flowers is much esteemed and considered very nutritious and wholesome in Scotland.

CLOVER TEA. Make from dried flower heads, 1 teaspoonful to a cup of hot water.

CLOVER VINEGAR. Pour nine quarts of boiling water over one quart of molasses. When cool add one cake of yeast dissolved in a little warm water, and add also two quarts of clover blossoms. Cover for a week let set then strain and bottle.

POT LUCK
AT A FIFTH AVENUE FLORIST'S

I never witnessed such a thing
    As potted four-leaf clovers till
I saw them stocked by Mr. Schling,
    Each ornamented with a frill

Clover

Labelled "Good Luck." How glib, how bold
    Of him to think that luck's a thing
That can be snared and reared and sold.
    How impudent of Mr. Schling!
        Margaret Fishback, One to a Customer

The Red Clover is the state flower of Vermont.

PICKLED FLOWERS FOR SALLETS. Take after picking clean from their stalks any wholesome flowers whatever. Put a layer of sugar in a pot, and then a layer of flowers, after well washing and drying them and dreeing them from any stalk and any white ends; then alternately more sugar and flowers till the pots be filled. Press them well down and then fill up with the best distilled vinegar. Cork tightly and keep for use in a dry place. They will last a year.

Brer Rabbit included clover in his diet, along with calamus root and Winnianni-mus grass. He was also very fond of camomile.

Sapsago cheese is a hay cheese, flavored with melilot. It comes from Switzerland and is made of skimmed milk and herbs. Grate some into a rich cream sauce and serve hot on toast. The fragrance is delightful — as fresh as a field of clover mixed with Alpine blooms.

SERENDIPITY. Take a slice of good white bread and lavish sweet butter on it, then a slice of one of the flower cheeses, lastly grate a bit of Sapsago on top. Add "serendipity" to your vocabulary and life—you'll have more fun.

CLOVER BUTTER. Take fresh petals of clover and make in the same way as other flower butters.

Bring me an unguent made of scented roots,
Pomander of Green herbs, and scarlet fruits,
Verbena leaves, mallow and melilot
And balmy Rosemary.
        Mary Webb

To Make A Bath For Melancholy. Take Mallowes, pellitory of wall, of each three handfuls; Camomile flowers, Melilot flowers, of each one handful; Senerick seed, one ounce, and boil them in nine gallons of water till they come to three—then put in a quart of milk and go into bloud warm or something warmer. The Fairfax Stillroom

Clover

Let the multitude perish them, which was born in vain; and let my grape be kept, and my plant; for with great labour have I made it perfect. Nevertheless, if thou wilt cease yet seven days more, (but thou shalt not fast in them, but go into a field of flowers, where no house is builded, and eat only the flowers of the field; taste no flesh, drink no wine, but eat flowers only;) and pray unto the Highest continually, then will I come and talk with thee.
So I went my way into the field which is called Ardath, like as he commanded me; and there I sat among the flowers, and did eat of the herbs of the field, and the meat of the same satisfied me. After seven days I sat upon the grass, and my heart was vexed within me, like as before.

Apocrypha, 2 Esdras, 9:8—27

CLOVES

"Mr. Trotter acquiesced in this agreeable proposal: and having deposited his book in his coat pocket, accompanied Mr. Weller to the top, where they were soon occupied in discussing an exhilarating compound, formed by mixing together in a pewter vessel, certain quantities of British Hollands and the fragrant essence of the clove."

Dickens, Pickwick Papers

Nothing will grow under a clove tree, as it absorbs all moisture. It has bright green leaves, peach colored buds and blue flowers.

"The Portugal women that dwell in the East Indies draw from the cloves when they be green a certain liquor of distillation of a most fragrant smell which comforteth the heart and is of all cordials the most effective."

William Coles, Adam in Eden

38

Cloves

FLOWERING CLOVE SYRUP. Pick 1 lb. of fresh-gathered cloves, and put the petals in a jar closing hermetically: Boil 3 lbs. of distilled water, pour it boiling over the flowers, close the jar, and let them steep therein for six hours: Strain the whole through a broth-napkin, and filter the liquid: Put 3 lbs. of loaf sugar, broken in pieces, into a sugar boiler: add the filtered infusion, and boil until the syrup registers 30 degrees on the saccharometer: When cold bottle the syrup, and keep it in a cool place.

Jules Gouffe, Book of Preserves

In the Eleventh Century a pound of cloves was equal in barter to two cows.

Cloves are such a common ingredient in modern cooking, it would be impossible to name all its uses, but a few are: in baked ham, various vegetables, especially candied sweet potatoes, mincemeat, preserves, spice cakes, cookies, doughnuts, gingerbread, game, sausages, and many other good things.

CLOVE SYRUP. Put three or four ounces of cloves in a mortar and bruise them well, mix with a pint of white wine and set on the back of the stove or in a warm place for several days, strain through a cloth, add three cups of sugar and boil until it reaches a syrup constituency.

✒ *"It is a pity that the meaning of this word is lost in English. It conveys the most vivid description of the spice to which it refers, for the word is no other than the French* clou de Girofla — *that is, a nail of the* caryophyllum. *One of the charms of gastronomy is in its names and the interesting associations which they awaken. It is always to be regretted, therefore, when on the one hand, as too often happens, names are multiplied without reason, and when on the other hand happy names are forgotten or lost in corruption.*
✒ *It may be added that a clove of garlic does not mean a nail; it means something cloven.*

Auguste Kettner, The Book of the Table 1877

COLTSFOOT

"Though sin and Satan hath plunged mankind into an ocean of infirmities, yet the mercy of God which is over all His works maketh grass to grow upon the mountains and herbs for the use of man and hath not only stamped upon them (as upon every man) a distinct forme, but also given them particular signatures, whereby a man may read even in legible characters the use of them. Heart Trefoyle is so called not only because the shape is triangular like the heart of a man, but also because each leaf contains the perfect icon of an heart and that in its proper colour, viz. flesh colour.

Hounds tongue hath a form not much different from its name which will tye the tongues of hounds so that they shall not bark at you.

William Cole, Art of Simpling

It is a pity that all fruits and flowers, and animals too, except those with good names, could not be passed in review before somebody with a genius for christening, as the creatures did before Adam in Paradise, and so have new names given them, worthy of their creation.

Leigh Hunt, A Flower For Your Window

COLTSFOOT WINE.
2 qts. Coltsfoot flowers
1 gallon of water
3 lbs. sugar
1 tea-cupful of raisins to 4 gallons
3 Seville Oranges
2 Lemons

The flowers should be measured when freshly gathered, then spread out on trays to dry. When quite dry put them into a pan and pour the boiling water on them and let them stand for three days, stirring three times each day. Then strain off the liquor, add the sugar, and boil well for half an hour. When cold put some yeast on a piece of toast into the liquid and let it ferment. Next day, remove the toast, put the liquor into a cask and add the raisins, oranges, and lemons, cut up. Let it stand for three months, and then it will be ready to bottle.

Dr. Fernald in Edible Wild Plants of Eastern North America recommends coltsfoot-candy, a delicious confection, and "one of the few medicines which one wholly craves." The foliage and the young inflorescenes of the sweet colts-foot (petasites palmatus) he says are frequently cooked and are very good. Why not take up the study of wild flowers as a hobby? You will find yourself immersed in the mysteries of nature—for instance you will discover that the Coltsfoot takes its name from the shape of its leaf, it is supposed to resemble a donkey's hoof. If you have lost the sense of wonder it will return and spiritual horizons will retreat into space. Also, it is your right. Aldo Leopold believed "the chance to find a pasque flower is a right as inalienable as free speech."

Coltsfoot

In the 18th Century pancakes were made using Coltsfoot, particularly those for Shrove Tuesday.

Coltsfoot Rock is now made in fluted sticks and flavored with anise or dill.

COSTMARY ～～～～～～～～～～～～～～～～～

Fresh Costmary and breathful Camomile
Dull poppy and drink quickening Setewale.
Vein heating Verven and head purging Dill
Sound savory and basil harty-hale.
        Michael Drayton

During medieval times the plant was associated with St. Mary and was cultivated for salads.

COSTMARY CONSERVE. Pick the flowers when they are dry, only use the petals, weigh them and to every pound of petals take two pounds and a half of loaf sugar. Beat the two together in a stone mortar, adding the sugar by degrees. When well incorporated press into gallipots without first boiling. Tie over paper and leather on the top of the paper and it will keep seven years.
        Mrs. Glasse

The symbolical meaning is impatience.

Costmary has a peppery lemonish flavor and at one time the English used it extensively to flavor ale. It is also one of the plants that Charlemagne had in his garden. It is particularly good with game, and is also good to flavor cakes and jellies.

Costmary

There are one hundred and thirty different herbs in Chartreuse and this is probably one of them.

COWSLIPS ～～～～～～～～～～～～～～～

And I serve the fairy queen
To dew her orbs upon the green;
The cowslips tall her pensioners be,
In their gold coats spots you see;
These be rubies, fairy flavours,
In those freckles live their savours:
> *I must go seek some dew-drops here;*
> *And hang a pearl in every cowslip's ear,*
> *Farewell, thou lob of spirits, I'll be gone,*
> *Our queen, and all her Elves, come here anon.*

> William Shakespeare, A Midsummer Nights Dream
> Act II, Scene I

SYRUPE OF COWSLIP. Instead of running water you must take distilled water of Cowslips, put thereto your Cowslip flowers clean picked, and the green knobs in the bottome cut off, and therewith boyle up a Syrupe. It is good against the Frensie, comforting and staying the head in all hot Agues.

A Book of Fruits and Flowers, 1653

COWSLIP SYRUP. Three pounds of the fresh blossoms infused in five pints of boiling water, and then simmered with sugar to a syrup.

Dr. Fernie, Herbal Simples, 1897

PICKLED COWSLIPS. Pickt very clean; to each pound of Flowers allow about one pound of Loaf Sugar and one pint of White Wine Vinegar, which boil to a Syrup, and cover it scalding hot.

John Evelyn, Acetaria, 1699

Cowslips

COWSLIP CONSERVE. Gather your flowers in the midst of the day when all the dew is off, then cut off all the white, leaving none but the yellow blossome so picked and cut, before they wither, weigh out ten ounces, taking to every ten ounces of them, or greater proportion, if you please, eight ounces of the best refined Sugar, in fine powder, put the Sugar into a pan, and candy it, with as little water as you can, then taking it off the fire, put in your Flowers by little and little, never ceasing to stir them till they be dry, and enough; then put them into glasses or gallypots, and keep them dry for your use. These are rather Candied than Conserved Cowslips.

A Book of Fruits and Flowers, 1653

COWSLIP TART. Take the blossoms of a gallon of cowslips, mince them exceedingly small, and beat them in a mortar; put to them a handful or two of grated *Naples* biscuit, and about a pint and a half of cream, boil them a little over the fire, then take them off, and beat them in eight eggs with a little cream; if it does not thicken, put it over again till it does; take heed that it does not curdle. Season it with sugar, rose-water, and a little salt; bake it in a dish or little open tartes. It is best to let your cream be cold before you stir in the eggs.

The Court and Country Confectioner, by an
Ingenious Foreigner, now head Confectioner to the
Spanish Ambassador in England-London, 1770

COWSLIP WINE. Take two pounds an half of powder sugar, and two gallons of water; boil them half an hour, taking care to skim it as the scum rises; then pour it into a tub to cool, adding to it the rind of two lemons. When cold put four quarts of the flowers of cowslips to the liquor, and with it the juice of two lemons. Let it stand in the tub two days, observing to stir it every two or three hours. Then put it in the barrel, and after it has stood about three weeks, or a month, bottle it, not forgetting to put a lump of sugar into each bottle.

Mrs. Mary Cole, The Ladies Complete Guide
London, 1791

RAINBOW TART
A roasted Ant that's nicely done
By one small atom of the Sun;
These are Flies' Eggs in moon-shone poached
This is a Flea's thigh in Collops scotch'd.
'Twas hunted yesterday i' th' Park,
And like t'have scap'd us in the dark.
This is a dish entirely new
Butterflies' brains dissolv'd in Dew;
These Lovers' vows, these Courtier's hopes,
Things to be eat by microscopes:
These sucking mites, a Glow-worm's heart,
This is a delicious Rainbow-Tart.
Dr. William King, Orpheus and Euridice, 1776
(Original works of William King, LLD. Vol. 3 First printed in 1704)

Cowslips

A CORDIAL TO PROCURE SLEEP AND REST. Take a quart of the best unsophisticated Claret wine; put into it a handful of Cowlip flowers, one handful of Borage-flowers & a slip of Rosemary; set it on the fire & when it is ready to burn, smother it in the first flame, & keep it in the pot till it is cold; then strain it, & put thereto three ounces of Clove gilly-flowers well mingled together, & every night at your going to Bed, take a Wine glass of it, you must not warm it the second time.

George Hartman, The True Preserver, 1682

SYRUP OF COWSLIPS.

Take of fresh cowslip flowers, twelve ounces
Boiling water . . . one pint.
Infuse for twenty-four hours and strain; then add
White sugar . . . half a pound.
Boil gently to the consistence of a syrup.

Richard Brooks, A New Family Herbal
London, 1871

COWSLIP CREAM. Take the Cowslips when they are green, and in Blossom, and bruise them in a Mortar; and to be a good Handful or two so done, put a Quart of Cream, and boil it up gently with them; put in a blade of Mace; season with fine Sugar and Orange-Flower water; strain it, and draw it up with the Yolks of two or three Eggs, and clip off the Tops of a Handful of the Flowers, and draw it up, and dish it as you please.

Charles Carter, the Practical Cook
London, 1730

LEGEND. Peter let his keys drop when he was told that a duplicate key to Heaven had been made. Where the keys fell the Cowslip broke from the ground.

In flower language COWSLIP means Winning Grace.

"Smiled like a knot of Cowslips on the cliff."
Blair

Cowslips

COWSLIP PASTE. Cowslip paste or cheese was much made and relished by our ancestors. Its deep yellow colour makes it very attractive, and it is supposed to be a cure for giddiness.

COWSLIP CHEESE. Infuse the heads of the flowers in boiling water (five pints of hot water to three pounds of flowers). Leave them for twenty four hours, and then strain and boil the liquid with enough sugar to make a thick syrup; reduce till a thick paste and pour into small glasses.

HONEYCOMB CAKES OF COWSLIPS. Take about ½ pound of sugar. Sift it through a hair sieve. Wet it a little more than for a candy with a little water; boil it almost to candy height, then put in the petals of the flowers. Boil them a little in the candy or it will be too thin, then put in card coffins.
Mrs. Eales, Confectioner to King William III and Queen Anne

COWSLIP VINEGAR. Cowslip 'pips' 2 pints; white wine vinegar 1 pint; lump sugar 1 lb; brandy 1 wineglassful; soda water.
Gather the cowslips on a dry day; pick all the flower 'pips' from the stalks, put them into a basin. Pour on white wine vinegar. Let them remain 3 days to infuse; wet a piece of muslin with vinegar, strain off the liquor from the 'pips' into a stone jar; add 1 pound sugar to every pint of liquor. Stir from time to time until the sugar is dissolved, then cover the jar. Set it on the fire in a saucepan of boiling water. Let boil for one hour. Add 3 ozs. brandy to each pint. Bottle when cold and seal. Dilute it with soda water as a cooling drink.

Children delight in making Cowslip Balls, or 'tosties' from the flowers. The umbels are picked off close to the top of the main flower-stalk and about fifty to sixty are hung across a string which may be stretched for convenience between the backs of two chairs. The flowers are then pressed carefully together and the string tied tightly so as to collect them into a ball. Care must be taken to choose only such heads or umbels in which all the flowers are open, as otherwise the surface of the ball will be uneven.

"I'll drown all high thoughts in the Lethe of Cowslip Wine."
Pope

COWSLIP CREAM. Take two ounces of Syrup of Cowslips and boil up in your Cream and season it as before. Thicken it with the Yolks of three or four Eggs, and put in two ounces of candy'd Cowslips when you draw it up. Dish it in Basons and Glasses, and strew over some candy'd cowslips.

> Joseph Cooper, The Receipt Book, Cook to Charles I, 1654

Cowslips

TO KEEP COWSLIPS FOR SALATES. Take a quart of White Wine Vinegar, and halfe a quarter of a pound of fine beaten Sugar, and mix them together, then take your Cowslips, pull them out of the podds, and cut off the green Knobs at the lower end, put them into the pot or glasse wherein you mind to keep them, and well shaking the Vinegar and Sugar together in the glasse wherein they were before, powre it upon the Cowslips, and so stirring them morning and evening to make them settle for three weeks, keep them for your use.

> A Book of Fruits and Flowers, 1653

TO MAKE A COWSLIP-TART. Take the Blossoms of a Gallon of Cowslips, mince them exceeding small, and beat them in a Mortar, put to them a Handful or two of grated Naples-Bisket, and about a Pint and a Half of Cream, boil them a little over the Fire, then take them off, and beat them in eight Eggs with a little Cream; if it doth not thicken, put it over again till it doth; take heed that it doth not curdle. Season it with Sugar, Rose-water, and a little Salt; bake it in a Dish or little open Tartes. It is best to let your Cream be cold before you stir in the Eggs.   Patrick Lamb, Royal Cookery 1710

COWSLIP SALAD. Cook some cowslip (tender) leaves, and make a mold of lemon gelatine — add cowslip leaves. After it is set, unmold and garnish with mayonnaise, slices of hard-boiled eggs, cream cheese balls rolled in paprika, and finally, scatter with cowslip petals.

COWSLIP BUTTER. Follow the recipe for rose butter.

COWSLIP RED WINE.   18 Gallons cold water
40 lbs. Smyrna raisins
Ferment the above. Then mix
 3 lbs. sliced beet root
 2 ozs. red tartar
14 lbs. cowslip flowers
 1 oz. powdered cloves and mace
 1 gallon brandy
This will make 18 gallons.

> MacKenzie's 5,000 Receipts

COWSLIP WHITE WINE.   18 gallons water
35 lbs. Malaga raisins
Ferment the above. Then mix
 2 ozs. white tartar
16 lbs. cowslip flowers
 1 gallon white brandy
This will make 18 gallons.

Ibidem

Use cowslips for stuffing meats.

Cowslips   To Make A Tarte Of Marigoldes Prymroses Or Couslips. Take the same stuffe to euery of them that you do to the tarte of borage and the same ceasonygne.

A Proper Newe Booke of Cokerye, 1575

COWSLIP CREAM. First thicken some cream with whites of eggs beaten to a froth, then add a little Cowslip syrup and serve in glasses, garnishing with candied Cowslips.

Upon a mushroom's head,   *Our Table do we spread,*
A Corn of rye of Wheat   *Is Manchet which we eat,*
Pearly drops of Dew we drink
In Acorn Cups fill'd to the brink.
The Brains of Nightingales,   *The unctuous dew of Snails*
Between two nut-shells stew'd   *Is Meat that's eas'ly chew'd.*
The Beards of Mice
Do make a feast of wond'rous price.
On tops of Dewy Grass   *So nimbly do we pass,*
The young and tender stalks   *Ne'er bends when we do walk;*
Yet in the morning may be seen
Where we the night before have been.
The Grasshopper and Fly   *Serve for our Minstrelsie;*
Grace said, we dance awhile,   *And so the time beguile.*
And when the moon doth hide her head
The Glow-worm lights us home to bed.

Joshua Poole, English Parnassus, 1657

PRIMEROLLE. (Cowslips). To make primerolle in pasthe take blanched almonds and flour of primerolle grind it and temper it with swet wyne and good brothe drawinge into the thik mylk put it into a pot with sugar salt and saffron that it have colour like primerolle and boil it that it be stondings and alay it with flour of rise and serue it as a standinge potage and strawe theron flour of primerolle aboue and ye may diaper it with rape rialle in dressinge of some other sewe.

A Noble Boke Off Cookry Ffor a Prince Houssolde or
Any Other Estately Houssolde, A rare Ms. c. 1470

PICKLED COWSLIPS. Wash, dry the flowers, and remove the green knobs at the bottom. To each pound of flowers allow 1 lb. of syrup and 1 pint of vinegar. Boil all to a syrup, put into dry, warm jars, and seal.

Serve fresh cowslips on breakfast cereal as a decorative touch.

Cowslips

COWSLIP PUDDING. Take the blossoms of a Gallon of Cowslips, mince them small and beat them in a Mortar, put in them two handfuls of grated Naples Bisket, a pint and half of Cream, boil them a little on the Fire, then take them off, and beat in eight Eggs with a little Cream; if it do not thicken set it on the Fire till it does gently thicken a little, but take heed it don't Curdle; then take it off, and season it with Sugar and Rose Water, let it stand till it be quite cold before you put in the Eggs; butter your Dish, and put in your Pudding: a little more than half an hour bakes it; strow Sugar on, serve it up.

William Salmon, The Family Dictionary, London,
Printed for D. Rhodes, at the Star, the Corner of
Bride-Lane, in Fleet-street, 1705

Our grandmothers mixed conserve of cowslip petals with tea.

Cowslips have the odor of anise, because of the volatile oil identical with Mannite. They have soporific powers.

The old Saxon name is "Cusloppe". In the nineteenth century they were often called Paigles.

COWSLIP MEAD. Dissolve 5 lb. honey in 5 gallons water, and reduce by about a quart by boiling. Skim well, and pour a little of the boiling liquid over 5 lemons cut in slices. Pour the remainder of the liquid into a tub over 2½ pecks of cowslip pips and let it remain for 12 hours. Now mix the two liquors together and stir in 2 oz. compressed yeast creamed with a little sugar. Add some sprigs of *sweetbriar*. Stir frequently for 3 or 4 days, strain it, pour it into a clean cask. Let it stand for six months. Bottle and use as required.

CRYSTALLIZED COWSLIPS. Gather the cowslips when full blown, wash gently and then place them in the shade to dry. Cut the stems to within two inches of the heads, and put the heads upon the wire tray of a crystallizing tin, pushing the stalks through the holes so that the flowers shall be upright. When the tray is full put it in the tin, and fill up with crystallizing syrup: pouring it round the sides and not over the flowers or you will flatten them.

Cowslips

COWSLIP CAKE. It is the custom in country places to use both fresh and dried cowslip 'pips' (i.e. the yellow corolla of the cowslip) in cakes as flavoring instead of currants. Primrose petals were used in the same way for the same purpose.

CORDIAL WATER OF COWSLIPS. Take two Quarts of Cowslip-peepes, a Slip of Balm, two Sprigs of Rosemary, a Stick of Cinnamon, half an Orange-peel, half a Lemon-peel, a Pint of Brandy, and a Pint of Ale; lay all these to steep twelve Hours, then distil them in a cold still.

E. Moxon, English Housewifry, 1758

COWSLIP PUDDING. Gather the flowers of a Peck of Cowslips, cut them small and pound them with Half a Pound of Naples Biscuit (lady fingers) grated and three Pints of Cream. Boil them a little; then take them off the Fire, and beat up sixteen Eggs, with a little Cream and a little Rosewater. Sweeten to your Palate. Mix it well together, butter a Dish and pour it in. Bake, and when it is enough, throw fine Sugar over and serve it up.

Mrs. Glasse

In the eighteenth century cowslip puddings were considered to be "Very Elegant".

COWSLIP PUDDING. For this you will need two ounces of sirup of Cowslips boiled in one quart of cream, seasoned with a blade of Mace, fine sugar and orange-flower water, thickened with the yolks of 3 or 4 eggs. Put this into small dishes and strew the top with candied cowslips.

Joseph Cooper, Cook to Charles I 1654

TO MAKE COWSLIP OR PRIMROSE WINE. Take three Gallons of fair water, put into it six Pounds of the finest Sugar, boil them together half an hour, or more, taking off the Scum carefully as it rises, then pour it into a Pan or Tub to cool; when it is almost cold take a Spoonful of Ale Yeast, and beat it well with six Ounces of Syrup of lemon, mix this with the Liquor by tossing it up and down; then take a Gallon of picked Cowslips or Primroses, bruise them in a Marble Mortar, and put them into the Liquor; let them work together two or three

Days; then strain it off, and put it into a Vessel that is just fit for it; Two or Three Days after stop it close, and three Weeks or a Month after that bottle it off, putting a Lump of Sugar into every Bottle. If it is well corked it will keep a Year.   Mrs. Martha Bradley, late of Bath, The British
Housewife, or the Cook, Housekeeper's and
Gardiner's Companion, London 1770

The Cowslip is a fairy flower and is sometimes known as Fairy Cups.

Cowslips

A FLOWER PUDDING. Mince cowslip flowers, clove, gillyflowers, rose petals and Spinach of each a handful, take a slice of Manchet (white bread) and scald it with cream. Add a pound of blanch'd Almonds pounded small with Rose-water, a quarter of a Pound of Dates sliced and cut small, the yolks of three eggs, a handful of Currants and sweeten all with Sugar. When boiled pour Rose-water over and scrape Sugar on. Then serve up.

John Nott, Receipt Book, Cook to the Duke of Bolton, 1723

Chloris of Greek descent, or Flora of Roman descent, is the goddess of spring and flowers. The West Wind or Zephyrus is her husband.
"Rise, and put on your Foliage, and be seene
To come forth, like the Spring-time, fresh and greene,
And sweet as Flora."

CYCLAMEN

I of the gout remove the very seed
And all the humours which that torment breed,
Thorns, splinters, nails I draw, who wondering stand
How they could so come forth without a hand.
Abraham Cowley

DOLMA OF DISTINCTION.

1 lb. minced lamb	chopped parsley
1 cup cooked rice	chopped mint (or ⅛ teaspoon cinnamon)
2 medium sized tomatoes	2 chopped Bell peppers
1 teaspoon lemon juice	¼ cup pinenuts
chopped garlic	salt and coarse-ground pepper
a pinch of coriander	A dozen cyclamen leaves

Blanch the cyclamen leaves. Mix the other ingredients and roll up in cyclamen leaves, add lemon juice and cook in a casserole for half an hour. The usual way is to roll in vine leaves, which are packed in brine, canned or bottled, and easy to procure.

Samuel Chamberlain in "Bouquet de France" speaks of "the mountain hams from the flower-fed pigs, with the overtones, real or fancied, of cyclamen."

Cyclamen

The tubers of cyclamen, which are given to swine for food, therefore commonly known as sow-bread, are also baked or made into cakes and are supposed to be aphrodisiacal in effect.

In flower symbology cyclamen represents diffidence.

DAISY

Trampled underfoot,
The Daisy lives and strikes its root
Into the lap of time; centuries may come
And pass away into the silent tombs
And still the child, hid in the womb of time
Shall smile and pluck them, when this simple rhyme
Shall be forgotten; like a churchyard stone,
Or lingering he, unnoticed and alone.
            J. Clare, The Eternity of Nature

Proverb: When you can put your foot on seven daisies summer is come.

DAISY WINE. Over four quarts of daisy blossoms, picked off the stalks, pour one gallon of boiling water. Let it stand all night; then drain the liquid off and boil it for ten minutes. When it is lukewarm add one yeast cube, two lemons and two oranges sliced, a cupful of raisins and three pounds of white sugar. Cover the crock with a cloth and let it stand three weeks to ferment. Skim it, strain and bottle it.

"And then last week I had a dinner party and told the twins and Christopher not to go in the living room, not to use the guest towels in the bathroom, and not to leave the bicycles on the front steps. However, I neglected to tell them not to eat the daisies on the dining-room table. This was a serious omission, as I discovered when I came upon my centerpiece — a charming three-point arrangement of green stems."
Jean Kerr, Please Don't Eat the Daisies

Daisy

In the 15th Century daisies were used extensively in salads, and in one of the troubadour romances it states that they are good to allay hunger. Vicomte Mauduit, five hundred years later, also finds the daisy good for salads.

Dark ages clasp the daisy root.

James Joyce, Finnegan's Wake

After reading a detailed account of the daisy, Walter de la Mare said, "Much thus aided, concerning our daisy, we have now shared with Rousseau, but, as poets repeatedly urge, we are no nearer the secret of its very being, of its 'life', of its unique individuality, of the intention of its creation, and of the ultimate destiny and appearance and purpose of its children's children to the n-th generation than, apart from what our faith and reason declare, we are concerning our own."
Walter De La Mare, Pleasure and Speculations
London, 1940

The botanical name for Daisy is *Bellis Perennis* but some of the common names are:

A Thousand Charms, Bachelor's Buttons, Bairnwort, Banwood, Banwort, Benner-gowan, Bennest, Bennet, Benwort, Bessy-Banwood, Billy Button, Boneflower, Bonwort, Briswort, Bruisewort, Catposy, Cockiloorie, Confery, Less Consound, Cumfirie, Day's Eye, Daiseyghe, Shepherd's Daisy, Dog Daisy, Children's Daisy, Dazey, Dickdaisy, Ewegowan, Gowam, May Gowan, Gowlan, Mary Gowlan, Hen- and chickens, Herb Margaret, Little Easter Flower, March Daisy, Margaret's herb, Marguerite; Maudlinwort, Measure of Love, Mother of Thousands, Silver Penny, and Sweep.

Daisy: Innonence and fidelity.

DANDELION ⤮⤮⤮⤮⤮⤮⤮⤮⤮⤮⤮⤮⤮⤮

Star-disked Dandelions, just as we see them,
Lying in the grass, like sparks that have leapt
From kindling suns of fire.
> Oliver Wendell Holmes, The Professor
> at the Breakfast Table

DANDELION JELLY SALAD.

2 tablespoons gelatin	5 tablespoons vinegar
¼ cup cold water	1 teaspoon salt
4 tablespoons sugar	¼ teaspoon paprika
½ teaspoon celery salt	1 small onion sliced thin
1 teaspoon onion juice	1 can sweet red pepper, minced
1 hard cooked egg	1 cup inner tender leaves of dandelion

Soak gelatin until soft in cold water. Dissolve in hot water. Add all other ingredients except egg, and mix well. Cut white of egg in rings, arrange around side of mold, rinsed with cold water. Pour in mixture and chill until firm. Turn jelly from mould, garnish with fresh dandelion leaves and blossoms. Serve with salad dressing.
> New York State College of Agriculture at Cornell
> Ithaca, N.Y., 1917

DANDELION SOUP.
1 cupful dandelion pulp
1 tablespoon butter
1 tablespoon flour
1 cup milk
salt and pepper
yolk of hard cooked egg

Make a white sauce and add to it the dandelion pulp. Just before serving add yolk of egg which has been pressed through a sieve.
> Ibidem

DANDELION TIMBALES.
2 eggs beaten
1¼ cup milk
2 tablespoons melted butter
½ teaspoon salt
pinch of pepper
1 teaspoon onion juice
1 cup chopped cooked dandelion greens

Mix ingredients in order given. Turn into buttered molds, place molds in pan of hot water and bake in moderate oven, bake until firm. Remove, serve with tomato sauce.

Ibidem

(This mixture would also be good served on bread fried in butter.)

Dandelion DANDELION OMELET. 1 cup dandelion hearts, 4 eggs. Fry the hearts of very white dandelions in butter or butter substitute, and mix them with the well-beaten eggs. Cook like an ordinary French omelet. The taste resembles an asparagus-top omelet.

The New Butterick Cookbook, revised by Flora Rose
Butterick Publishing Company, 1924

DANDELION AND BEET SALAD.
Salde de Pissenlit
aux Betteraves

If you have a garden you can easily grow dandelions. In fact you cannot help their growing. Cover them with a flat stone or a tile and they will get beautifully white. Use only the hearts, add about the same quantity of beets and dress with plain oil and vinegar, salt and pepper. It is really a very good winter salad, though it is not much thought of in England.

X. Marcel Boulestin

Symbolic of----Rustic oracle.

DANDELION STOUT.   1 oz. balm
                    5 ozs. dandelion herb
                    5 ozs. ground ginger
                    2 ozs. yellow dock
                   35 grns. Saccharine 550
                 2½ lbs. sugar
                   10 galls. water

Directions. Boil the ingredients in half the amount of water for 15 minutes, then pour through a strainer on to the sugar and saccharine. Stir until dissolved, then add the remainder of the water. Add a sufficient quantity of yeast and allow it to work for 12 hours at a temperature of from 65 to 70 degrees F. Skim off the yeast and bottle for use.

DANDELION SHRUB. (Good for Midsummer) Two quarts of blossoms. Wash and pour on them one gallon of boiling water. Let it stand over night, strain through double cheesecloth, add juice of three lemons and four pounds of granulated sugar. Heat until sugar is dissolved. Strain and bottle in airtight bottles. Serve in glasses with a little chipped ice. A delicious, healthful drink.

Wild flowers are the philanthropists of nature.

Dandelion

DANDELION BEER.

> 4 or 5 qts. dandelions
> 2 ounces root ginger, bruised
> 2 lemons
> 2 ounces cream of tartar
> 2 pounds brown sugar
> 1 ounce yeast
> piece of toast
> 2 gallons water

Put the water into a pan, then the freshly gathered dandelion roots, leaves, etc., and the bruised ginger. Boil for 10 minutes. Pour the liquid over the sugar and cream of tartar and divided lemons in an earthenware pan. When nearly cold, put in the yeast on a piece of toast. Leave for 12 hours. Strain carefully, and bottle in 3 days. Ready for use in a week and onwards.

ANOTHER DANDELION OMELET: Take very small dandelion buds—which are just about to open and toss them in butter over a low low heat. Then add eggs. By that time the buds will be open (caused by the heat). Served with hot buttered toast you have a very delicious luncheon dish.

EASTER PUDDING (ENGLISH STYLE). Take a handful of dandelion leaves and a handful of nettles and cook about 20 minutes. Strain and chop. Add some cooked barley (or oatmeal), a diced hard-boiled egg, and season with salt, pepper and butter. Put into a casserole and heat before using.

YUBLO CAKE. In the chapter on Arabian cooking Jean Conil, in the fine book "Haute Cuisine", mentions "Yublo" cake, made of honey, olive oil, flour, rose petals and dandelion flowers.

Hecate entertained Theseus with dandelion water.

Dandelion has some Vitamin B and a great deal of Vitamin C.

DANDELION SALAD. Gather young dandelion leaves, wash and pick carefully. Drain and dry well, place in salad bowl and add a dressing of oil and vinegar, and two tablespoons of chopped chives. Decorate with petals. If a bacon dressing is preferred, then cut bacon slices in small pieces, fry until desired crispness is attained, then add a little vinegar to the pan and pour all over the salad.

Dandelion

Although Europe and America recognized the tonic effect of the dandelion, England was slow in appreciating it, which prompted Dr. Culpepper to write in 1770: "You see here what Virtues this common Herb hath, and that's the reason the French and Dutch so often eat them in the Spring; and now if you look a little farther, you may see plainly, without a pair of Spectacles, that Foreign Physicians are not so Selfish as ours are, but more communicative of the Virtue of Plants to People."

Lord Macaulay "hated dandelions savagely".

DANDELION WINE. To every quart of blossoms allow:—

> 1 quart of water
> a little ginger root
> 3 Cloves
> 5 Chillies

Boil all the ingredients for half an hour and then strain. Allow 5½ lbs. of sugar to every 6 quarts of liquid, add the rind of a lemon and the juice, strained, then boil it all up again for half an hour. When lukewarm, place yeast in it spread on a piece of toasted bread. Put the liquid into a stone vessel and let it ferment for 14 days, then pour into a stone jar or bottles, and cork up. It will be ready for use in 6 months' time.

DANDELION WINE. 2 quarts Dandelion flowers

> 1 gallon water
> Juice and rind of two oranges
> Juice and rind of one lemon
> 2 tablespoonsfuls of yeast
> 3 lbs. loaf sugar

Put the flowers in the water and bring to the boil; then add the rind of oranges and lemon and the sugar and boil for an hour. Strain and, when nearly cold, add the yeast, bottle the next day, adding juice of oranges and lemon, also a few raisins. Do not cork down until it has done working, which will be in about three weeks.

DANDELION DINNER

Dandelion omelet
Dandelion and beet salad
Dandelion Greens
Dandelion wine
Dandelion coffee (made from roots)

Dandelion

DANDELION SANDWICHES. Use a slice of whole wheat and a slice of white bread for each sandwich. Butter with sweet butter and spread with finely chopped very young dandelion leaves.

ELDER ~~~~~~~~~~~~~~~~~~~~~~~~

Fresh Elder Flowers hung in a vessel of new wine and pressed every evening for seven nights together, "giveth to the wine a very good relish and a smell like Muscadine."

Parkinson

ELDERFLOWER AND RHUBARB JAM. Peel and cut six pounds of rosy rhubarb in 2 inch lengths and place in a large bowl. Take a pint of elder flowers, tie in a nylon net bag and place in the middle of the fruit and add six pounds of sugar. Cover, and leave for 12 hours, then stir, cover it and leave for twelve hours more. Place all in saucepan and heat to boiling point, but do not boil. Replace in bowl for another 24 hours, remove the flowers and add two tablespoons of grated lemon rind and half a cup of lemon juice. Boil until jam is done.

Elder flowers are fatal to turkeys.

ELDER FLOWER AND VINE LEAF FRITURES. Those of Elder Flowers are made while they are in bloom; and those of Vine Leaves, by breaking off the tops of the small tender shoots in little bunches; both are to be marinated as the Apples on Pedestals: When drained, dip them in good thick Batter to fry, and serve with rasped Sugar as most usual.

B. Clermont, The Professed Cook, MDCCLXXVI, London

ELDER FLOWER WATER, "FRONTIGNAC" — When elders are in flower gather them on a dry day. They should be in full but fresh blossom. Put the flowers in a preserving pan with sufficient water to cover them, and boil for ½ hour. Then strain through a fine sieve, or woollen bag, and let it stand. When cold put again in the pan, and allow ½ lb. of sugar for each pint of the flavoured water. Boil 10 minutes, skimming well all the time.

Elder

 ❧ When cold, bottle for use, corking the bottles tight and sealing them down.

 ❧ For an ordinary shape of ice use a breakfastcupful of this syrup and make like any other ice, but use less sugar.

The Cookery Book of Lady Clark of Tillypronie

ELDERFLOWER WINE.

> 1 quart elderflowers
> 1 lb. halved large raisins
> 2 gallons water
> 4 lb. loaf sugar
> 2 tablespoons yeast
> 2 oranges
> 2 lemons

Only fully blown elderflowers should be used. Gather them on a dry day just before their petals begin to fall. Shake off the blossoms on to a paper towel. To do this first press the heads lightly to loosen the flowers without breaking off the buds, as they would make the wine slightly bitter. Place the flowers, raisins and sliced lemons and oranges, water and sugar in a barrel. Stir frequently till the sugar is dissolved, then add the yeast. Allow to ferment for 7 days, stirring every morning. Leave for 3 months, then strain and bottle. Close tightly.

ELDERFLOWER VINEGAR. Take of Elder flowers, half a pound, the flowers of red roses, rosemary, and lavender, each four ounces, of nutmeg and cloves each two drams, of cinnamon three drams, pour upon them five pints of the sharpest white wine vinegar, let all infuse a month or six weeks, and after having pressed it out well, and the liquor is settled, put it into bottles and keep it well stopped for use.

Culpeper

FLAVOURING (ELDERFLOWERS) — Make a syrup of white sugar and a little water. When boiling throw in a handful of fresh elderflowers and let it remain for three or four minutes. Then strain off the syrup and bottle. Cork. (This tastes like Muscat grapes.)

Elder

Elderflowers have a peculiar and agreeable flavor. Beaten up in the dough of cakes, boiled in a gruel, distilled to flavor vinegar, buds are used as capers, or in a salad. The elder blossom is five fingered like ourselves; in every bloom there is an unvarying number of five branches. These detached, dipped in batter, fried lightly, sprinkled with sugar are an afternoon tea dainty in some parts of Germany.

> Charles Cooper, English Table in History and
> Literature, London, 1929

Costain in his book "The Moneyman" mentions curds and whey baked in a coffin of crust and flavored with elder flowers.

TO PICKLE ELDER BUDS. Get them the size of hop buds, put them in salt and water nine days, stir them two or three times a day, put them in a saucepan with wine leaves pour the water that came out of them, set them on a slow fire till they are quite green; take vinegar, mace shalots, and ginger, boil them three minutes and pour it on; then tie them down as usual.

> The Court and Country Confectioner, by an
> Ingenious Foreigner, now head Confectioner
> to the Spanish Ambassador in England—
> London, 1770

Legends of the Elder:

It must not be burnt, if you put it on the fire you will see the devil sitting on the chimney-pot.

Judas hanged himself upon an Elder, in token of this the ear of Judas, 'Jew's Ear' grows on the bark.

The Cross of Christ was made of the Elder.

If Elder wood was used in making a cradle, the child would sicken or the fairies would steal it.

ELDERFLOWER CHAMPAGNE.

1 quart elderflowers
1 gallon cold water
1 lemon, sliced and thinly peeled
2 pounds sugar
¼ cup white wine vinegar

Elder

✐ Put all ingredients into a crock and steep for 48 hours, strain into bottles and firmly cork. In two months time you will have a nice bubbly drink.

To PICKLE ELDER TOPS. Break the Tops of young Sprouts of Elder, about the middle of April, six inches long, let them have half a dozen walms in boiling Water, then drain them; make a pickle of wine water, salt, and bruised pepper, put them into the Pickle, and stop them up close.

> Receipt Book of John Nott, Cook to the
> Duke of Bolton, 1723

ELDERFLOWERS FRITTERS. A dozen clusters of flowers; mix ¼ cup cognac with ½ cup honey.

✐ Dip into a thin beer batter and delicately brown. Dip into cognac and honey mixture and convey to mouth.

Pour elderflower syrup on strawberries.

When making gooseberry jelly, add elderflower heads to each glass.

Elder buds are pleasantly tart and very good in salads.

MORE ELDERFLOWER FRITTERS. Take a cup or two of elderflowers and bruise in a mortar, and mix with cream cheese, an egg, a quarter teaspoon of cinnamon and a teaspoon of rose-water. Mix well and form into balls, fry in butter and serve hot, sprinkled with sugar or dribbled with honey.

ELDER VINEGAR.
Take of dried elder-flowers . . . one part;
        Vinegar . . . twelve parts;
Macerate for twelve days, clarify with milk, and filter.

> Richard Brooks, A New Family Herbal, London, 1871

The French use elder flowers when they pack apples, as the flowers enhance the flavor.

MUSCADINE ICES. Take one ounce of elder flower, which you put in a *fabotiere*, pour upon it about half a pint of boiling water, cover your *fabotiere* with its lid, thus let it draw about half an hour, make then a composition precisely, as it were to make a plain lemon ice; to that composition add your infusion of elder flower, pass the whole through a sieve, and put it in the *fabotiere* to congeal as we have explained.   The Court and Country Confectioner, by An
Ingenious Foreigner, London, 1770

Elder

(Fabotiere is an icing pot.)

The Ingenious Foreigner has written a fascinating treatise on distilling and has given some beguiling recipes, but since it involves special equipment will not give the details. Included are Orange Flowers, Roses, Lily, Carnation, Jessamine, Violets and Jonquils. In all recipes he emphasizes that flowers must be gathered immediately after the rising of the sun. (If any reader would like to have these recipes I would be glad to send them).

Diet watchers — remember saccharine cannot be used in wine making — It will not ferment.

FRIED ELDERBERRY FLOWERS. Make a batter of ½ cup flour, ½ cup milk, 1 egg, ½ teaspoon sugar, and ¼ teaspoon salt. Then, holding the stem, dip the flower umbels into the batter and fry in deep hot fat until light brown. Sprinkle with cinnamon and sugar. Make some crullers of the remaining batter and place on same platter with the flowers. If desired it could be served with a boiled custard.

GRAPE-ELDER SAUCE. Melt one jar of wild grape jelly; add a small amount of powdered sugar and one cup of elderflower wine. Mix well over low heat. Serve cold with cold game.

ELDERFLOWER PANCAKES. Take a pancake mix, add an extra egg, and ½ to 1 cup of flowers. Fry these in butter, lay on a paper towel covered with sugar and squeeze a taste of lemon juice on them.

ELDERFLOWER AND GOOSEBERRY WATER ICE. Make a syrup of five pounds of sugar and a quart of water. Add three cups of gooseberries and cook about five minutes. Tie 2 cups of elder flowers in a nylon net bag, put into syrup and let it set for five or six hours. Remove flowers and pour mixture into a pan for freezing.

ELDER FLOWER LEMONADE.
1. Put into an earthenware bowl fine, full elder flower blooms, and for every cluster of flowers, pour in 4 quarts of fresh cold water.
2. Add 1 lemon (cut in four) and 2 tablespoonfuls white vinegar.
3. Sweeten with 1½ lb. granulated sugar.
4. Let it stand 24 hours, stirring occasionally.
5. Strain, boil up and bottle, tying the corks down well. Use in about three weeks.

Elder

ENGLISH BAMBOO. There is a fine and much esteemed foreign pickle which is made of the tender shoots of the bamboo cane, and in England an imitation of it may be made with young shoots of elder. They are as tender, and by the time they have been four or five months pickled are very little different in taste. They are to be done thus:

❧ Cut some of the fine young shoots of elder, that appear towards the end of May. Mix up a strong brine of salt and water, and set it by you in a pan. Cut the shoots into lengths and peel them carefully; as they are peeled, throw them into water, and let them lie there twenty-four hours.

❧ Then take them out, wipe them with a napkin, and lay them to be perfectly dry on the outside.

❧ While they are drying, prepare the pickle thus: mix together equal parts of white wine and beer vinegar, and to two quarts of this put two ounces of white pepper, two ounces of black pepper, and three ounces of sliced ginger; half an ounce of mace and the same quantity of allspice. Set all upon the fire, place the shoots regularly in a large jar, and when the pickle boils, pour it upon them. Stop the jar with a bung, and set it before the fire to keep it hot, for two or three hours, often turning it about, that it may everywhere heat equally. Then set them away to cook, and tie the jar over for keeping.

Mrs. Martha Bradley, The British Housewife, 1750

TO DRY ELDER FLOWERS. The blossoms should be gathered before sunrise; put all together in a wooden bucket, cover with a thick cloth, and let them remain thus until their own heat has ripened and opened every blossom; sift through a cane sieve. The blossoms should not be left too long in the bucket or they will redden and lose their aroma.

Jules Gouffe, The Book of Preserves

Elderflowers were often added to the posset of the christening feast.

A conserve of elder buds is good with cold game.

Elder

ELDER FLOWER FRITTERS. Gather four Bunches of Elder Flowers just as they are beginning to open, for that is the Time of their Perfection, they have just then a very fine Smell and a spirited Taste, but afterwards they grow dead and faint. We complain of these Flowers haveing a sickly Smell, but this is only when they are decaying; when fresh and just open they have the same Flavour, but it is spirited, and just the Contrary of what it is afterwards.

The Elder Flowers being thus chosen, break each Bunch into four regular Parts, lay these carefully in a Soup Dish, break in a Stick of Cinnamon, pour to them a Wine Glass of Brandy, and when this has stood a Minute or two add half a Pint of Sack; stir the Flowers about in the Liquor, cover them up, and let them soak about an Hour, uncovering and stirring them about at Times, to see how they are kept moist.

Put a Handful of the finest Flour into a Stewpan, add the Yolks of four Eggs beaten, and afterwards their Whites beat up quite to a foam, add some White Wine and a little Salt, and put in the Whites of the Eggs last.

Let all this be very perfectly and thoroughly mixed.

When the Batter is thus made set on a Quantity of Hog's Lard in a Stewpan, when it is very hot fry the Fritters. The Method is this:

The Elder Flowers are to be taken out of their Liquor and put into the Batter and the Quantity for each Fritter is one of the Bunches of Elder, with as much Batter as agreeably covers it and hangs well about it.

While they are frying heat the Dish they are to be sent up in, rub a Lemon upon it not cut, and lay in the Fritters as they come out of the Pan, strew a little of the finest Orange-Flower Water over them, and serve them up.

Mrs. Martha Bradley, The British Housewife

A DELICIOUS MILK DRINK. Take a quart of milk and simmer with a cup of elderflowers. Beat the yolks of two eggs with a half cup of sugar and add to milk drink—after straining out the flowers. For a light, foamy drink, beat the egg whites until peaks form and mix with milk mixture. Chill, and when serving add a dash of cinnamon or nutmeg.

Another variation of elder fritters is to sprinkle them with orange juice and roll in granulated sugar.

GERANIUM 〜〜〜〜〜〜〜〜〜〜〜〜〜〜〜

"Genteel geranium
With a leaf for all that come."
                                    —*Hunt*

In the East the geranium almost reaches the proportions of a tree, and there it was first created.

For once when the prophet Mahomet had washed his shirt, he threw it over a plant of mallow in the sun to dry. It was not long in drying, but even in that short time a marvellous change took place in the mallow, which was transformed by contact with the sacred garment into a tall and lovely plant, covered with bright scarlet flowers, its leaves giving out an exquisite scent. The mallow had become a geranium, the first ever seen on earth, in honor of the virtues of the Prophet.

ROSE GERANIUM PUNCH

> 1 quart apple juice
> 4 limes
> 6 leaves of rose geranium
> 1 cup sugar
> 6 drops green vegetable coloring

Boil apple juice, sugar and geranium leaves for five minutes and add limes thinly sliced and crushed. Cool, strain and add coloring. Pour into glasses half filled with cracked ice and garnish with rose geranium petals.

Puddings are more delicious — and beautiful — when garnished with geranium leaves and blossoms.

Make a rose geranium sugar to use when dusting cookies.

Rose geranium butter made with sweet butter makes a delicious sandwich spread.

GLADIOLUS ⟨∿∿∿∿∿∿∿∿∿∿∿∿∿∿∿∿∿∿∿∿⟩

'Coarne flagge or Coarne-gladdyn, I have yt in my garden.
Mr. Morgan gave ut to me anno 1578 at London. . .'
                                    Lyte, Nievve Herball, 1578
In France during the Middle Ages, Gladiolus were used as a strewing flower.

Maison Rustique recommends the gladiolus or corn flag among the plants on the site of bee hives.

SCARSDALE SALAD.

> Red, yellow and purple gladiolus
> Lettuce
> French dressing, vinagrette

⟨∿⟩ Toss the flowers in the French dressing lightly, then arrange on lettuce. It was a great success.
                      Ford Frick, Commissioner of Baseball

Hassoldt Davis the explorer, was a guest at the same luncheon, where each guest had been asked to contribute a special dish. He related that Mr. Frick came in with a large bunch of gladioli and pockets bulging with prepared dressing. When asked what he had brought to *eat,* Mr. Frick answered that he had brought the salad, and to everybody's surprise began to remove the gladioli blossoms.

"At Fiesole, the crimson Gladioli in the cornfields had given place to poppies and blue corn-flowers. Fields of Sainfoin stained the hillsides with patches of dusty pink; and here and there, at the border of fields and copses, the tall blue irises unfurled their resplendent banners, heraldic flowers flaunting the brave insignia of Florence and the Medicis.
                      Jocelyn Brook, A Mine of Serpents

GOAT'S BEARD ⟨∿∿∿∿∿∿∿∿∿∿∿∿∿∿∿∿∿∿∿∿⟩

The goat's beard, which each morn abroad does peep
But shuts its flowers at noon and goes to sleep.
                      Abraham Cowley

SALSIFY. Goat's Beard (tragopogon) is now (June) as well as in May fit for boiling. It is eaten like asparagus, and dress'd the same way, the part which is eaten is the blossoming bud, a little before it would flower with about six inches the stalk to it.
                      R. Bradley, The Country Housewife, 1732

Goat's Beard

OMELETTE AUX FLEURS DE SALSIFIS. While these flowers are a little hard to come by, and the best is the Spanish variety, with black roots and yellow flowers, they make a very delicious omelette. Nip them literally in the bud, and wash them well in several waters to get rid of the kind of milk which oozes from them when you break them. Then dry them in a cloth for a few minutes, after which cook them in butter till they are brown, with salt and pepper. Mix them with the beaten eggs, and make your omelette in the ordinary way. Do not be surprised to see the buds open in the hot butter. It affects them more quickly than the sun Some show a few already yellow petals; it is a pretty sight; also the taste is delicious.

Marcel Boulestin, Simple French Cooking

EVELYN BECOMING INDIGNANT IN 1706. "Goats-beard, *Trago-pogon*; but of late they have *Italianiz'd* the Name, and now generally call it *Salsisix*; and our Seed-Sellers, to disguise it, being a very common Field Herb, growing in most parts of *England*, would have it thought an Exotick, and call it *Salsify* and *Sassify*. . ."

GORSE

The gorse-field dark, by sudden, gold caprice,
Turns, here and there, into a Jason's fleece.

Coventry Patmore, *The Odes*

Symbolizes anger.

GORSE WINE. Gather a pint of the yellow flowers and put into 2 quarts of water with 3 thinly sliced lemons. Add two pounds of honey, stir and add a half pound of raisins cut in half. After simmering for a half hour, cool and add a cup of barley and two packages of yeast. Let stand for three weeks, skim and strain into a container. Let stand for another ten days and strain again and put into bottles. Fasten tightly and in six months you will have a golden champagne.

In another recipe ginger is listed as one of the ingredients.

Elizabeth Barrett Browning says gorse has a vigorous sound.

Gorse

To Pickle Gorse Buds. Make a stronge pickle of white wine vinegar and salt, able to bear an egg. Stir very well till the salt be dissolved, clearing off the dregs and scum. The next day pour it from the bottom, and having rubbed the buds dry, put them up in a pickle glass, which should be frequently shaken until they sink under it, and kept well stopt and covered.

J. Evelyn, Acetaria, 1622

Gorse Tea. Use the buds and make as other flower teas.

GRAPE-BUDS

The culture of the vine is not desirable in lands capable of producing anything else. It is a species of gambling, and of desperate gambling too, wherein, whether you make much or nothing, you are equally ruined. The middling crop alone is the saving point, and that the seasons seldom hit. Accordingly, we see much wretchedness among this class of cultivators. . . . It is a resource for a country, the whole of whose good soil is otherwise employed, and which still has some barren spots, and surplus of population to employ on them. There the vine is good, because it is something in the place of nothing.

—Thomas Jefferson
(Letter to William Drayton-Paris, July 30, 1787)

Vine-Bud Potage: They sometimes make a Vine-Bud Potage in the Countries abounding with Vineyards; in order to do which they cut off the largest Leaves of the Buds, taking Care that none of the Wood be left; then they scald them in boiling Water, and trying them up in Bunches, stew them in a little Pot, with a Carrot, a few Turneps cut in Quarters, and a Clove of Garlick; they add to these as they are dressing a little thickening Liquor; and garnish the Potage with other Buds, and a Loaf in the middle.

Dictionnaire Oeconomique, M. Chomel,
translated by R. Bradley, 1725.

HAWTHORNE ⟨⟨⟨⟨⟨⟨⟨⟨⟨⟨⟨⟨⟨⟨⟨⟨⟨⟨⟨⟨⟨⟨⟨⟨⟨⟨

And then I returned to my Hawthorns, and stood before them as one stands before those masterpieces of painting which one imagines one will be better able to 'take in' when one has looked away, for a moment, at something else; but in vain did I shape my fingers into a frame, so as to have nothing but the hawthorns before my eyes; the sentiment which they aroused in me remained obscure and vague, struggling and panting to free itself, to float across and become one with the flowers. They themselves offered me no enlightenment, and I could not call upon any other flowers to satisfy this mysterious longing.

Marcel Proust, Remembrance of Things Past

Since before Christ the hawthorn has symbolized fertility and marriage in Greece and Rome.

HAWTHORN CORDIAL OR LIQUEUR. Take about two cups of hawthorn flowers, no leaves or stalks and put into a large bottle. Cover with good brandy and let stand for at least three months. If you like it sweeter, add a bit of sugar or capillaire. Strain into bottles. Excellent for seasoning puddings or custards.

The Hawthorn, in flower language, means Hope.

Hawthorn flowers contain trimethylamine, a stale, sweet odor, which somehow suggests sex.

The almond scent of the hawthorn flowers is delightful in compotes, blancmanges and jellies.

Jellies and marmalades are made from the fruits, Wood in 1634 writes in New England's Prospect, "the white thorne affords hawes as bigge as an English Cherrie, which is esteemed above a Cherrie for his goodnesse and pleasantnesse to the taste." And for those of us trying to reduce it is comforting to know that Haw jelly requires comparatively little sugar.

HAWTHORN WINE. Take a gallon of hawthorn flowers, 2 lemons and 2 oranges, and four pounds of sugar. Mix, stir, and let stand for two weeks. Skim and stir again and let stand for another week and then strain and bottle. Put it out of temptation's way for a year.

Hawthorn and White Thorn are the same.

When Charlemagne knelt before the Holy Crown, it blossomed again and perfumed the room with the odor of hawthorn.

FLOWRYS OF HAWTHORN. Take Flowrys of Hawthorn, boyle hem, presse hem, bray hem smal, temper hem uppe with Almaunde mylke, or gode Cowe Mylke, allay it with Amydoun or Flowre of Rys; take Sugre y-now, and putte there-to, or hony in defaute; coloure it with the same that the flowrys be on y-peyntid a-above.

Hawthorne

(And what is Amydoun? It is wheat flour, steeped, strained, and dried in the sun.)

> Two Fifteenth-Century Cookery-Books, ed. Thomas
> Austin, London 1864, from Harleian Ms. c. 1430

HAWTHORN HONEY. Flowrys of Hawthorn putte with sugre or hony, coloure it with the same dat be the flowrys.

> Ibidem

.1xxv. Spyneye. — Take ye Flowberys of Hawthorun; boyle hem — presse hem, bray hem smal, temper hem vppe wyth Almaunde Mylke, & lye it with Abyndoun & Gratyd brede and flowre of Rys; take Sugre y-now & put it jam or Hony in defawte, & coloure it wyth ye same get ye flowrys ben, & whyle forth.   Ibidem

HAWTHORN SYRUP. Clip your flowers and take their weight in Sugar; then take a gallypot, and put a row of flowers and a strewing of sugar, till the pot is full; then put in two or three spoonsfuls of the same syrup or still'd water; tie a cloth on the top of the pot, put a tile on that, set your gallypot in a Kettle of water over a gentle fire, and let it infuse till the strengh is out of the flowers, which will be in four or five hours; then strain it through a flannel, and when it is cold bottle it up.   E. Smith, The Compleat Housewife, 1736

Glastonbury Abbey was long famed as possessing a hawthorn that was in full leaf and flower each Christmas-day. The legend is that it sprouted from the staff of Joseph of Arimathea, as during his mission to England he arrived at Glastonbury in midwinter, for some reason he stuck his staff into the ground and it budded at once. This tree was considered to have great virtue and sanctity and the sale of blossoms to pilgrims was very lucrative, some were even exported to Europe.

HAWTHORN COCKTAIL. Pour into the bowl a bottle of sauterne, a whole bottle, then half a bottle of red wine. Add a sliced orange, some lemon thyme and two borage flowers. Scatter hawthorn flowers on top of the mixture. Cover with a cloth and let it stand twenty-four hours.

HEATHER ～～～～～～～～～～～～～～～～～

From the bonny bells of heather,
*   They brewed a drink longsyne,*
Was sweeter far than honey,
*   Was stronger far than wine.*
                              Robert Louis Stevenson

A famous ale was made by the Picts who lived in Scotland during the 6th Century, Boethius says that from the honeyed flowers of the purple heather they made a sweet beer, though its secret was hereditary and even under threat of death they refused to reveal it, the legend is that the secret perished with them.

HEATHER ALE. Follow any good ale recipe. Fill whatever vessel you are going to use with heather blossoms and cover with water. Boil for an hour, strain and measure. To each gallon of liquid add ½ ounce of ground ginger, a spoonful of hops and a pint of syrup. Boil again and strain, when warm add two packages of yeast, strain and bottle after 24 hours. It will be ready to drink in 2 or 3 days.

The Scots also have another ancient and famous drink called Athol Brose. It is made of oatmeal, water, Drambuie, heather honey and cream. The oatmeal is not cooked but mixed with the water and let stand for an hour or so, after which the liquid is pressed out, (again the nylon net bag) or it could be hung and allowed to drip out in the manner of farmer's cheese, and then mixed with the other ingredients. Since it is used in giving toasts serve in wine glasses.

HEATHER HONEY. Heather honeys are produced from the blossoms of both ling (calluna vulgaris) and bell heather (Erica cinerea). Bell heather honey which is the less viscid, may be extracted by rotary action and granulates, or "sets". Ling honey is a glutinous, "non-setting" honey, which on account of its high viscosity, is usually extracted from the comb by crushing between cheesecloths in a honey press.

Both bell heather and ling honeys are dark brown, the section cappings usually being white. It is almost impossible to get rid of the air bubbles in ling honey, and the extracted honey has a characteristic bubbly appearance.

                    Ministry of Agriculture and Fisheries, 1931

HOLLYHOCK ❧❧❧❧❧❧❧❧❧❧❧❧❧❧❧❧❧❧❧❧

The Holihock disdains the common size
Of Herbs, and like a tree do's proudly rise;
Proud she appears, but try her, and you'll find
No plant more mild, or friendly to mankind.
She gently all obstructions do's unbind.
                              Abraham Cowley

In the language of flowers the hollyhock means ambition and fecundity.

In China, which is its natural home, it has been a part of the cuisine for thousands of years.

HOLLYHOCK FLOWERS FOR SALAD. There is a surprising choice of flowers, almost unknown to French cooks, but very much appreciated by gourmets and constantly used in Chinese cooking, one of the most valuable being the hollyhock, so rich in nutritive elements. The Chinese cooks use the fresh buds and petals with a salad dressing, and the tender stalks are cooked in the same way as salsify; what a precious suggestion for the cottage and farm household! I have seen many country houses with those pretty rosemallows framing the small windows and growing in the gardens. Why not gather them for the cook, and also the fragrant *verbena* and the *wallflower*, the *sweet-pea* and the *marigold*, even the *hyacinth* and the aristocratic magnolia. They will all mingle most happily their aroma and the beauty of their colourings with the contents of the salad bowl.   Comtesse Berjane, French Dishes for English Tables

RECIPE FOR OBTAINING A SIGHT OF THE FAIRIES (year 1660). We have a precious ungent, prepared according to the receipt of a celebrated alchymist, which, applied to your visual orb, will enable you to behold without difficulty or danger the most potent fairy or spirit you may encounter. This is the form of the preparation:—R. A pint of sallet-oyle, and put it into a vial-glasse; but first wash it with rose-water and marygolde water; the flowers to be gathered towards the East. Wash it till the oyle becomes white; then put it into the glasse, and then put thereto the budds of hollyhocke, the flowers of marygolde, the flowers or toppess of wild thime, the budds of young hazle, and the thime must be gathered neare the side of a hill where fayries use to be; and take the grasse of a fayrie throne; then all these put into the oyle into the glasse; and sette it to dissolve three dayes in the sunne, and then keep it for thy use.
                    Reverend Hilderic Friend, Flowers and Flower Lore

Evelyn in his *Book of Sallets*, says that Nonius has commended "the tall Holi-hock that bears the broad flower" for the best, and that it is laxative:

"Nulla est humanior herba,
Nulla magis suavi commoditate bona est:
Omnia tam placide regerat, blandeque relaxat,
Emollitque vias, nec sinit esse rudes."

Hollyhock

HOLLYHOCK TEA. Gouffe recommends hollyhock tea, made in the usual manner.

HONEYSUCKLE ~~~~~~~~~~~~~~~~

"Where the bee
Strays diligent, and with th' extracted balm
Of fragrant woodbine loads his little thigh."
                                        Thomson

Woodbine symbolizes fraternal love.

"Oh how sweete and pleasaunte is Woodbinde in Woodes or Arbours, after a tender soft rain: and how friendly doe this herbe if I maie so name it embrace the bodies, armes and branches of trees, with his long windying stalkes and tender leaves, openyng or spreding forthe his swete Lilles, like ladies fingers, among the thornes or bushes. Is this Woodbinde so profitable as pleasant I praie you tell me?"
                    Bullein's Bulwarke of Defence . . . Which is kepte
                    with Hillarius the Gardener 1562

SYRUP OF HONEYSUCKLE. Take of fresh petals of honey suckle, four pounds; boiling water . . . 8 pints. Infuse for twelve hours in a covered vessel; express lightly, set aside the liquor for a few hours, decant and add twice the weight of white sugar, and make a syrup.
                    Richard Brooks, A New Family Herbal
                    London, 1871

The honeysuckle is the third flower of the Song of Solomon: *"I am the rose of Sharon, and the lily of the valleys. As the lily among thorns, so is my love among the daughters."*

HYACINTH

Come home, come home O centuries
Whose saints come down this winter morning's iris
Whose soundless islands ring me from within,
To wait upon our prayers with hyacinths.

> *Thomas Merton, Sign of Jonas*
> *(January 20 — Eve of Saint Agnes)*

Burns sang of constancy, the symbolical meaning of hyacinths.

The Hyacinth's for constancy,
Wi' its unchanging blue.

BAGHDAD RECIPE. (Rutab Mu'assal). Take fresh gathered dates, and lay in the shade and air for a day: then remove the stones, and stuff with peeled almonds. For every ten ratls of dates, take two ratls of honey: boil over the fire with two uqiya of rose-water and half a dirham of saffron, then throw in the dates, stirring for an hour. Remove and allow to cool. When cold, sprinkle with fine-ground sugar scented with musk, camphor and hyacinth. Put into glass preserving jars, sprinkling on top some of the scented ground sugar. Cover, until the weather is cold and chafing dishes are brought in.

> Professor Arberry, A Baghdad Cookery Book, 13th Century

A CURIOUS WATER, KNOWN BY THE NAME OF THE SPRING NOSEGAY. Take six ounces of Hyacinths, a quarter of a pound of picked Violets, the same quantity of Wall Flowers, picked, and Jonquils; an ounce of Florentine Orrice bruised; half an ounce of Mace grossly powdered, and two ounces of Quintessence of Orange. Put the whole (the Jonquils, Wall Flowers, and Lilies of the Valley excepted) about the end of March, into a glass body, with a gallon of strong Spirit of Wine: bruise the Hyacinths, Violets, Orrice and Mace; and towards the end of April, add the Jonquils when in their perfection, that is to say, when full blown. A few days after, put in the Wall Flowers, the Petals only; then add the Lilies of the Valley, carefully picked; and shake all the ingredients well: Eight days after having put in the last Flower, empty the infusion into an alembic, lute on a head and receiver, which must be placed in cold water, and distil in a water bath, with a gentle fire. From the above quantity three quarts of excellent Spirit may be drawn off, that justly deserves the appellation of the Spring Nosegay.

> The Toilet of Flora

Grape hyacinth pickles are popular on the island of Crete.

HYSSOP ~~~~~~~~~~~~~~~~~~~~~~~~

Purge me with Hyssop and I shall be clean
Wash me and I shall be whiter than snow.

Hyssop symbolizes cleanliness.

QUEEN ELIZABETH'S CORDIAL ELECTUARY OF HYSSOP. Boil a pint of the best honey; and having carefully taken off all the scum, put into this clarified liquid a bundle of Hyssop which has been well bruised before being tied up. Let them boil together till the honey tasts strongly of the Hyssop—then strain the honey very well and add a quarter of an ounce of pulverized liquorice root and the same of aniseed, with half the quantity of pulverized elecampane root and angelica root, and a pennyweight each of pepper and ginger. Let all boil together for short time and stir well—then pour into gallipots and stir till cold. Keep covered for use and whenever troubled with straightness at the stomach, or shortness of breath, take some of the electuary, which will very soon give relief.

The New London Family Cook

The plant has red, white, and blue flowers and a flavor of mint, with a slightly bitter taste. It is good for soups, broth, candies and especially game.

The fresh flowers and tops are used for flavoring sausage, and also make a welcome addition to fresh fruit pies.

HYSSOP SYRUP. Take four ounces of hyssop petals, put them in a covered jar boil 2 and a half pints of water; pour it boiling onto the flowers; let it steep for six hours, keeping the jar closed. Strain and filter, then add 3½ pounds of sugar; close the jar and melt the sugar *au bain marie*.

Paris Pharmacopoeia, 1866

HYSSOP HONEY. Is deemed one of the world's finest, Make by boiling a pint of honey with a small bundle of well bruised hyssop. Strain, bottle and store.

HYSSOP DESSERT. Make boiled custard and flavor with hyssop syrup, beat sweetened egg whites stiff and fold into it.

Hyssop flowers are not only decorative on salads, but add a delicious flavor.

JASMINE ⟿⟿⟿⟿⟿⟿⟿⟿⟿⟿⟿⟿⟿⟿⟿⟿

The ointment Jessamine without abuse
Is gain'd, yet grave old Scots condemn the use
Tho' Jove himself, when he is most enrag'd
With thy ambrosial odours is assuag'd.
                    Cowley

WHITE JESSAMINE LIQUEUR. Pick a quarter of a pound of jessamine blossoms, put them into two quarts of spirit of wine and let them steep for two days. Prepare 1½ pints of clarified syrup, strain the spirit and mix with the cold syrup, filter, pouring the liqueur through and through until it is quite clear, and bottle it for use.

                    Jules Gouffe, The Book of Preserves, 1871

JASMINE FONDANT. Make a white fondant and flavor with the essence of jasmine.

VIOLET OR JESSAMIN CAKES. Prepare after the manner of violet cakes, the only difference being in the quantity of Sugar; one pound and a half of Sugar prepared as the former to half a pound of Jessamin Flowers.

                    B. Clermont, The Professed Cook, MDCCLXXVI, London

GLACE DE JASMIN. Pound a handful of Jessamin Flowers, and pour about a pint of hot Water upon them; let them infuse about an hour, adding about half a pound of Sugar; when it is properly dissolved, sift through a Napkin. To make the liquid taste more of the Flowers, pour it several times from one Pan into another before sifting. The infusion may also be mixed with Cream instead of Water.

                    Ibidem

Add to Pomona's riches Flora's treasure,
Then rose and jasmine, lily and carnation
Change staid desserts to gardens plann'd for pleasure;
And nature-lovers shout for joy to see
Your blossom jam and candied picotee.
                    Berchoux (Gastronomy, Canto 4)
                    (Real French Cooking by Savarin, Doubleday 1957)

The Italians make many flower liqueurs, including jasmine, iris, and many others which appeal to the imagination.

JESSEMAIN WATER. Take two handfuls of Jeseme flowers and put them into a flagon or earthen pot, put to them about a quart of fair water and a quarter of a pound of Sugar, let this stand and steep about half an hour, then take your water and flowers and pour them out of one vessell into another till such time as the water hath taken the scent and tast of the flowers, then set it in a cool place and you will find it a most excellent scented water.

Jasmine

> A Perfect School of Instructions for the Officers
> of the Month by Giles Rose, one of the Master Cooks
> to Charles II, 1682

JASMINE SYRUP. Take a glass jar or pyrex dish with cover, then place a layer of flowers and a layer of sugar until about an inch from the top, then cover with a damp napkin and cover, put in a cool place and let it set for several hours, when the sugar will have absorbed the flower essence, then take the sugar and make syrup in the usual way.

The white jasmine symbolizes amiability; the yellow, grace and elegance.

The Chinese often use flowers to scent tea, among those most used are jasmine, oleanders, gardenias, peonies and roses. To every hundred pounds of tea they use about forty pounds of flowers; they let the fresh flowers mingle with the tea for about twenty-four hours, then winnow out the flowers.

In Grasse on the French Riviera, pralined jasmine blossoms are one of the many flower delicacies.

CANDY OF JESSAMINE (PETIT CANDI DE JASMIN). Take two handsful of jessamin; have a pound of sugar at the *fort perle*; when it is half cold, put in the flowers, and set the pan upon hot cinders for two hours; put it through a search; rub the flowers in sifted sugar to dry them; put them into the stove till next day; then search them to take out the superfluous sugar; put the candy into moulds, and cover the surface with flowers, without making them too thick in pressing them in with a fork, that the flowers may attach to the sugar, and that they should be well covered; put the moulds into the stove for five hours without heating it too much; drain them to take off the syrup: when cold, take them out of the moulds, put a sheet of paper upon the table, and turn them quickly over as with a stroke, to make the candy fall.

> Beauvilliers, Art of French Cookery

JASMINE BOBBONS: Take a cup of apple sauce (what would we do without apples!). Stir into it about a pound of jasmine flowers until it is very smooth. Meanwhile make a syrup of water and sugar, about two cups of water and a pound of sugar and cook to the hard-boiled stage. Add the jasmine and apple mixture and boil for 10 minutes, stirring constantly. Pour onto a cookie sheet or shallow pan and dry out in the oven with very low heat at first and then with the oven off.

Jasmine

JASMINE JELLY: Take apple jelly liquor and add sufficient blossoms to flavor. Cook as any jelly & store in jelly jars.

JONQUIL

His brooks run down from the hills to feed my lilies
His clouds drift up from the sea to redden my rose,
He scatters his broken sun through the grass of the orchard
Where the jonquil laughs with delight and the daffodil glows.
The Remembering Garden—Alfred Noyes

Symbolically means: "I desire a return of affection."

CANDIED JONQUILS: Fill the moulds with Sugar a la grand Plume, (ninth degree) when it is half cold, put Jonquil Flowers in it, with a little Skewer, and dry it in the Stove (put on white paper).

> The Professed Cook by B. Clermont
> (Who has been many Years Clerk of the Kitchen
> in some of the first Families of this Kingdom,
> and lately to the Right Hon. the Earl of ABINGDON)

JONQUILL CONSERVE: Take any quantity of jonquills, which you pick carefully from their stalk, put them in a little mortar and pound them well, take them out with a card and put them in a saucer; then take a little clarified sugar, boil it to the ninth degree, take it off from the fire, add your jonquils to it, and stir it well with a spoon, till you see your sugar begins to thicken, pour it in a paper mold and let it cool; but before it is quite cold, make with the point of a knife the different drops or *pastils* you intend to make of it, that you may afterward break them with more facility, and take them off from the paper. Do not let it harden too much when working with the spoon, for your conserve would not be so well melting in the mouth.

Jonquil   The Court and Country Confectioner by an Ingenious Foreigner, now head Confectioner to the Spanish Ambassador in England—London 1770

JONQUIL WATER. Let a good handful of these Flowers be well pick'd, and infused in water with Sugar, from Morning to Noon, or from Noon till Night; and one hour before the Liquor is served up, let it be cool'd and iced, after having strain'd it through a Sieve or a Linen Cloth. The work may also be more speedily done by beating up the water, with the Flowers and Sugar, after they have been steeped as long as the time will admit; then strain off the Liquor and pour it into the Cistern to be Iced.

The Family Dictionary by William Salmon
London, Printed for D. Rhodes, at the
Star, the Corner of Bride-Lane, in Fleet-street, 1705

(He also uses the same for tuberoses, jessamins, pinks, musk roses, and violets.)

CANDYED JONQUILLE FLOWERS—(Jonquille Entiere)—Take the double jonquille; cut the stalk within a quarter of an inch of the flower; boil them in prepared sugar; take them off the fire, and leave them a quarter of an hour in it; throw them into sifted sugar; in mixing them lightly, care must be taken that the leaves are kept in their places, that the flower retains its form, and that it is equally covered with sugar; put paper into a search, and sift sugar over it, and lay in the flowers; put them into a stove to dry, and keep them in a box in a dry place.

Flowers done in this way could be put into candy in having little grills made for the moulds, upon which they might be put; and one above with a weight sufficient to keep them in the sugar. This might be done with all the flowers that are preserved, whether in leaves or entire; and the candies could be had at all seasons.

Art of French Cookery, Beauvilliers

FLOWERING JUDAS ⌇⌇⌇⌇⌇⌇⌇⌇⌇⌇⌇⌇⌇⌇⌇⌇

Laura sees her world fall to pieces and suddenly discovers that she is a traitor to herself as well as the oppressed. Laura dreams.

"Without a word, without fear she rose and reached for Eugenio's hand, but he eluded her with a sharp, sly smile and drifted away. This is not all, you shall see— Murderer, he said, follow me, I will show you a new country, it is far away and we must hurry. No, said Laura, not unless you take my hand, no; and she clung first to the stair rail, and then to the topmost branch of the Judas tree that bent down slowly and set her upon the earth, and then to the rocky ledge of a cliff, and then to the jagged wave of a sea that was not water but a desert of crumbling stone. Where are you taking me, she asked in wonder but without fear. To death, and it is a long way off, and we must hurry, said Eugenio. No, said Laura, not unless you take my hand. Then eat these flowers, poor prisoner, said Eugenio in a voice of pity, take and eat: and from the Judas tree he stripped the warm bleeding flowers, and held them to her lips. She saw that his hand was fleshless, a cluster of small white petrified branches, and his eye sockets were without light, but she ate the flowers greedily for they satisfied both hunger and thirst."

Flowering Judas, by Katherine Anne Porter
Harcourt, Brace and Company (1958)

The flowers have a sharp, acid flavour, and are not only mixed with salads to render them more grateful, but are also picked in the bud, in the manner of Capers.

Charles Bryant, Flora Diaetetica, 1783

Horace Kephart, in "The Book of Camping and Woodcraft" recommends the buds, flowers and young pods be fried in butter, or made into fritters.

Flowering Judas (redbud) are very delicate, and the first settlers found the Indians using them, fried or boiled. The North American Indians used flowers in their diet extensively.

LAVENDER ～～～～～～～～～～～～～～～～～～

Lavender, sweet blooming Lavender,
Six bunches a penny to-day.
Lavender, sweet blooming Lavender,
Ladies buy it while you may.

Old London Street Cry

CONSERVE OF THE FLOWERS OF LAVENDER. Take the flowers being new so many as you please, and beat them with three times their weight of White Sugar, after the same manner as Rosemary flowers; they will keep one year.

W. M., The Queen's Closet Opened, 1655

LAVENDER TEA. One pint of boiling water poured on half an ounce of the young leaves. Mint or rosemary may be added. Serve hot or iced.

LAVENDER WINE. Made similar to other flower wines. Simply substitute lavender flowers, either 1½ pints of distilled water from the flowers or 1 pint of flowers

"I judge that the flowers of Lavender quilted in a cap and dayly worne are good for all diseases of the head that come of a cold cause and they comfort the braine very well."

William Turner, A Newe Herball, 1551

TO CANDY ALL MANNER OF FLOWERS IN THEIR NATURAL COLOURS. Take the flowers with the stalks, and wash them over with a little Rose-water, wherein Gum Arabick is dissolved; then take fine searsed sugar, and dust over them, and set them a drying on the bottom of a sieve in an oven, and they will glister as if it were Sugar-Candy.

William Rabisha, The Whole Body of Cookery Dissected
London, 1675

TO PICKLE FLOWERS. Take Flowers of any sort, put them into a Gallypot with their weight in Sugar, and to each pound of sugar put a pint of Vinegar.

Ibidem

Fresh flowers of lavender garnish hot weather beverages. Very good in fruit punches, lemonade, limeade, jellies and wine cups.

Lavender

ASPIC JELLY. And now it may be asked: Why is it called aspic? There is upon this point the most curious ignorance, though the explanation lies upon the surface . . . It means lavender . . . in old French, espic or spic; in good old English, spike, lavender-spike, and spikenard; Lavender-spike is to be found in the sauces of Roman cookery; it is mentioned among the pot-herbs used in France five hundred years ago; one of the spikes—the spikenard of Spain— is in English books of the same period mentioned as a flavouring ingredient of Hippocras.

> Kettner, Book of the Table
> Republished in 1912

LAVENDER JELLY. Use apple jelly, and while it is hot, pour over lavender petals which have been placed in the bottom of jelly glasses, cover with paraffin and seal while hot.

LAVENDER HONEY. That which is gathered by the bee is best of course, but it may be made as other flower honeys.

"And then she took him into a room of the eighteenth century, which no longer exists there, or elsewhere save in name. It was the Still-room, and on its shelves stood the elixirs, and cordials of ancient time: the Currant-gin to fortify the stomach on a raw morning before crossing the Roads; the Cherry Brandy for a cold and stormy night; the Elder-berry wine, good, mulled, and spiced at Christmas-time; the Blackberry wine; the homemade Distilled waters, Lavender water, Hungary water, Cyprus water, and the Divine Cordial itself, which takes three seasons to complete, and requires all the flowers of Spring, Summer, and Autumn."

> *Armorel of Lyonese by Walter Besant, Harpers, 1890*

DISTILLED LAVENDER VINEGAR. Put into a stone cucurbit any quantity of fresh-gathered Lavender Flowers picked clean from the Stalks; pour on them as much distilled Vinegar as is requisite to make the Flowers float; distil in a vapour-bath, and draw off about three fourths of the Vinegar.

In the same manner are prepared the Vinegars from all other vegetable substances. Compound vinegars are made by mixing several aromatic substances together; observing only to bruise all hard woody ingredients, and to let them infuse a sufficient time in the Vinegar before you proceed to distillation.

> Toilet of Flora

LAVENDER SUGAR. Pound freshly picked Lavender flowers into three times their weight in sugar.

To Make Baggs And Sweet Water. Take Storax, Calamint one ounce, Labdanum two ounces, half an ounce of Lemon Pills dryed, six Oranges stuck with Cloves (but not too thicke), half an ounce of gallingall, much Orris powder, 2 grains of musk, 2 grains of amber greece, 4 grains of Civitt; to all these add 2 shillings of Damask powder mingle all these together and it will be 6 or 7 Baggs, then take rose tops, Lavender, sweet Margerum, Brazill, 3 Nutmeggs bruised, some Pink Clove Gilliflowers ye leaves pulled from ye stalk. Mingle ye herbs & flowers together, strew some of ym among your Clothes.

Lavender

Mary Doggett, Book of Receipts

LAVENDER means Acknowledgement.

"She sent him Lavender, owning her love."
Shakespeare

Lions love lavender.

LEMON BLOSSOMS

Lemon blossoms signify discretion and meekness.

Lemon Blossom Icecream. One pint of heavy cream (unbeaten), ¼ teaspoon salt, ½ cup sugar, two ounces lemon flowers (ground), and 8 slightly beaten egg yolks. Scald the cream with salt and slowly pour over the egg yolks, beating constantly, and lastly add the lemon flowers. Then cook in a double boiler until it coats a spoon, strain, cool and pour into pan for freezing, or better still freeze in hand freezer.

Lemon Flower Butter. Made as other flower butters. Alternate layers of butter and flowers, close tight and set aside so that the fragrance may permeate the butter.

Sweet-Sour Tart. Boil a quarter of a Pound of Sugar in a Glass of Verjuice (Crabapple) or Lemon-juice, and when it is wasted half, put to it some Cream, with the Yolks of half a dozen Eggs, Lemon-flowers, Lemon-peel candy'd, grated; a little beaten Cinnamon, and a little Butter. Put these into a Tart made of fine Paste, and bake it without a Lid.

John Nott, Receipt Book, 1723

LEMON FLOWER PUDDING. Nuts, lemon-peel and lemon flowers combined with milk, sugar and eggs. (An old Italian recipe.)

LEMON BLOSSOM JAM. Make and clear a syrup by putting the whites of two fresh eggs in an enamelled or clean copper saucepan, whisk them well and throw in four tumblerfuls of cold water, and two pounds of lump sugar. Mix this well with a clean wooden spoon, let it come to the boil, and then draw it to the cooler part of the stove, and let it simmer till it has thickened and is of the consistency of honey. All this time scum will rise to the top; this should be taken off as it rises. When there is no more froth or scum it is ready for use.

Lemon Blossoms

Weigh one pound of well and carefully washed lemon blossoms to one pound of sugar, and add them to the syrup. Cook slowly until done.

Cherries stoned and preserved in this way take about two hours to cook but the lemon blossoms cook more quickly.

Euterpe Craies, Recipes from East to West

SALAD DRESSING. Mix lemon flower water and lemon flowers with five table-spoons honey and 2 cups flower vinegar.

LEMON FLOWER FRITTERS. Follow the recipe for acacia flowers.

TEMER (Stewed Dates). Peel two dozen fresh dates, remove their stones, pound their pulp, and pass it through a sieve; give sugar to this puree, add a few drops of extract of roses or lemon, spread it in a layer on a pie dish, and mask the puree immediately with a stiff sauce of good arrowroot or rice flour, prepared with milk, perfumed with lemon flowers.

Robert H. Christie, Banquets of the Nations
Edinburgh, 1911

WANMORE BOWL. This is a Japanese dish containing shrimp, lotus root, and lemon flower, mentioned in "Haute Cuisine" by Jean Conil, but the recipe is not given, simply the above ingredients. Of course novices should not attempt to use this book.

Louis Golding in "Good-bye to Ithaca" says that lemon flower jam is called anthos, and is specially made on the Island of Chios, and that it smells like hair oil and tastes like ambrosia.

LILAC ∽∽∽∽∽∽∽∽∽∽∽∽∽∽∽∽∽∽∽∽

Just now the lilac is in bloom
All before my little room;
And in my flower beds I think,
Smile the carnation and the pink;
And from the borders, well I know,
The poppy and the pansy blow.
        Rupert Brooke

The purple lilac is symbolical of first emotions of love, while the white variety means joy of youth.

LILAC CANDY. Make a fondant and flavor with the essence of lilac and tint it a pale heliotrope.

LILAC MARZIPAN. Soften the marzipan with sufficient orange-flower water and mix with it crystallized lilac blossoms and leaves. Roll out to a medium thickness (between ½ and 1 inch thick) and cut into one inch lengths. Dip into pale lilac-colored fondant and decorate each with a lilac blossom.

LILAC ICE. Make as other flower ices, coloring it a pale heliotrope. At a large gathering a group of flower ices colored as the flower represented would be a conversation piece.

Men become passionately attached to women who know how to cosset them with delicate titbits.
        H. de Balzac

The Lilac various in array, now white,
Now sanguine, and her beauteous head now set
With purple spikes, studious of ornament,
Yet unresolved which hue she most approved,
She chose them all.
        Cowper, Winter's Walk at Noon

Some students of flower symbology say that the lilac represents fastidiousness.

LILAC CRYSTALS. Take small bunches of lilac and dip in a gum arabic mixture of ½ cup hot water and 1 oz. gum arabic. Let dry and meanwhile mix 1 tablespoon corn syrup, ½ cup water, and 1 cup sugar; cook to the softball stage. Dip bunches of lilacs carefully into mixture and lightly sprinkle with granulated sugar.

LILIES ⟨∼∼∼∼∼∼∼∼∼∼∼∼∼∼∼∼∼∼∼∼∼∼⟩

The Bright Lily
Have you seene but a bright Lillie grow
  Before rude hands have toucht it?
Have you mark'd but the fall of the Snow
  Before the soyle hath smutch't it?
Have you felt the wool of Beaver?
Or Swan's Downe ever?
Or have smelt o' the bud o' the Brier?
  Or the Nard in the fire?
Or have tasted the bag of the Bee?
O so white! O so soft! O so sweet is she!

  Ben Jonson, Charis: Her Triumph

SPIRIT OF LILLEY OF THE VALLEY (from Norway). This is very good in puddings and cakes, though in Norway it is drunk as a Dram. Gather your Lilley-of-the-Valley Flowers, when they are dry, and pick them from the Stalks; then put a Quarter of a Pint of them into a Quart of Brandy, and so in proportion, to infuse six or eight Days; then distil it in a cold still, marking the Bottles, as they are drawn off, which is first, second, and third, etc. When you have distill'd them, take the first, and so on to the third or fourth and mix them together, till you have as strong as you desire; and then bottle them and cork them well, putting a lump of Loaf-Sugar into each Bottle.

  The Country Lady's Director, 1732

The lily of Kamschatka furnishes food for the natives. The field mice do the work of collecting the roots, the natives then collect these hoards and boil the roots.

PORK AND GOLDEN LILY BUDS.

1 cup sliced pork	Mix:
¾ cup dried golden lily buds	1 teaspoon salt
1½ cups dried fungi	2 teaspoons sugar
3 tablespoons oil	1 tablespoon sherry
¼ cup water	2 tablespoons soy sauce

Soak fungi and lilly buds separately in 1 cup water each for 20 minutes. Wash thoroughly. Heat pan, add oil, and saute pork 1 minute. Add mixture of salt, sugar, sherry, and soy sauce. Add lily buds, fungi, and water. Mix well and cook 1½ minutes. Serves 6.

Mary Sia's Chinese Cookbook
University of Hawaii Press, 1956

Lilies

The White Lily — Purity and Beauty. White is the color of innocence and immortality. Lady Godiva rode a white horse, Sir Galahad was clad in white armor, and when Undine was given the kiss of immortality, her gown "turned lily white".

"There is required only a divine understanding and knowledge . . . which shall blossom in the time of the lily."

Jacob Boehme, The Signature of All Things

CHICKEN WITH LILY BUDS. Take a chicken and cover with a sauce made of 4 tablespoons soy sauce, 2 teaspoons sugar, 3 tablespoons sherry and a half teaspoon salt. Then fry with half cup of oil. Remove and drain, add a bit more oil and fry a dozen yellow lily buds, with a few mushrooms. Return chicken to pan, add water and cover. Simmer until chicken is tender.

Both the day lily and the tiger lily are widely used in the orient for food, either fresh or dried, and are frequently added to soups, meat dishes or noodles. In Japan the bulbs are especially relished and it is thought that the extreme height of the natives of the island of Ainu can be traced to the constant use of this food. Lewis Carroll gave the tiger lily a bad character, when it talked to Alice in the looking-glass garden it was neither good tempered nor polite.

In China the day lily is known as the plant of forgetfulness.

The strict Chinese cook will rub the stove with water-lillies and burn an abundance of the best food as an offering to his god, and while it burns he will offer a prayer.

This is the correct dish to offer a sweetheart:

> *Water-lilies, long or short ones,*
> > *Seek them left and seek them right*
> *For the chaste and modest maiden*
> > *I have sought for, morn and night.*
> > > *"The Odes of Chow and of the South"—1200 B. C.*

STEAMED SOLE WITH WATER-LILY. Mix water-lily with a glass of wine or sherry, a little vinegar, Chinese sauce and ginger. Pour this mixture over the soles and steam for from ten to fifteen minutes, according to size.

Townley Searle, Strange News from China—1932

Lilies

RICE COOKED IN EIGHT PRECIOUS SHADOWS. Wash thoroughly one pound of rice—preferably soaked overnight, and cook in an iron saucepan, in nut oil, adding a quarter of a pound of sugar.

Now mix in another saucepan a mixture consisting of two ounces of ginger, a few grains of lotus flower, half an ounce of lychees, a few jujube fruits, a few cherries and flowers of cinnamon, a number of dates, plums and oranges. Divide this mixture into as many parts as are required. Place each portion in a cup, adding a little of the rice already cooked.

Now place all the cups in a saucepan half-filled with rice and cook until the saucepan is dry. Surround with water again, and cook until the saucepan is almost dry. Then serve hot.

This dish is said to inspire dreams, but you must be careful not to dream of a banquet: "Those who dream of a feast may wake to lamentation and sorrow."

Ibidem.

"Coming suddenly upon the cottage where the magician compiles his edible poems, Mr. Blythe and I were greeted by Mrs. Mallen, who appeared on a wide veranda in a setting of blossoms. "George," said she, setting a tray of long-stemmed lilies on a service table, "has a passion for eating out of doors, where sunlight filters through foliage. Make yourselves comfortable. Here comes his majesty, right from the kitchen."

Enter Saint George, cool as a cucumber, garbed in pongee trousers and a sport shirt open at the neck. Lifting the tray, he offered the lilies. Within each alabaster chalice a light sherry trembled like a living jewel. "Gentlemen, your health. Welcome to Honolulu."

Armitage, Fit for a King

Some Hessian townships have to pay a bunch of Lilies of the Valley every year for rent.

After frying fish add lily buds. A new adventure in taste.

The name "Susannah" signifies a lily.

St. Dominic is always represented as holding a lily.

Pliny says that the root of the white lily steeped in purple wine will produce a purple flower.

Lilies

GREEK EASTER FEAST. Cottage cheese in the form of a Cross. Roast sucking pig or young lamb. Hard-boiled Eggs marked with a Cross. New Honey. Unleavened Bread, Jellied fish in a Cross-shaped mould. Dolmas. Callalou. Stuffed Cucumbers, Lemon Sauce. Tcheureks. Rose-Petal Jam. Black Coffee.

Tcheureks are Greek Easter Cakes sold on the street at the season during Passion and Holy Weeks. Mix four and a half ounces butter with an equal amount of sugar, add five eggs well beaten, one cup of milk, two ounces Yeast, and ten ounces of flour. Let it rise for two hours, form into shape of a large fleur-de-lis, to represent the Trinity, ice with sugar, and bake one hour.

A suggested table decoration—Arrange with garlands of laurel, interwoven with violets and roses in clusters and "lyles entermellyed and graciously arrayed." Old China and silver.

Adelaide Keen, With a Saucepan Over the Sea, 1902

LILY OF THE VALLEY FONDANT. Flavour with the essence and tint a pale cream.

GOLDEN WATER. Take the flowers of lily of the valley and steep them in New Wine for the space of a month; which being finished, take them out again and distil the wine three times over in a Limbeck. The wine is more precious than gold, for if any one that is troubled with apoplexy drink thereof with six grains of Pepper and a little Lavender water they shall not need to fear it that moneth.

Coles, 1657

Golden Water, known as Aqua Aurea was preserved in vessels of gold and silver.

"A Glasse being filled with the flowers of May Lilies and set in an Ant Hill with the mouth close stopped for a month's space and then taken out, ye shall find a liquor in the glasse which being outwardly applied helps the gout very much."
Joachim Camerarius of Nuremberg, 1560

In Germany a wine is made from the flowers, mixed with raisins.

TIGER LILY ⟪⟫⟪⟫⟪⟫⟪⟫⟪⟫⟪⟫⟪⟫⟪⟫⟪⟫

O'er her blue dress an endless blossom strayed;
About her tendril curls the sunlight shone;
And round her train the tiger lilies swayed,
Like courtiers bowing till the Queen be gone.
                                            Austin Dobson

The symbolical meaning of the tiger lily is—"For once may pride befriend me."

The specific name of lily-of-the-Valley is Majalis, signifies that which belongs to May, and the old astrological books place the plant under the dominion of Mercury, since Maia, the daughter of Atlas, was the mother of Mercury or Hermes.

OIL OF LILLIES. As touching the oile of Lillies, which is the most subtile and thinnest of all other, it is made of Lillies, Ben, sweet Calamus, Honie, Cinnamon, Saffron, Myrrhe.

                            Pliny, Naturall Historie

Dr. Roberta Ma, assistant to Dr. William J. Robbins of the New York Botanical Garden, who is an authority on Chinese matters, gives the following recipe for using flowers of the hemerocallis fulva in soup:

1. Fresh buds (just before opening) for six, 2 cups cut or left whole.
   4 cups of meat broth
   1½ cups of meat or chicken
   Salt to taste

   Cook meat in broth until tender; add salt, then the buds; cook for a few minutes before serving.

2. Dried buds.
   Similar to above, but cook dried buds and meat together until both are tender, add salt and some green vegetables, such as watercress or cabbage leaves, cook a few minutes longer.
                            The Herbarist, 1944

YELLOW TIGER LILIES. Place duck in sufficient water to nearly cover. Cook slowly 2½ to 3 hours. At the end of half an hour add tiger lily petals, scattering them over the duck. When done remove duck and slice. Make paste of Chinese Sauce (soy) and flour to thicken soup. Cook two minutes. Pour over sliced duck and garnish with fresh tiger lily blossoms.
                            Alice Moore to Ethel Moore Rock, Long Island, 1923

The flowers of the yellow water-lily are used by the Arabs in a delicious drink called "nufu." As the Mussulman raises the nufu vase to his lips, those present exclaim "May it benefit thee!" "Praise be to Allah!" is the devout response, and he passes the cup with the further ejaculation, "May Allah benefit thee!" The word is a corruption of the Arabic "nonfu," whence is derived from nuphar, the name of the genus.

The Table, by M. B. Flint, May 4th, 1922

Tiger Lily

Gioacchino di Fiore, mystical theologian who founded the community of 'The Flower', writing in the last decade of the 12th Century, divided life of humanity into three periods. In the first, during the reign of the Father, men lived under the rule of the Law; in the second, reigned over by the Son, men live beneath the rule of grace; in the third, the Spirit shall reign and men shall live in the plentitude of Love. The first saw the shining of the stars; the second sees the whitening of the dawn; the third will behold the glory of the day. The first produced nettles; the second gives roses; the third will be the age of lillies.

Elizabeth Haig, Floral Symbolism of
the Great Masters, 1913

WATER LILY. The herb is under the dominion of the Moon, & therefore cools & moistens like the former. The leaves & flowers of the Water Lilies are cold & moist, but the roots & seeds are cold and dry.

Nicholas Culpeper, The Complete Herbal, 1653

ANGELS OF THE EIGHTEEN DISCIPLES OF BUDDHA. Take equal quantities of the following ingredients—honey dates, ginger, Chinese "Come Quick" orange, jujube fruit, lychee, persimmons, lily flower, plums, prunes, preserved tangerine, lily seeds, melon seeds, almonds, nuts, apricots, lemon ground rice and cherries. Cut all up finely and well mix, adding sugar.

Now mix flour and eggs as for an ordinary cake, add the ingredients above and bake in a buttered tin for thirty-five minutes.

Townley Searles, Strange News from China

SWEET LOTUS FLOWER DESSERT. Peel, clean and mince a quarter of a pound of roots of lotus. Place in a saucepan one ounce of ground nut. When sufficiently hot add two ounces of white sugar. When the sugar is melted, add the lotus roots. Stir well and cook for one minute. Turn into a dish and sprinkle with cinnamon.

This is a favourite dish in the Chinese teashops outside which the professional story-tellers, who go from town to town, and from village to village, tell again the popular tales of the mighty heroes of the past.

"The Leyle is an herbe wyth a whyte floure. And though the levys of the floure be white: yet wythin shyneth the lykenesse of golde."

> Bartholomaeus Anglicus, De Proprietatibus Rerum
> 1280 A.D.

LILY-HONEY. Steep the flowers in honey for a week.

Tiger Lily

LILY VINEGAR. An ounce of flowers dried in 1 pint vinegar. Closely stop bottle and infuse 15 days in the sun.

"A lily blossoms upon the mountains and valleys in all the ends of the earth. Ye that seeketh findeth. Amen."

> Jacob Boehme, Signatura Rerum

DUCK AND DRIED LILY BUDS.
  1 duck (3½ pounds)
  ½ cup dried lily buds
  ½ cup dried fungi
  1 cup oil
  ½ cup sliced bamboo shoots
  ½ cup sliced mushrooms
  2 cups water

Mix:
  2 teaspoons sugar
  1½ teaspoons salt
  4 tablespoons soy sauce
  3 tablespoons sherry
  ¼ cup ginger juice
  ¼ cup garlic juice

Rub duck with mixture of sugar, salt, soy sauce, sherry, ginger juice, and garlic juice. Let stand 20 minutes. Soak lily buds and fungi separately 10 minutes in 2 cups warm water each. Wash and pour off water. Heat pan, add oil, and brown duck. Remove duck and pour off oil. Reheat pan, add 2 tablespoons oil, and saute' lilly buds, fungi, bamboo shoots, and mushrooms 1 minute. Add remaining soy sauce mixture and water and simmer 1 minute. Remove to large pot, add duck, and simmer until tender.

∽ Bamboo shoots and mushrooms may be omitted if desired.

> Mary Sia's Chinese Cookbook, Honolulu, 1956

Lily buds should not be more than two inches long, otherwise they will be bitter.

Tiger lilies have a slightly acid flavor and are quite palatable.

One and one half fresh lily bulbs are equal to 97 calories, over sixty-six percent is water. Lily flowers have only 37.5 calories in three-fourths of a cup, with more than ten per cent of it in proteins. The Lotus root has 204 calories in one and a half medium sections.

Tiger Lily

In France on May 1st lilies of the valley (muguets) are worn and sent to friends to wish them luck.

A "Pottys of lylys" was served during the post-coronation banquet of Henry IV in 1399. The recipe? I hope a reader can find it and send it to me. In another early cook book Turk's-cap lilies are mentioned for their savour, but again, no recipe.

"The flowerbuds of the common fragrant water-lily, which abounds from Labrador to Manitoba, south to Florida and Texas, are cooked and relished by the Ojibwa Indians."

Dr. Huron H. Smith

. . . And up and down the people go
Gazing where the lilies blow,
Round an island there below,
The island of Shalott.

Tennyson

The Lotus symbolizes Purity being so beautiful and stainless, yet rising from slime.

In ancient China wine was poured into small golden cups, placed in the center of a lotus flower and passed to the guests.

Dip buds (or open blossoms) of the day lily in a rich batter, then into hot fat and fry a golden brown.

The tiger flower is from Mexico, and while they do not look it they are fierce. They are known as shell flowers and were grown profusely in the ancient gardens of Mexico (elcacomite). They furnished two kinds of feasts, one for the eye and the other to allay hunger, having the flavor of chestnuts.

LIME FLOWERS ∿∿∿∿∿∿∿∿∿∿∿∿∿∿∿∿∿∿

In the early 5th Century, recognizing the lime as a tree of love, sang, "Under the lime tree on the daisied ground, two that I know of made this bed . . . There you may see heaped and scattered round, grass and blossoms broken and shed . . . Taradaradei — sweetly sang the nightingale."

Walther von der Vogelweide

LIME FLOWER TEA. Put half an ounce of lime flowers, fresh or dried, into a tea pot and pour over a cup of boiling water. Let it steep for five minutes, and if desired, add milk and sugar.

Cold lime flower tea is a noted thirst quencher. This is a popular drink in Iraq and also France where stocks of dried lime-flowers (linden) are kept by most families for making Tilleul.

In flower symbolism they mean conjugal love.

LIME FLOWER HONEY is regarded as the best flavored and the most valuable in the world.

LIME FLOWER WINE. Use the recipe for making Clary Wine.

LIME BLOSSOM CONSERVE. The Siamese are skilled in making this conserve, made as follows: Take 1/4 pound of lime blossoms and chop fine, add 1 tablespoon lemon juice. Make a syrup of 2 lbs. of sugar, boil until it feathers, cool slightly and add the flowers.

Linden sap contains a great deal of sugar, but one of the strangest uses made of this tree was in the making of a substitute for chocolate. Nissa, a French chemist discovered it by making a paste of flowers and fruits. Although the results were good it would not keep. The Iroquois Indians liked to nibble the young spring buds.

LOTUS ~~~~~~

In the square pool the
Lotus are tall,
Countless beauties dazzle
  each other.
The recluse rising from his
  night's sleep,
Wonders whether the wilderness
  is on fire.

                    Yao Ho, T'ang Dynasty

The Lotus symbolizes Purity.

Every part of the lotus plant has a name and is made use of by the Chinese. The tubers are eaten as a vegetable, also sliced and candied. Chinese arrow-root made from dried and powdered stems, and the kernels are eaten in soup, roasted, or eaten raw.

The lotus is the emblem of the Past, Present and the Future.

❧ It is believed to be the first flower to appear on earth and was the floral emblem of Mu.

LILY-ROOT PUDDING. 2 cups lily-root powder, 1 cup sugar, 6 cups of water. Dissolve lily-root powder in a small quantity of cold water and mix well, add the balance of the water and sugar. Stir and place in a suitable pan for steaming. It will be done in about an hour.

LOTUS-ROOT SOUP. Take 12 cups of stock, 6 cups of roots (either fresh or dried), 6 very thin slices of fresh ginger, tangerine rind (a third or fourth of a whole rind), 2 cups of meat (pork, veal, beef, oysters, fish, duck, chicken—or a combination), 2 teaspoons MSG, 1 tablespoon soy sauce, salt and pepper to taste. If you can get the fresh roots, skin and slice 1/4 inch thick. If you use the dried roots, soak first in warm water. Also soak the dried tangerine skin in warm water for 20 minutes. Add roots, tangerine and ginger to boiling stock-simmer for an hour. Add meat and simmer for another 20 minutes, then add MSG, soy sauce, salt and pepper. Cook all together for another ten minutes and serve very hot.

Lotus

LOTUS SEED TEA. 1 cup candied lotus seeds, ½ cup sugar, 3 cups water and 1 tablespoon cornstarch. Mix sugar, cornstarch and water — boil for a few minutes and add lotus seeds. Serve hot.

LOTUS ROOT SOUP. 1 lotus root, peeled and sliced, 1 pound beef-sliced thin, salt to taste and 4 cups of water. Place beef and lotus root in water, bring to a boil and cook for 30 minutes. Add salt and serve.

ALMOND TEA. ½ cup ground almond powder, 1 tablespoon lotus flour, ½ cup sugar, ¾ cup milk, 4 cups of water and a few toasted almonds. Put the sugar, lotus flour and almond powder in a saucepan, gradually add milk and water. Simmer for 10 minutes and serve hot with toasted almonds.

I bring thee the flower which was in the Beginning, the
glorious lily of the Great Water.
Text from Denderah

Stuffed Lotus Stems

Take 10-12 slices of lotus stem and make a filling of minced pork, chopped onion, 1 slice ginger chopped, 2 tablespoons soy sauce and 1 tablespoon corn starch which have been sauteed together. Spread this mixture between 2 slices of lotus stems, dip in fritter batter and fry in deep fat until golden brown. Drain on paper towel. Serve hot.

Lotus seeds are also good to flavor winter melon soup.

During Chinese New Year the seeds are served candied.

Moon Cakes (Harvest Moon)

Mix 3 or 4 chopped preserved cherries, ½ cup chopped jujubes, ½ cup chopped green plums, ¼ cup chopped walnuts, ¼ cup chopped preserved ginger, ½ cup pine nuts, ½ cup brown sugar, ½ cup red wine, 1 cup chopped cooked beef with a tablespoon suet, 6 lotus seeds, ½ teaspoon ground ginger and ¼ teaspoon salt. Cook for an hour and cool. Make piecrust and line tart tins, fill ⅔ full and cover with crust. On top of this cut crescents from remainder of pastry. Cook in 450 degree oven for 20-30 minutes. Serve either hot or cold.

Candied lotus seeds are one of the ingredients in the famous Eight Precious Pudding.

Lotus Roots

Lotus

  Take a quarter pound of lotus roots (cleaned, peeled, and sliced thin), a quarter teaspoon of sugar, 1 teaspoon cornstarch, quarter cup water, 1 tablespoon soy sauce, 2 tablespoons gin, a quarter pound meat (either pork or beef, sliced thin), salt to taste and two tablespoons cooking oil.

  Heat oil in a saucepan or skillet, add salt and meat. After meat is slightly browned add soy sauce and gin, then the lotus roots. Cover and cook five minutes, then add the sugar and cornstarch which has been blended with water. Stir and cook until translucent. (A popular March dish.)

In ancient Egypt wine from the Nile Delta was rare. Beer was made of grain ground in stone mortars, then moistened, stamped in a cask, laid in a sieve, and kneaded till it dripped. This was the daily intoxicant and was kept in earthenware jars closed with plugs of Nile mud. Both wine and beer jars were decorated with the lotus. Tables were lavishly decorated with the lotus and women put them in their hair, as men were enticed by their fragrance. These gay parties led Aristotle to note that those drunk with wine fall forwards, and those drunk with beer fall backwards.

Today on Delta channels the blue lotus blooms as in the days when they laid the blossoms beside the dead; but the nekheb, the true, sacred lotus, has vanished from Egypt.

Lotus-Root Salad. 1 pound of lotus root, peeled and sliced, 2 tablespoons vinegar, 2 tablespoons soy sauce, 1 tablespoon sesame oil, 3 hot red peppers—chopped, and 2 tablespoons cooking oil or olive oil. Soak the roots in cold water for 10 to 15 minutes, then dip in boiling water and change again to cold water. In the meantime heat the oil and fry the peppers. Remove and add all other ingredients—including the lotus roots. Cook for 3 or 4 minutes then chill in refrigerator before serving.

Lotus Seed And Rice Dessert. 1 cup rice, ½ cup dried lotus seeds, and ½ cup sugar. Soak seeds in hot water and remove skins and the green hearts, which are very bitter. Wash and boil in 3 pints of water for 30 minutes. Wash rice and add to seeds, when rice is done add the sugar. Serve hot.

Bitter as the plumule of the Lotus seed,
    —Chinese proverb

  This plumule—a small green hook—represents the nth degree of bitterness, which the Chinese extract and use in the treatment of fever.

Lotus

Fried Rice In Lotus Leaves. Take 3 cups cooked rice and ½ cup of sliced mushrooms, 1 cup each of diced pork and shrimp, a tablespoon soy sauce, 2 tablespoons sesame oil, ½ teaspoon each of sugar and salt, and 6 lotus leaves which have been parboiled.

  Saute all ingredients, except the lotus leaves, and divide into six portions—one for each leaf. Wrap in the leaf and tie with the stem. Steam for 10 minutes—the rice will absorb the flavor of the leaf. Serve hot, let each guest open the leaves, which are then discarded.

  Herodotus, an historian who lived circa 500 BC, went to Egypt and wrote the following: "But to obtain food more easily, they have the following invention when the river is full . . . they gather and dry in the sun then having pounded the middle of the lotus, which resembles a poppy, they make a bread of it and bake it. The root also of this lotus is fit for food, and is tolerably sweet, and is round and of the size of an apple. There are also other lilies, like roses, that grow in the river, the fruit of which is contained in a separate pod that springs up from the root, in form very like a wasp's nest; in this there are many berries fit to be eaten, of the size of an olive stone, and they are eaten both fresh and dried."

The Chinese often flavored rice with lotus flowers.

MALLOW

With many curve my banks I fret
By many field and fallow
And many a fairy foreland set,
With willowweed and mallow.
      —Tennyson

  In the first century B. C. a Chinese poet wrote: "I'll pluck the mallows and make soup."

Mallow Soup. Take the young leaves and make as you would spinach soup. They blend well with other tender garden or wildflower greens. Serve garnished with hard-boiled eggs, or even nuts would be good.

  In this chapter I decided to combine mallow (malva), marsh-mallow (althaea officinalis), and marsh-marigold (caltha palustris).

MARSHMALLOW

These flowers are white or pale purple and were the base of a famous confection—Pate de gimauve. The marshmallows we buy in the supermarkets today have long-since had a base of gelatine or agar-agar.

Mallow

MARSHMALLOW SYRUP. Take 4 ounces dried marshmallow roots, bruise; add two ounces of raisins and seven pounds of water. (Remember a pint is a pound the world around.) Boil it down to five pounds and strain.

The Paris Pharmacopoeia has more or less the same recipe but adds 15 drops of orange-flower water.

TO DRY MARSHMALLOW FLOWERS. Gather the flowers before sunrise; pick them off the stalks and spread them on a table in a shady place. When the flowers are perfectly dry put them in tins or paper bags and keep them in a dry place.

Paris Pharmacopoeia

MARSHMALLOW TEA. Gather some purple marshmallow flowers and dry them in the sun until they are quite crisp. Put the dried flowers into a teapot, one tablespoonful for two people, and pour on boiling water and drink hot. This is an excellent cure for colds.

Recipes from East and West by Euterpe Craies, 1912

MARSH-MARIGOLD

This is known in America as the "Cowslip", but don't confuse with the English cowslip.

MARSH-MARIGOLD PICKLES. Use the unopened flower buds. First soak in salt water and then cook in spiced vinegar. They make a good substitute for capers and at one time were very popular in South Carolina.

CREAMED "COWSLIPS": Cook the cowslips and add salt. Drain and chop fine. Into a saucepan put a tablespoon of butter, mix with same amount of flour, and salt and pepper to taste. Add greens and a half-cup of milk. Mix well and serve on toast.

I don't have many recipes but I have found some beguiling names for the marsh-marigold. Bassinet, Blobs, Boots. Bull flower, Butter blob, Carlock cups, Chirms, Clout, Cow cranes, Crazy Bet, Crow flower, Drunkard, Fire o'Gold, Gitcup, Water goggles, King cups, Meadow bright, Moll blob, Publicans and Sinners, and Soldier's buttons.

Symbollically it means: Desire for riches.

Mallow

MARSH MARIGOLD WINE.
1 gallon marsh marigold blossoms
Lemons, 2
Orange, 1
Brandy, 1 quart
Water, 1 gallon
Sugar, 3 lbs.
Yeast, 1 package

Boil the sugar and water together for 20 minutes. Meanwhile put the grated rind of the lemons and the orange into a crock and pour the boiling syrup over them. Let cool, strain, and pour it over the marsh marigold blossoms. Add the yeast. After several days, skim and pour into a cask. Add the brandy and seal tight. Bottle after 2 months, and it can be served then, but it is better to wait for 6 months.

MARIGOLD

Open afresh your round of starry folds
Ye ardent marigolds!
Dry up the moisture from your golden lids,
For great Apollo bids
That in these days your praises should be sung
On many harps, which he has lately strung.
                    —John Keats

SCRAMBLED EGGS WITH MARIGOLDS. Beat 4 eggs with 4 tbsp. milk, add $\frac{1}{8}$ teaspoon each salt, pepper, nutmeg. Scramble in 1 tbsp. butter. When almost done, add 2 washed, chopped marigolds. Serve on French toast made of pumpernickel. Garnish with marigold petals. Serves 2.

CHEESE MADE WITH MARIGOLDS. To Make a Cheese (Mrs. Bennet). Take ye night's milke of seven cows, & take ye creame of it; then take morning milk of 7 cows, & ye morning milke and ye night's creame together. Then take a handfull or two of marrigold flowers well picked & bruised; then boile the marrigolds in a gallon of water a whill; then strain the water into ye said milke & creame & put as much runnet as will make it com. Covere it close with a blanckett and it may com hard; & when it is com take two cheese cloaths and lay them in two stands & give your curd one stirr & lay in your curd without breaking of it or sinking of it; then let it stand one houre; then crush it with bords, till ye whay is all out; then lay it in water halfe an houer; then crush it with boards till ye whay & water is all out. Then make it up into ye vatt & put a little salt in ye midle of it; then sett a fifty pound weight on it for an houer, then shif it into fresh cloaths every houer for 3 or 4 houers, then put it into ye press & when you take it out of ye press, salt it, but not tow much; then pinn a cloath about it to keep it upright till it is stiffe.

Marigold

The Receipt Book of Ann Blencowe, 1694

Marigold petals can be used fresh or dried, in salads, braised beef, chowders, chicken soup, and broths. The secret of the famous Dutch soups, color and flavor, was the use of the marigold. Mediaeval French and English cooks liked it too.

Marigolds give a piquant flavor to custards, cookies, muffins and buns, puddings and some beverages.

MARIGOLD CUSTARD. Bruise a cup of marigold petals in a mortar and add to a pint of scalded milk flavored with vanilla. Add the slightly beaten yolks of three eggs, 1/4 teaspoon salt, 1/2 cup of sugar, a generous pinch of nutmeg and allspice. Cook until it coats a spoon and then add a dash of rosewater. Serve with whipped cream garnished with marigold petals.

MARIGOLD RICE. Dissolve half a teaspoon powdered marigold into half a cup of chicken broth. Set aside. Then take 1 cup uncooked rice (if minute rice cook in chicken broth) for 5 minutes. Fry a bit of minced onion in butter and add. Mix the dissolved marigold powder with all ingredients and sprinkle grated Parmesan over top. Other ingredients may be added to the rice, such as shrimp, mushrooms, or chicken livers, or all three.

Marigold

CALENDULA OFFICINALIS by Marjorie Gibbon

📖 The plant soon strayed from the "Apothecarie's" to the "Dame's Garden". The temptation is irresistible to suggest a Marigold Meal for a compleat and courageous hostess. The dinner begins with mutton broth, and "none", says Gerard, "are well made without Marigold petals, and Marigold buns with golden yellow butter." Next, the main dish of "good fat beef, garnished with a few Marygold flowers . . . and serve up with sippets." The proper vegetable to go with this will be the "buds before they be floured. Boiled and eaten with butter . . . they are exceeding pleasant." Then a salad decorated with the blossoms, "for Marigolds *should* be present at the last rites of the crab that meets its end in a salad, for all to gaze upon and not to eat." Accompany this with a Farmhouse Marigold Cheese, "Mix the new milk of seven cows with the cream from the milk of seven more cows. . . . Add to this three or four handfuls of Marigolds bruised a little. . . ." Top off with a "Tart of Marygold, Primrose or Cowslips" and wash down with Marigold wine, "very golden and pleasant".

📖 If this dinner of herbs fails to induce the proverbial contentment, why, *similia, similibus curantur*—just take a potion of the petals pounded in vinegar for "they strengthen the heart exceedingly and are very expulsive."

The Herbarist, No. 7, 1941
A Publication of the Herb Society of America
Boston, Massachusetts

HOW TO CANDY ROSEMARY-FLOWERS. ROSE-LEAVES, ROSES, MARIGOLDS, ETC. WITH PRESERVATION OF COLOUR. Desolve refined or double-refined sugar, or sugar candy itselfe, in a little Rose-water; boyl it to a reasonable height; put in your roots or flowers when you sirup is eyther fully cold, or almost cold: let them rest therein till the sirup have pierced them sufficiently: then take out your flowers with a skimmer, suffering the loose sirup to run from them as long as it will: boyl that sirup a little more, and put in more flowers, as before; divide them also; then boyl all the sirup which remaineth, and is not drunke up in the flowers, putting in more sugar if you see cause, but no more Rose-water, put your flowers therein when your sirup is cold, or almost cold, and let them stand till they candy.

Delights of Ladies

GOLDEN SAUCE. Cream together 1 egg, 1 cup of softened butter, 1 cup sugar, $\frac{1}{2}$ teaspoon lemon juice, a bit of lemonpeel and a cup of marigold petals. Add a bit of boiling water and cook until thick.

The Marigold symbolizes grief, sorrow and cares.

MARYGOLD WINE. Mix 24 pounds of granulated sugar, four pounds of honey with 10 gallons of water and boil. Remove from fire and add 12 well-beaten egg whites. Boil again for an hour, scum, and add a bushel of marigold petals and five pounds of raisins. Cover and leave for 24 hours. Then put into a dry, clean cask and add the peel of half dozen Seville oranges. Put aside two gallons of the mixture to be added as the fermentation decreases the wine. Stir three packages of yeast into the wine and leave until fermentation ceases. Stop it close and leave for a year, then add a quart of brandy and leave for another year.

Marigold

EGGS WITH MARIGOLDS. Chop a few marigold flowers and have ready for the required number of poached eggs. While they are cooking sprinkle with the flowers and a bit of nutmeg and pepper and salt to taste. Then fry some bread, which has first been soaked in milk, serve eggs on top garnished with powdered marigolds and fried parsley.

MARIGOLD PUDDING. Ingredients: Dry cherries, pistachios, almonds, fine white breadcrumbs ½ lb.; sugar 1 tablespoon, boiling milk 1 teacupful (or ¼ pint); suet, finely chopped 4 oz.; 1 to 1½ cups marigold petals; eggs 3; champagne sauce or some other not quite so expensive.

Butter a mould well and decorate it with the cherries and nuts. Put the breadcrumbs into a basin, stir in the sugar and pour the boiling milk over the mixture. Stir in the suet and marigold petals. Whisk up the eggs to a very light froth and whisk them into the mixture a little at a time, so that the pudding may be light. Pour the mixture carefully into the mould so as not to disturb the decorations. Cover with buttered greaseproof paper and steam for one hour and a quarter. Serve with champagne or other wine sauce.

The yellow leaves of the floures are dried and kept throughout Dutchland, against winter, to put into broths, in such quantities that in some grocers or spice sellers are to be found barrels filled with them and retailed by the penny more or lesse insomuch as no broths are well made without dried marigolds.

Gerarde, Herball

MARIGOLDS IN MUTTON BROTH. Take a neck of mutton about 6 lb., cut it in two. Boil the scrag in a gallon of water. Skim it well. Put in a little bundle of sweet herbs, an onion and a good crust of bread. Let it boil one hour, then put in the other part of the mutton. Take a turnip or two, some dried marigold flowers, a few chives chopped fine, a little parsley chopped small. Put these in about a quarter of an hour before your broth is enough. Season with salt. Or you may put in ¼ lb. barley or rice at first. Some love it thickened with oatmeal and some with bread: and some love it seasoned with mace instead of sweet herbs and onions; all this is fancy and different palates. If you boil turnips for sauce, do not boil all in the pot; it makes the broth too strong of them.

Marigold

> Mrs. Hannah Glasse, The Art of Cookery
> Made Plain and Easy. First edition
> 1747. Last edition, 1803.

Marigolds were the favorite flowers of Margaret of Angoulême. It was worn by Huguenot soldiers in battle, and picked from her Navarre garden as a distinctive badge for her warriors.

TO STEW BEEF WITH MARYGOLDS. Take good fat Beef, slice it very thin into small pieces, and beat it well with the back of a chopping knife. Then put it into a pipkin, and cover it with wine and water, and put into it a handfull of good herbs, and an onion and an anchovie. Let it boil for two hours; a little before you take it up, put in a few Marygold-flowers; and so season it with what spice you please, and serve them up with sippets.

☙ Garnish your dish with Marygold-flowers or barberries.

> Sir Kenelm Digby, Queen's Closet Opened
> 1669

CRAB SALAD AND MARIGOLDS. "I shall half-fill the bowl with cool watercress and lettuce; then, having broken my crab's claws with discrimination, I lay dainty fragments of the 'meat' atop my greenery. Two kinds of leafage is sufficient: many flavours, a mistake.

☙ "Next, keeping a watchful eye on 'deaf ears' (are they its ears, and is it deaf!) I shall remove the jaw-part from my crustacean, the better to make a dressing in the shell. To this I shall put a teaspoonful of salt, a saltspoonful of pepper, and a tablesponful each of vinegar and olive oil. If I have chilli vinegar I shall use no mustard. If this condiment is plain, a teaspoonful of made mustard will give my dressing zest. When it is properly blended, I shall pour it into the bowl and toss all lightly.

Marigold

    "Lastly, I shall place slices of hard-boiled egg on my crab salad, and if my marigolds are flowering then, alternate circles of the blooms and thin cucumber rings.

    "For marigolds *should* be present at the last rites of the crab that meets its end in a salad—for all to gaze upon, and not to eat."

Crab Salad, by an Old Maid.

MARYGOLD BUNS. Dry one pound of flour, and work into it 3 oz. of lard and the same weight of butter. When well mixed with the flour stir in a teaspoonful of baking powder, 1/4 lb. of sugar, and a tiny pinch of salt.

    They can be made without fruit, but they are much better with fruit. Wash and dry a handful of sultanas and cut up some candied peel into small chunks and throw into the mixing bowl. Put some dried marigold petals into a small muslin bag and set to soak in a small cup of very hot milk. While the milk is cooling an egg should be well beaten. Remove the marigold petals from the milk and add the beaten egg to it.

    Then stir the mixture into the bowl containing the dry ingredients, and the whole should be beaten for some minutes—the longer the better. The mixture should then be put into bun tins and baked in a moderate oven.

DRIED MARYGOLD PETALS. Only the ray florets are to be used and they must be dried quickly, out of the sun and in a current of warm air. They must be placed loosely on large sheets of paper, care being taken that they should not touch each other or they will become discoloured. When the flowers seem quite dry rub the petals from the flowers and bottle for use.

"The first herbe is called with the men of Chaldea, Elois, with the Latynes, Eliotropium, with Englysh men, Marigolde, whose interpretation, is of Elion, that is the Sone, and Tropos, that is alternation, or chaunge, because it is turned according to the sunn. The vertue of this herbe is mervelous: for if it be gathered, the Sunne beyunge in the Sygne Leo, in August, and be wrapped in the leafe of a Laurell, or baye tree, & a wolves tothe be added thereto, no more shalbe able to have a word to speak agaynst the bearer thereof, but wordes of peace. And yf anything be stolne, yf the bearer of the thynges before namen, laye them under hys head in the night he shall see the thefe and al his conditions. And moreover if the aforesaid herbe be put in any churche, where eomen be, which have broken Matrymonye, one theyr parte, they shall never be able to go forthe of the churche, excepte it be put awaye. And this last poynt hath bene proved, and very true. The Boke of the Secrets of Albertus Magnus, 1560*

"Calendula is an herbe called ruddes . . . It groweth most in gardyns & numerous places. Maydens make garlands of it when they go to feestes and brydeales because it hath fayre yelowe flowers and ruddy. And it is called Calendula because it beareth flowers all the kalendes of every month of the yere.
The Grete Herball, 1526

Marigold

CONSERVE OF MARIGOLD. Take one pound of marigold petals and three pounds of sugar and boil together with a quart of water, until a syrup is formed and then pour into glasses.

Markham trying to explain the difference between PRESERVES *and* CONSERVES:
"I understand by this preserve, taken properly, the preserving of things whole and not stampt and beaten into one bodie.
. . . Roses, Mints . . . and such like be preserved: the flowers of Marigolds, Succorie, Violets, Broome, Sage and other such like: and such preserves are more acceptance than conserves, because the flowers and laves do in better sort retaine and keepe their natural smell thus, than in conserves . . ."

BEST ORDINARY POTTAGE. Violet leaves, Succory, Strawberry leaves, Spinage, Langdebeef (a variety of bugloss), Marygold flowers, Scallions, and a little Parsley. (He also added oatmeal.)

Gervase Markham, English Housewife   1615

AN EXCELLENT CORDIAL. Take the flowers of Marigolds, and lay them in small spirit of Wine, when the tincture is fully taken out, pour it off from the flowers, and vapour it away till it come to a consistency as thick as any Electuary.

Elizabeth Grey, Countess of Kent, A Choice
Manuall of Rare and Select Secrets in Physick
and Chirurgery, 1653

TO PICKLE MARYGOLD FLOWERS. Strip the Flower-leaves off, when you have gathered the Flowers at Noon, or in the Heat of the Day, and boill some Salt and Water; and when that is cold, put your Marigold-Flower-Leaves in a Gallypot and pour the Salt and Water upon them; then shut them up close till you use them. And they will be of a fine Colour, and much fitter for Porridge than those that are dry'd.

R. Bradley, Country Housewife and Lady's
Director, 1732

MARIGOLD WINE. To every gallon of water put two pounds of sugar, let it boil for an Hour, then set it to cool; make a good brown toast, spread it well on both sides with yeast; but before you put it in, put an ounce and half of Syrup of Citron to each Gallon of Liquor, and beat it well in, then put in the Toast while it is of a proper warmth for working and let it work which it will do for two Days; during which time put in your marygold flowers a little bruised, but not much stamp'd, a Peck to each Gallon, and add a Pint of White or Rhenish wine to each Gallon, and let it stand two Days, then tun it up in a sweet cask.

Marigold

Charles Carter, Cook to the Duke of Argyll, 1731

CORDIAL. Take a large still with marigold-flowers, and strew on it an ounce of case-nutmegs, that is, the nutmegs that have the mace on them; beat them grossly, and take an unce of the best English saffron, pull it and mix it with the flowers; then take three pints of Muscadine, or Malaga sack, and with a sprig of Rosemary dash it on the flowers; then distil it off with a slow fire, and let it drop on white sugar candy, draw it off till it begins to be sour, have a pint of the first running to mix with other matters on an extraordinary occasion.

This cordial is excellent in fainting.

E. Smith, The Compleat Housewife

TO CANDY DOUBLE MARIGOLDS, ROSES, OR ANY OTHER FLOWERS. Take a little piece of your Arabrick and lay it in steep in a little Rose water and then take some sugar Candy and bruise it in little small pieces like small sparks of Diamonds, then take your flowers in ye height (heat) of ye day & wett ym over with gum water and lay ym upon ye bottome of ye sive, & strew ym over with sugar candy and sett ym in ye sun to dry & when ye one side is candied of ym turn ym and candy ye other side of ym in ye same manner and so keep ym for your use.

Mary Doggett, Book of Receipts, 1682

MARIGOLD CORDIAL OR LIQUEUR.
½ peck marigold petals
1 pound honey
6 quarts of water
4 pounds of brown sugar (or white sugar)
1 pound raisins, cut in half
3 oranges
1 package of yeast
2 envelopes of unflavored Knox gelatine

Marigold

⤴ Mix petals and raisins and pour over them a boiling liquid made of the sugar, honey and water. Clear while boiling with the whites and shells of three eggs. Cover and let set for twenty-four hours. Strain and put into a wooden keg and add the grated orange rind and another pound of sugar, add the yeast, and when the fermentation is stopped add a pint of brandy and the gelatine as a clearing agent. Bung tightly and at the end of six months, bottle and keep another six months.

MARIGOLD PUDDING. Take a pretty quantity of marygold flowers very well shred, mingle with a pint of Cream or New Milk and almost a Pound of Beef Suet chopt very small, the gratings of a Twopenny loaf and stirring all together put into a Bag flower'd and tie it fast. It will be boil'd within an hour—or bake in a pan.

John Evelyn, Acetaria, 1699

EVELYN'S PUDDING RECIPE MODERNIZED FOR 1965.
Take a cup of chopped marigold petals, 1 cup of marjoram-chopped, 1 cup of currants, 1 cup of sugar and 2 eggs. Meanwhile make a dough of 2 cups of flour, 4 teaspoons baking powder, salt, and ¼ pound of butter or suet and mix other ingredients, plus a cup of water. Put into a floured bag, tie and steam for 2 hours. This can be served with orange or tangerine sauce, and garnished with fresh petals.

In the Middle Ages the marigold was the emblem of jealousy.

The marigold that goes to bed with the sun
And with him rises weeping; these are flowers
Of middle summer, and I think they are given
To men of middle age.
                    Pericles.   Act iv, Scene 1

The French call the marigold Souci, meaning worry.

The marigold is one of the flowers which gives flashes of intermittent light, usually occurring at twilight time in clear weather.

October 18th is St. Luke's Day, and was regarded as lucky for lovers. Mother Bunch said to Margaret, "Let me see, this is St. Luke's day, which I have found by long experience to be fitter for this purpose than St. Agnes's, and the ingredients more excellent. Take Marigold flowers, a sprig of Marjoram, Thyme, and a littel Wormwood; dry them before a fire, rub them to powder, then sift it through a fine piece of lawn; simmer these with a small quantity of virgin

honey in white vinegar over a slow fire; with this anoint your stomach, breasts, and lips lying down, and repeat these words thrice:—
> "St. Luke, St. Luke, be kind to me,
> In dreams let me my true love see!"

This said, hasten to sleep; and in the soft slumber of your night's repose the very man whom you shall marry will appear before you.

Reverend Hilderic Friend, Flowers and Flower Lore
Nims & Knight, Troy, N.Y. 1889

Marigold

An Old Flower Riddle
"What flower is that which bears the Virgin's name,
The richest metal joined with the same?"

Answer: MARY-GOLD

John Gay, 1728

MARIGOLD CHEESE. Take two cups of marigold petals and tie in a nylon net bag and then pound in a mortar, saving the juice. Add rennet and this juice to milk, then when set stir and break it gently and hang in another nylon net bag so that the whey can drip out.

MARIGOLD POSSET. Take a fair scoured skellet, put in some milk and marigold petals. After boyling, strain out the marigolds, add ale or beer and some sugar, or leave out the sugar.

Robert May, 1671

"The fruitful or much-bearing marigold, is likewise called Jackanapes-on-horse-backe: it hath leaves stalkes and roots like the common sort of marigold, differing in the shape of his floures; for this plant doth bring forth at the top of the stalke one floure like the other marigolds, from which start forth sundry other small floures, yellow likewise and of the same fashion as the first; which if I be not deceived commeth to pass per accidens, or by chance, as Nature often times liketh to play with other flowers; or as children are borne with two thumbes on one hande or such like; which living to be men do get children like unto others: even so is the seed of this Marigold, which if it be sowen it brings forth not one floure in a thousand like the plant from whence it was taken."

Gerard

Marigold Sandwich: Layer on thinly sliced whole-wheat bread (1) a slice of cheddar cheese (2) liver wurst (3) marigold petals (4) mayonnaise. Sprinkle with sesame seeds.

MEADOWSWEET

Where is the girl, who by the boatman's door
Above the locks, above the boating throng
Unmoored our skiff when through the long Thames flats
Red loosestrife and blond meadowsweet among
And darting swallows and light water gnats
We track'd the shy Thames shore.

Matthew Arnold

"The flowers and leaves of Meadowsweet farre excelle all other strowing herbs
for to decke up houses, to strawe in chambers, halls and banqueting-houses in the
summer-time, for the smell thereof makes the heart merrie and joyful and delight-
eth the senses."
Gerard

In flower symbology meadowsweet means uselessness.

MEADOWSWEET TEA. A quart of boiling water poured on an ounce of the fresh or dried leaves and flowering tops.

A little meadowsweet is an excellent flavor for soup.

MEADOWSWEET SYRUP. Take 2 ounces of Meadowsweet, Betony, Raspberry leaves and Agrimony, boil in eight quarts of water for fifteen or twenty minutes, strain and add 2 pounds of sugar. Bottle. This makes a good drink poured over ice. (This can be made into beer by adding yeast.)

Culpeper recommends adding it to claret cup, it has a pleasant almond like taste.

MIGNONETTE

The invisible garden is that of scents, Jason Hill uses various adjectives—
cold, intense, complex, evocative, interesting, hearty, luscious. But, "Mignonette
has the dusty odor of antiquity."
—Hill, The Curious Gardener

A MIGNONETTE BOWL. One bottle of white wine, fifteen or twenty fresh sprigs of mignonette and a cup of sugar. Remove the blossoms and stir into the wine.

✍ Mignonette flavored salt is used frequently in Turkish cooking, especially with veal and lamb dishes.

Mignonette

Symbolical meaning: Your qualities surpass your charms.

MIMOSA

"Les Mimosas" the flower-girls cry as they offer us branches
Along the curve of their sea a-bloom in the sunlight;
Like dust, like foam are the blooms, but many and golden
On branch that I hold in my hand . . .
—Flower Pieces by Padraic Colum
The Orwell Press, Dublin 1938

✍ In Grasse, on the French Riviera, they praline the blossoms of mimosa. The little fluffy balls, solidified in sugar, are particularly delicious in flavor.

MIMOSA CRYSTALS.
1 cup flowers
1 oz. gum arabic
1 cup water
1 tablespoon corn syrup
1 cup sugar
✍ Dry flowers. Dissolve gum arabic in ½ cup hot water and cool. Carefully coat the petals with this mixture. Put them on wax paper so they will not touch and mix the corn syrup and sugar in ½ cup water and cook to a soft ball. Dip petals into syrup and dry. Sprinkle with finely granulated sugar.

MOTHERWORT

✍ *Venus owns the herb and it is under Leo; there is no better herb to drive away melancholy vapours from the heart.*
—Nicholas Culpeper

Symbolizes: Concealed love.

✍ Motherwort is a herb of life to the Japanese. They have a Motherwort Festival on the ninth day of the ninth month. The month is known as Kikousouki, "Month of Motherwort fllowers."
✍ Saki has as one of its ingredients this herb, as its flowers are dipped into

the liquor. At festival time it is drunk along with rice mixed with the flowers. Cups of saki are dressed with the flowers which neighbors pass from hand to hand with wishes for a long life.

Motherwort

* There is a village there whose inhabitants drank from a stream which flowed over a hill covered with motherwort, and it is said that many of them lived to one hundred and thirty and longer. It is said that one lived to be three hundred.

MOTHERWORT CONSERVE. To one pound of flowers add two pounds of sugar. Crush and stir in the sugar gradually. Store in a tightly covered jar.

MOTHERMORT SYRUP. To three pounds of flowering stems use one gallon of boiling water. Let it set overnight. In the morning squeeze herbs and add more. Heat and again let it set. Keep doing this until it is strong enough to suit you, then to every quart of water add four pounds of sugar. (Or one pound to every cup of liquid.) Make a syrup and bottle.

NASTURTIUMS ෴෴෴෴෴෴෴෴෴෴෴෴

The Indian cress our climate now do's bear,
Call'd Larksheel 'cause he wears a horse-man's spur,
This gilt-spun knight prepares his course to run
Taking his signal from the rising sun,
And stimulates his flow'r to meet the day
So Castor mounted spurs his steed away
This warrior sure has in some battle been
For spots of blood upon his breast are seen.
                    Abraham Cowley

GENERAL EISENHOWER'S RECIPE FOR NASTURTIUM VEGETABLE SOUP

* The best time to make vegetable soup is a day or so after you have had fried chicken and out of which you have saved the necks, ribs, backs, un-cooked. (The chicken is not essential, but does add something.)

* Procure from the meat market a good beef soup bone—the bigger the better. It is a rather good idea to have it split down the middle so that all the marrow is exposed. In addition, buy a couple pounds of ordinary soup meat, either beef or mutton, or both.

Nasturtiums

✎ Put all this meat, early in the morning, in a big kettle. The best kind is heavy aluminum, but a good iron pot will do almost as well. Put in also the bony parts of the chicken you have saved. Cover it with water, something on the order of 5 quarts. Add a teaspoon of salt, a bit of black pepper and, if you like, a touch of garlic (one small piece). If you don't like garlic put in an onion. Boil all this slowly all day long. Keep on boiling till the meat has literally dropped off the bone. If your stock boils down during the day, add enough water from time to time to keep the meat covered. When the whole thing has practically disintegrated pour out into another large kettle through a colander. Make sure that the marrow is out of the bones. Let this drain through the colander for quite awhile as much juice will drain out of the meat. (Shake the colander well to help get out all the juice.)

✎ Save a few of the better pieces of meat just to cut up a little bit in small pieces to put into your soup after it is done. Put the kettle containing the stock you now have in a very cool place, outdoors in the winter time or in the ice box; let it stand all night and the next day until you are ready to make your soup.

✎ You will find that a hard layer of fat has formed on top of the stock which can usually be lifted off since the whole kettle full of stock has jelled. Some people like a little bit of the fat left on and some like their soup very rich and do not remove more than about half of the fat.

✎ Put the stock back into your kettle and you are now ready to make your soup.

✎ In a separate pan, boil slowly about a third of a teacupful of barley. This should be cooked separately since it has a habit, in a soup kettle, of settling to the bottom and if your fire should happen to get too hot it is likely to burn. If you cannot get barley use rice, but it is a poor substitute.

✎ One of the secrets of making good vegetable soup is not to cook any of the vegetables too long. However, it is impossible to give you an exact measure of the vegetables you should put in because some people like their vegetable soup almost as thick as stew, others like it much thinner. Moreover, sometimes you can get exactly the vegetables you want; other times you have to substitute. Where you use canned vegetables, put them in only a few minutes before taking the soup off the fire. If you use fresh ones, naturally they must be fully cooked in the soup.

❧ The things put into the soup are about as follows:

1 qt. can of canned tomatoes

½ teacupful of fresh peas. If you can't get peas, a handful of good green beans cut up very small can substitute.

2 normal sized potatoes, diced into cubes of about half-inch size.

2 or 3 branches of good celery.

1 good-sized onion. (sliced)

3 nice-sized carrots diced about the same size as potatoes.

1 turnip diced like the potatoes.

½ cup of canned corn.

A handful of raw cabbage cut up in small pieces.

❧ Your vegetables should not all be dumped in at once. The potatoes, for example, will cook more quickly than the carrots. Your effort must be to have them all nicely cooked but not mushy, at about the same time.

❧ The fire must not be too hot but the soup should keep bubbling.

❧ When you figure the soup is about done, put in your barley which should now be fully cooked, add a tablespoonful of prepared gravy seasoning and taste for flavoring, particularly salt and pepper, and if you have it, use some onion salt, garlic salt and celery salt. (If you cannot get the gravy seasoning, use one teaspoonful of Worcestershire sauce.)

❧ Cut up the few bits of the meat you have saved and put about a small handful into the soup.

❧ While you are cooking the soup do not allow the liquid to boil down too much. Add a bit of water from time to time. If your stock was good and thick when you started, you can add more water than if it was thin when you started.

❧ As a final touch, in the springtime when nasturtiums are green and tender, you can take a few nasturtium stems, cut them up in small pieces, boil them separately as you did the barley, and add them to your soup. (About one table-spoonful after cooking.)

Dwight David Eisenhower

STUFFED NASTURTIUMS. Take tuna fish and mix with chopped parsley, capers and sweet pickles, then blend with mayonnaise. Go into your garden and pick the largest and most perfect nasturtiums you can find and stuff each with a teaspoonful of this mixture. Put on a dish and pour over French dressing. This can be garnished with other flowers, a very striking one would be borage.

Nasturtiums

NASTURTIUM CIGARETTES. Make a fish relish and add anchovies and spread on nasturtium leaves, sans stems. Roll into cigarettes and tie with thread. Steep in vinegar season with bayleaf, thyme and salt. White wine can take the place of the vinegar. Garnish with nasturtium flowers.

Nasturtiums

Comtesse Berjane recommends serving stuffed nasturtiums with Sauce Chantilly —mayonnaise thinned slightly with whipped cream. The mayonnaise should be made with lemon juice, not vinegar.

LATIN CHICHEGHI SALATASSI (Nasturtium Salad). Put a plate of flowers of the nasturtium in a salad-bowl, with a tablespoonful of chopped chervil; sprinkle over with your fingers half a teaspoonful of salt, two or three tablespoonfuls of olive oil, and the juice of a lemon; turn the salad in the bowl with a spoon and fork until well mixed, and serve.

Turab Effendi, Turkish Cookery Book, 1862

Try sliced apples trimmed with nasturtium flowers.

Mix nasturtium flowers with butter or creamed cheese and spread on orangenut bread, good at any time.

Drop a nasturtium seed into a cup of tea.

TO PICKLE NASTURTIANS. The Part of the Nasturtian that is pickled is the Bud of the Flower; People usually call it the Seed of the Nasturtian, which they also call the *Stertion*, but this is all erroneous.

Gather a Parcel of the largest and fairest Buds of the Nasturtian that can be found, just before their opening into Flower, throw them into a Pan of Cold Water, stir them well about, then pour off the Water, and put on fresh; stir them about again, and pour it off as before, and then lay them on a Sieve to dry; set the Sieve, supported, by a Couple of Bricks, or otherwise, in an airy Place, and now and then turn the Buds: They will fade a little, and they will soon be as dry as when just gathered; and being thus faded they will take the vinegar better than if they had been quite fresh.

The Buds being ready prepare some wide-mouthed Bottles, scrape down two or three Nutmegs, and break a few Blades of Mace; set by you also some Pepper whole, and a few Cloves.

~ Put a little of each of these Spices into the Bottom of each Bottle, and then fill the Bottle a third Part full of the Buds.

~ Put in some more of the Spices of all the Kinds, and then more of the Buds, and thus proceed till the whole Quantity is in.

~ Then pour into each Bottle as much fine white Wine Vinegar as will fill it up, and tie them over; let them stand six weeks before they are opened, and in that Time the Vinegar will have penetrated them thoroughly, and the Taste of the Spices will be got into their very Substance, so that they will be one of the finest Pickles in the World.

Nasturtiums

Mrs. Martha Bradley

NASTURTIUM SANDWICHES. Cut up tender nasturtium leaves, mix with dressing and spread on thin buttered bread.

NASTURTIUM SAUCE. Take a quart of nasturtium flowers and pour over them a mixture of a quart of vinegar, six shallots, six cloves, a teaspoonful of salt, and half a teaspoon of pepper (which has been boiled together for ten minutes). Keep the flowers covered with this mixture for a month and then strain into bottles. A little soy sauce could be added if desired.

NASTURTIUM PUNCH. Take 2 dozen nasturtium flowers, half a cup of claret, a pound of sugar and ½ cup of lemon juice. Make a paste of the flowers and half the sugar. Reserve the balance of the sugar for syrup and add the lemon juice and flower paste. When cold add the claret.

NASTURTIUM ICE. Add one quart of water to the punch and another ½ cup sugar. Free and garnish with flowers.

"Those who make wry faces when they taste mustard-oil or Water-Cress should appreciate the generic name NASTURTIUM. *from the latin* NASUS TORTUS, *a convusled nose. This generic name, for centuries belonging to Watercress, has in popular usage, been transferred to the wholly different South American* TRO-PAEOLUM, . . . *Ask any non-botanical seedsman for* NASTURTIUM; *you will surely get* TROPAEOLUM! *One who uses the latter name is a "prig."*
Edible Wild Plants of Eastern North America
Merritt Lyndon Fernald and Alfred Charles Kinsey

Nasturtium symbolizes patriotism.

To Pickle Nasturtium Berries. When blossoms are off, gather the berries and put in cold water and salt for three days, changing the water each day. On the last day make a pickle of white wine vinegar, mace, nutmeg, six small onions, 2 cloves of garlic, peppercorns, salt, and horseradish. Drain berries and dry and put into bottles and cover with pickle mixture. Cover tightly.

Nasturtiums

Nasturtium Sauce With Cold Lamb. Make a sauce of butter, flour, water, salt, pepper and nasturtium seeds. Cook until thick and add nasturtium seeds.

Nasturtium Salad. Gather nasturtium leaves, seeds and flowers. Take lettuce and mix with lightly chopped nasturtium leaves. Use a salad dressing of oil and vinegar mixed with the nasturtium seeds, mix with lettuce and leaves and garnish with flowers.

Nasturtium Vinegar. Take a gallon jar and fill with nasturtium flowers. Add 1 tablespoon of chopped shallots, 2 cloves garlic, and small pieces of hot red peppers. Fill with white wine vinegar and close tightly and let stand for two months. At that time add a teaspoon salt and strain through nylon net (several thicknesses if necessary). Store in sterilized bottles.

Nasturtium Butter. Buds, flowers, leaves, even the succulent stems of nasturtiums, serve for mincing fine and whipping into fresh butter without any other seasoning.

Nasturtium Sandwich. Spread small squares of whole wheat bread with nasturtium butter. Pinch out the bitter pistils from several nasturtiums and use only the sweet flowers for filling, with a little mayonnaise and a dash of cayenne.

Nasturtium leaves contain ten times as much vitamin C as lettuce.

Peoples of the Orient have for centuries enjoyed nibbling the flowers of nasturtium.

Trimalchio said that the soul of festivity is in cookery, and the soul of cookery in the sauce.

Nasturtium Pepper. Gather ripe seeds and grind. Salt added will add to the flavor. Store in dry, closely-stopped bottles. (This was a substitute for pepper during World War II when pepper was very expensive and at times unobtainable.)

To Pickle Nasturtium Buds. Gather your little Knobs quickly after your Blossoms are off: put them in cold Water and Salt for three Days, shifting them once a day; then make a Pickle (but do not boil it at all) of some White-wine, some White-wine vinegar, Eschalot, Horse-radish, Pepper, Salt, Cloves, and Mace whole and Nutmeg quartered; then put in your seeds and stop them close; they are to be eaten as capers.

E. Smith, Compleat Housewife, London 1739

Nasturtiums

(The garden nasturtium has 8 males and 1 female in the blossom)

Beef Tongue With Nasturtiums. Take a beef tongue and soak in salted water for an hour. Drain and trim, and simmer in salted water, skimming every few minutes. When tender serve with a sauce of ½ cup almonds-chopped, brown in 2 tablespoons with cinnamon and cloves. In another pan fry a minced onion, garlic and 2 cups of peeled tomatoes, salt and pepper. Add a half cup of sherry and some guava jelly, combine with nut mixture and pass with sliced tongue. Garnish sliced tongue with nasturtium flowers and leaves.

Salmagundy. This is a very delightful seventeenth and eighteenth century salad. It was sometimes most amusingly called Solomon Gundy. There are many ways of making it; Mrs. Glasse gives three, and this is one of them:
1. Mince some cooked veal or fowl very small.
2. Bone a pickled herring and pick that small.
3. Mince small some cucumber, apples, a little boiled onion, some pickled red cabbage, parsley and celery, laying each ingredient separately.
4. Mince some cold pork, or duck or pigeon small.
5. Chop small some white or hard-boiled eggs: also the yolks.
6. Butter the outside of a small china basin and turn it over into the centre of your dish.
7. Lay round it, so as to completely cover it, rings of the different ingredients according to their contrasting colours and flavours.
8. Surround them with what pickles you have, and sliced lemon nicely cut: a bunch of Nasturtium flowers and leaves if you can get them on top of the basin, and a few at each end and each side of the dish.

"This," says Mrs. Glasse, "is a fine middle dish for supper; but you may always make salmagundy of such things as you have according to your fancy."

PEACH SALPICON WITH NASTURTIUMS. 3 cups of ripe peaches—sliced, 1 cup orange juice, 1½ cups sugar, ½ cup lemon juice. Pour blended orange and lemon juice over the peaches in a dish, and sprinkle with sugar. Let stand on ice until perfectly chilled. Garnish with nasturtium blossoms.

Make a mixture of cream cheese, raisins and nuts, I like walnuts better, roll up in nasturtium leaves, and tie with a long-stemmed flower.

Nasturtiums

Pickled nasturtium seeds are good in martinis.

NASTURTIUM SOUP.
4 cups chicken stock
1 cup of nasturtium blossoms fried in butter
Salt and pepper to taste

Heat chicken stock, mix fried nasturtium blossoms, salt and pepper. Serve hot.

NETTLE

"One day he (Monsieur Madeleine) saw some peasants busy plucking out Nettles; he looked at the heap of plants uprooted and already withered, and said — 'They are dead. Yet it would be well if people knew how to make use of them. When the nettle is young, its leaf forms an excellent vegetable; when it matures, it has filaments and fibres like hemp and flax. Nettle fabric is as good as canvas. Chopped, the nettle is good for poultry; pounded it is good for cattle. The seed of the nettle mingled with fodder imparts a gloss to the coats of animals; its root mixed with salt produces a beautiful yellow colour. It is besides excellent hay and can be cut twice. And what does the nettle require: Little earth, no attention, no cultivation. Only the seed falls as it ripens, and is difficult to gather. That is all. With a little trouble, the nettle would be useful; it is neglected, and becomes harmful.' "

Victor Hugo, Les Miserables

Nettle Pudding. To one gallon of young nettle tops, thoroughly washed, add 2 good-sized leeks or onions, 2 heads of broccoli or small cabbage, or Brussels sprouts, and ¼ pound of rice. Clean the vegetables well, chop the broccoli and leeks and mix with the Nettles. Place all together in a muslin bag, alternately with the rice, and tie tightly. Boil in salted water, long enough to cook the vegetables, the time varying according to the tenderness or otherwise of the greens. Serve with gravy or melted butter. These quantities are sufficient for six persons.

In Saxon days nettle was called by the poetic name "wergulu".

NETTLE SOUP. Mix a cup of chopped nettles with 3 cups of chicken stock, salt and pepper, with a half cup of barley. Simmer until barley is done. For a more nourishing broth add two pounds of beef cut into one-inch cubes.

Nettles are rich in Vitamins A, B, and C.

Grated cheese and croutons fried in butter are very good with nettle soup.

NETTLE BEER. Take a peck—8 quarts or 2 gallons—of nettle tops, and 4 pounds of malt, boil in 2 gallons of water, add 2 ounces hops, 4 ounces sarsaparilla, 1½ pounds sugar, ½ ounce ginger. Strain it when nearly cold and add a little yeast. Bottle it while it is in a state of fermentation. Makes a pleasant beverage.

Also lemon juice, lemon rind, or lemon crystals can be used. Another recipe suggests the addition of pineapple mint or a bunch of well bruised balm. Still another recipe suggests adding dandelions and comfrey.

TO MAKE A SYRUP OF NETTLES. Pick the young red Nettles in April, and put them in a Pint-stoup; put the Stoup in a Pot of Water, and let them simmer for twelve Hours, then squeeze out the Tincture, and put it in a clean Pan, beat the Whites of Two Eggs and mix with it; and when it boils, skim it, and to every Mutchkin of Tincture put a Pound of brown Sugar-candy: When it is dissolved, set it on the Fire and boil it up to a Syrup, then let it cool, and bottle it, put no Water to the Nettles.

Elizabeth Cleland, A New and Easy Method of Cookery, 1755

"The flower of the dead nettle is like a weasell's face."
W. Coles, The Art of Simpling, 1626

The netle groweth somtyme next the rose.
John de Trevisa, 1387

NETTLE TEA. Gather the blossoms (White Nettle) when quite free from moisture, pick, and spread them out to dry in the shade. Keep in tins or paper bags.
Jules Gouffe, Book of Preserves, 1871

In his remarks on the use of infusions made of flowers, he advises that the beverage should not be made too strong.

Nettle

HERB PUDDING. To make it you take some young nettles and all kinds of green vegetables from the kitchen garden and wash all very thoroughly. Boil till tender and then tie in a pudding cloth with some barley and boil. When the barley is cooked, turn into a basin and beat in an egg.

Nettle   John Wesley in his Primitive Physick, 1747, advises that we take an ounce of nettle juice.

STCHI WITH NETTLES. Stchi is for Great Russia what Bortsch is for Little Russia. It is a kind of Bortsch without the beet root, and is generally a green color, which explains why it is named Green Bortsch.
Prepare a bouillon for Stchi. At same time cook two pounds of young shoots of nettles in the same way as one would cook spinach, and chop very fine. One half hour before dinner, incorporate one cup of thick cream into the nettles. Pour bouillon over this, allow to boil over a small fire and serve it with stuffed eggs.

> Marie Alexandre Markevitch, The Epicure in Imperial Russia, San Francisco, 1941

Put into a greased pudding basin and then steam for 1½ hours, just as for an ordinary boiled pudding. The pudding should, of course, be seasoned to taste with salt, pepper and, a pinch of sage.

Nettle pudding was Pliny's favorite.

If they would drink nettles in March,
And eat mugwort in May,
So many fine maidens
Wouldn't go to the clay.
> *Michael Denham, Proverbs, 1846*

Out of this nettle, danger, we pluck this flower, safety.
> *Shakespeare, Henry iv, ii, 3, 10*

NETTLE HAGGIS. Ingredients: Young nettles, boiling water; salt; oatmeal, 2 or 3 tablespoonfuls; pepper; rashers of bacon.
Boil nettles, cut off the rind from the rashers of bacon. Fry them. Pour the fat over the strained nettles. Chop them up. Put ½ pint of nettlewater in the frying pan, and when it boils, sprinkle in the oatmeal, stirring all the time. Season with pepper, and boil till it is of the consistency of properly cooked porridge. Stir in the chopped nettles. Taste. Serve very hot with the fried bacon.

120

RENNET. "In Arran, and other islands, a rennet is made of a strong decoction of nettles: a quart of salt is put to three pints of the decoction and bottled up for use. A common spoonfull of this liquor will coagulate a large bowl of milk very readily and agreeably, as we say and experienced.

John Lightfoot, Flora Scotica, London, 1777

Nettle

In Italy the "herb knodel" of Nettles made into round balls like dumplings, are esteemed as nourishing and purifying.

"To Mrs. Symons, and there we did eat some Nettle porridge, which was made on purpose to-day, and was very good."

Samuel Pepys Diary, February 25, 1660

The Nettle symbolizes cruelty, though in German mythology it is dedicated to the god, Thor, the patron of marriage.

The Nettle is also said to symbolize slander.

"Am I to have nettles cooked on holidays?"

Persius in Satire VI

"If with rich dishes ready for your food
You leave them and find grass and nettles good."

Horace to Agrippa's steward—Epistles, 1, xii, 8

ORANGE FLOWER

Next thereunto did grow a goodly tree,
With branches broad, and body great,
Clothed with leaves, that none the wood might see
And laden all with fruit, as thick as thick might be.

Spenser, Fairie Queene

The flowers symbolize chastity.

ORANGE FLOWER BUTTER. Take a quarter pound of best sweet butter and wash with orange flower water, then add to it the crumbled yolks of a half dozen hard-boiled eggs, when this is thoroughly mixed add two ounces of almonds, grated lemon peel and a cup of sugar. Arrange lady fingers in a glass dish and soak with white wine and cover with butter mixture.

ORANGE FLOWER BISCUITS. Follow the recipe for Rose Sugar Biscuits by John Conrade Cooke, but use the essence of orange-flower water in place of the essence of roses.

Orange Flower

ORANGE FLOWER PRAWLINGS. Pick half a pint of fresh orange flowers off the stalks and buds; boil a pint of syrup to a blow; boil the flowers to a blow in it, strain them off, rub them in fine sifted sugar, and dry in a drying stove till crisp.

> John Conrade Cooke, Cookery and Confectionary
> London 1824

JELLY OF ORANGE FLOWERS AND CHAMPAGNE. Gelee de Fleurs d'Orange au Vin de Champagne. Take a handful of orange flowers; take out the hearts, and put the leaves in fresh water; put water upon the fire; throw in the flowers, and give them one boil; drain them, and put them into syrup (au petit perle); when done enough, and nearly cold, add five or six small pots or glasses of *Champagne,* and as much isinglass as is prescribed for the orange jelly, and the juice of two lemons; mix all together, and pass it through a double tammy; shake it well; arrange little pots or cups as before directed, make them take and serve.

> A. B. Beauvilliers, The Art of French Cookery, 1827

ORANGE FLOWER MARMALADE. Marmalade de Fleurs d'Oranges. Take two pounds of orange flowers, fresh gathered; and very white; pick and throw them into fresh water; two pounds, when well picked, will not give more than one pound; drain, and put them into boiling water; give them one boil only; take them immediately off the fire; drain and throw them into fresh boiling water, with the juice of two or three lemons over a very brisk fire: when the flowers break easily with the fingers, take them out; put them into cold water, with the juice of a lemon; drain, and press them in a new cloth to take out the water; beat them very well in a marble mortar, wetting it with lemon juice; when it is enough beaten, put it in a small pan, and clarify two pounds and a half of the finest sugar; bring it to the *perle,* and put it by degrees to the flowers, and mix it with a spatula: when the half of the sugar has been put in, put the other half upon the fire to bring it to the *petit souffle,* and add it to the marmalade, stirring it always with a spatula; put it again upon the fire; heat it well without letting it boil, and pot it.

> Ibidem

ORANGE FLOWER ICECREAM. Take 1 quart orange blossoms, arrange in layers and cover each layer with powdered sugar. Let stand for at least an hour. Then pour over them 2 quarts of boiling water and the juice of two lemons. Cover and let stand for two hours. Strain and use the water to make icecream, which is made like vanilla, except omit the milk and vanilla. Freeze in deepfreeze or hand freezer.

Orange Flower

"Knowest thou the Land where groves of citron flower,
The golden Orange darkling leaves embower—
Know'st thou the Land? Oh there! Oh there!
I long with thee, my loved one, to repair.
                                        Goethe

ORANGE BLOSSOM HONEY. The bee does a better job, let the bee continue while we get on with other things.

Put two teaspoons orange flower water to brewing coffee.

Vicomte de Mauduit suggests adding a few drops of orange blossom extract to the water when making pastry for Pates De Foie Gras.

VINEGAR OF ORANGE FLOWER. Take one ounce of fresh orange flowers, put into pint bottle and cover with vinegar. Close tightly and set in the sun for fifteen days.
                                        MacKenzie's 5,000 Receipts

ORANGE-FLOWER BRANDY. Take a gallon of French brandy, boil a pound of orange flowers a little while, and put them in, save the water and with that make a syrup to sweeten it.
                                        E. Smith, The Compleat Housewife, 1736

FAIRY BUTTER. Take the Yolks of four hard Eggs, and half a Pound of Loaf Sugar beat and sifted, half a Pound of fresh Butter; bray them in a clean Bowl with two spoonfuls of Orange-flower Water; when it is well mixed, force it through the corner of a thin Canvas Strainer in little Heaps on a Plate. It is a very pretty Supper Dish.
                                        Elizabeth Cleland, Receipt Book, 1759

PRESERVED ORANGE FLOWERS. Spread the blossoms on a sheet of cloth and pour over them a boiling syrup. Make a syrup by combining 1 cup of water with 1 cup of sugar. Let the syrup boil rapidly for 3 to 5 minutes, or until it is clear. Let stand overnight, and bring to the boiling point on the next day. Spread on platters or trays. Put a sheet of glass over them and let them dry in the sun half a day. Then sprinkle well with powdered sugar. Pack in jars, seal hot in syrup. They are very delicate for flavoring drinks, desserts, and cakes.

ORANGE FLOWER COCKTAIL. Into a large champagne glass place a thin slice of lemon generously doused with orange-flower water. Add a couple of ice cubes, a dash of orange bitters and about 3 ounces of your favorite gin. Add a few drops of orange-flower water and decorate with blossoms.

Orange Flower

The Chinese like flower scented teas, most of which they keep for themselves. Orange Pekoe is perfumed with orange blossoms. The proportion of tea to blossoms is 60-40. Before packing the blossoms are winnowed out.

ORANGE FOWER CREAM. Put two ounces of candied orange flowers into a stew pan with two ounces of castor sugar and half a pint of milk; stir these over a slow fire until the sugar is melted, adding three ounces of sugar mixed with four yolks of eggs and a tablespoonful of orange-flower water. Stir this preparation over the fire to set the yolks of the eggs; add three-fourths ounce of gelatin, dissolved in half a gill of water, and one-half pint of stiffly whipped cream; mix well together, and then pour the cream into a mould set on ice.

> Charles Elme' Francatelli, The Modern Cook
> London, 1911

ORANGE BLOSSOM ICE. Paghoton Anthous Portokaleas. Bruise to a paste a pound of very fresh pistachios in a mortar, with a handful of sugar. Dilute with two pints of nearly cold English cream; let it infuse for half an hour: pass the preparation through a sieve, and freeze in the usual manner.

Ten minutes previous to dressing the ice, gradually introduce into it five or six tablespoonfuls of genuine orange-blossoms (eau de fleurs d'oranger), previously mixed up with a little cold syrup and a little of the preparation. Now dish the ice in a rock shape on a folded napkin.

> Robert H. Christie, Banquets of the Nations
> Edinburgh, 1911

Eau de naffe is a liqueur made with citron flowers.

ORANGE FLOWER SUGAR. Take ½ lb. of fresh orange flowers, pick off the petals and dry them gently in a hot-closet. When dry, pound the orange flowers in a mortar, together with 1 lb. of loaf sugar, sift through a silk sieve, and keep the sugar in a dry place.

> Jules Gouffe, Royal Book of Pastry and Confectionery

ORANGE FRANGIPANE CUSTARD CAKE. Make, bake, and glaze the cake, merely flavouring the custard with orange sugar. (Frangipane custard is like our boiled custard, more or less.)

Gouffe also suggests using candied orange flowers and orange flower sugar in tarts of various kinds. His "Precieuse Cakes" consist of a lining flavoured with almonds and then filled with a paste flavoured with almonds combined with orange flavour.

These flavours also combine well with anise seed.

Crushed candied orange flowers are very good as filling for Puff Paste tartlets.

Orange Flower

ORANGE BLOSSOM JELLY. Pick some orange blossoms so as to get ¼ lb. of the petals, put them in a basin, pour over them 1 quart of nearly boiling Clarified Syrup registering 30 degrees, cover the basin, and let the flowers steep for two hours, then strain the syrup through a jelly bag, mix it with 2¼ ounces of clarified Pork Rind Gelatine melted, and making 1¼ pint of liquid.

෴ Put a mould in the ice, fill it with the jelly; when this is set cover the mould with a baking-sheet with some ice on the top, and turn the jelly out of the mould at the end of two hours.

Jules Gouffe, Royal Book of Pastry and Confectionery
London, 1874

ORANGE BLOSSOM LIQUEUR. Take one-fourth pound orange blossom petals and mix in two quarts of brandy. Cover and let mixture stand for six weeks. Filter and add to it a syrup made of 8 cups of sugar and 1 cup of water. Skim and cool before bottling.

ORANGE FLOWER SYRUP. Put 2 lbs of loaf sugar, broken in pieces, into 1 lb. of Orange Flower Water, and dissolve it without warming.

෴ Filter the syrup, and keep it in well-corked bottles.

Paris Pharmacopoeia, 1866

ORANGE FLOWER MACAROONS. Two lbs dry sifted white sugar, 2 ozs. of the petals of freshly gathered orange blossoms, the whites of eight fresh eggs.

෴ Put the sugar — which must be *very* dry — into a basin. The moment the orange flowers come in, pick the petals off the stems, weigh them and chop them *at once* with a pair of scissors *into* the sugar; if there is any delay they will be discolored. Add the whites of the eggs and whisk the whole well together until it looks like snow; drop the mixture at once on to a sheet of paper in little cakes, the size of a walnut, and bake in a very cool oven for about twenty minutes or more. When they are ready they will be delicately colored a pale fawn color and dried through.

Dainty Dishes for Indian Tables, Calcutta 1879.

Orange Flower

BURNT ORANGE FLOWERS BAVAROIS CREAM. Pick sufficient orange blossoms to give 3 oz. of petals; Melt 3 oz. of pounded sugar in a copper sugar-boiler until it acquires a light brown tinge, add the picked orange blossoms, stir over the fire for a minute, and pour in 1 gill of water to melt the sugar;

☙ Break 8 yolks of egg in a stewpan, mix them with ½ lb. of pounded sugar, add 9 gills of boiled cream, and stir over the fire, without boiling, until the custard thickens and coats the spoon, then mix in the sugared orange flowers, and 2 oz. of drained gelatine, previously steeped in cold water; strain the whole through a pointed strainer into a basin, Put the basin on ice, stir until the contents begin to set, then mix in lightly 1 quart of well-whipped double cream. Set in ice and after two hours, turn the cream out of the mould and serve.

Gouffe, Royal Book of Pastry and Confectionery

When making egg custard flavour with orange flower water instead of vanilla.

ORANGE FLOWER TEA. Dry flowers and use one teaspoonful for a cup of tea.

Macaroon souffle is improved by candied orange flowers.

Queen Victoria liked to perfume whipped cream with orange flower water.

"Mrs. Pocket looked up from her book, and, smiling upon Pip, in an absent state of mind asked him if he liked the taste of Orange-flower water, this question not having any bearing, near or remote, on any foregone, or subsequent trans-action."

Charles Dickens, Great Expectations

Orange-flower water is frequently taken in France by ladies as a mild soporific at night, when sufficiently diluted with sugared water.

Dr. Fernie, Meals Medicinal

ORANGE BUTTER. The Dutch way. Take of new cream a gallon, beat this up to a thickness; then add four ounces of Orange-flower water, with the same quantity of red wine; and being thus become of the thickness of butter, it retains both the colour, and scent of an orange.

Closet of Rarities, 1706

Orange Flower

CONSERVE OF ORANGE-FLOWERS. Take a Quarter of a Pound of Orange-Flower-Leaves well pick'd, chop 'em as small as you can, and moisten them as you chop 'em with a little Lemon-juice; In the meantime clarify two Pounds of Sugar upon the Fire, which you are to boil till it is much feather'd, take it off, and let it stand a little, then stir it with a Silver Spoon all about the Sides and in the Middle of the Pan; then put your Flowers as before order'd into the Sugar, stir it readily with a Spoon; and having Paper-Moulds ready, pour Part of your Stuff into them, and for the other form it properly with the Spoon into Lozenges, upon some Paper; and for those in the Moulds, when the Conserve has taken, you are to mark with a Knife in what Bigness you would have 'em.

M. Chomel, Dictionnaire Oeconomique   1725

ORANGE-FLOWER PRESERVE. An Operation of the Confectioners performed in the following manner; first the Flowers must be thrown into Water and Salt, and for the Space of five Days left in their Pickle; then they are to be scalded in two Waters over the Fire, with a little Lemon Juice, in order to be put into Sugar, newly pass'd thro' the straining Bag, and already heated; let the Sugar next Day be boil'd a little smooth, and pour'd upon the Flowers, for they ought not to be set on the Fire any longer; on the third Day boil your Sugar quite smooth, and pour it likewise upon the Flowers; having afterwards set it all by to cool, let the Flowers be drained, and dried with Powder Sugar, laying them in order upon Sieves; On the Day following, they must be turned on the other Side, and strewing them likewise with Sugar, put into an Handkerchief, the Work is done.

M. Chomel, Dictionnaire Oeconomique

EGGS AFTER THE ITALIAN MODE. They prepare a Syrup with Sugar and a little Water for Eggs after the Italian Mode, and when above half made, take the Yolks of Eggs in a Spoon, one after another, and hold them in this Syrup to be poached. Thus as many may be drest as you think fit, continually keeping the Sugar very hot, and they may be serv'd garnished with orange quarters and covered with Pistachoes, Slices of Lemon Peel, and Orange-Flowers boiled in the rest of the Syrup, with Lemon Juice sprinkled upon them.

Ibidem

RATAFIA, AND ORANGE FLOWER SOUFFLE OMLET. Weigh 5 eggs in their, shells, allow an equal weight of sugar; break the yolks into one basin, and the whites into another, and whisk the whites to a stiff froth quite alone. Beat the yolks with a wooden spoon, adding the sugar and a good dessertspoonful of orange flower water. Beat for 20 minutes, then the frothed whites are added very carefully.

Orange Flower

☙ Your omelet should be in a metal dish which will bear going into the oven and is well buttered inside before the mixture is poured in. It should be only three parts filled, as the mixture will rise in the oven. Bake about 10 minutes in a moderate oven, and sprinkle over thickly with pounded ratafias well browned.

☙ The omelet should be quite set at the top, but underneath more like very firmly frothed Schaum sauce.

The Cookery Book of Lady Clark of Tillypronie,
Edited by Catherine Frances Frere, London 1909

ORANGE-FLOWER MERINGUES. Brown a handful of powdered sugar in a pan; then add a pound of sugar and a little water and cook it to the feather.

☙ Grill a number of orange-flowers and stir them in the syrup until it rises in the pan. Whip up the whites of eggs with a little sugar. Whip syrup and eggs together. Pour the mixture into a dish and brown quickly in a hot oven.

ORANGE-FLOWER ICE. Pound a handful of orange-flowers and pour about a pint of hot Water upon them; let them infuse about an hour, adding about half a pound of Sugar; when it is properly dissolved sift through a Napkin.

B. Clermont, The Professed Cook
London, MDCCLXXVI

ORANGE-FLOWER SUGAR CANDY. Sucre Candi en Terrine a la Fleur d'Orange, ou gros Candi. Prepare half a pound of very white orange-flowers; boil three pounds of sugar *au souffle'*; put in the orange flowers, and give them a dozen of boils; run it through a hair search to take out the flowers; return the sugar into the pan, and bring it to the *souffle';* skim, and take it off the fire; add a quarter of a glass of the spirit of roses; pour it into a basin; cover it and put it into the stove for eight days, taking care to keep it of an equal heat; drain off the syrup, as the candy remains fixed; heat the basin; it will fall off. Not to lose the flower, rub them well in sifted sugar, till they are dry with the hands; sift, and put them to dry in the stove.

Beauvilliers, Art of French Cookery

ORANGE FLOWER MARMALADE. After your flowers are properly picked, scald them near the space of a minute, then put them in water, that has had a little alum dissolved in it; boil some other water, in which you squeeze near half the juice of a small lemon, and boil the flower in it till they feel tender; then put

128

them into fresh water again, with the same quantity of lemon juice, and drain them in a napkin to pound; and mix two pounds of this marmalade with five pounds of sugar of the first degree, or any quantity in proportion; finish as usual.

The Court and Country Confectioner, by an
Ingenious Foreigner, London 1770

Orange Flower

GELATINA DI ORANGE BLOSSOM. Is made in the same manner as Gelatina Di Violette, substituting orange blossoms for violets.

ORANGE FLOWER BOMBOONS. Take dryed, burnt, or what we call *pralined* orange flower, which you pound in a mortar and pass through a sieve; then take half a pound of pounded loaf sugar, which you mix with your orange flower, and put in a pan over a slow fire, to melt it gently in stirring continually with a spoon; when it is all well melted, pour it on a tin plate, and so as we directed for the lemon bomboons. (These are the directions: butter the tin plate, spread bomboons with a rolling pin, and when cold cut in desired shapes and send it up.)

The Court and Country Confectioner, by
an Ingenious Foreigner, London, 1770

ORANGE FLOWER BISCUITS. Take twelve whites of eggs and six yokes, observing to let them be new laid; to which add a little grated or rasped green lemon, and beat them all well together; a quarter of a pound of fine flour; when all is properly mixed, bake in proper cakes and glaze. (The author evidently forgot to mention the orange ingredients, or perhaps the reader is supposed to know enough about cooking to mix orange flowers and orange water.)

Ibidem

TO MAKE FRESH ORANGE FLOWER PRALINED. Take any quantity of orange flowers, pick them carefully leaf by leaf; when that is done have a pan with what quantity of clarified sugar you need to have, boil it to the ninth degree then put your orange flowers in; you will see that it will spoil all your sugar by the water it will throw off; let it boil thus till your sugar recovers as far as the first degree, then take it from the fire, and stir it till your sugar turn sand or gravel like: should it not dry so well as you would have it, set it again on the fire, and keep stirring it perpetually, till you see your sugar begins to melt; take it off immediately, and continue by stirring to reduce it into a sand: better to have a little more trouble in working your sugar to reduce it in sand, because then the orange flower does not take so much sugar, and has a better flavour; after it is dried you throw it in a sieve to drain the sugar from it, and keep nothing but the flower; then you place it in that sieve, in the stove, to finish drying it quite, stirring now and then for fear it should stick together; when it is well dried put it in your boxes and keep it for use.

Ibidem

Orange Flower

CONSERVE OF ORANGE FLOWERS. Conserve de Fleur d'Orange. Take a little orange-flower; pick and hash it upon white paper, putting in some drops of lemon juice; have ready four ounces of sugar *au souffle';* add the flowers, and give them a little boil, to work it; mould it in paper cases.

Beauvilliers, The Art of French Cookery

ICE CREAM OF ORANGE FLOWERS. Glace de Creme a la Fleur d'Orange. To four pints of good cream, put the yolks of eight eggs, and half a pound of sugar, sifted or in lumps, with a small handful of orange flower *pralinee,* which has been well minced: do it over a slow fire, stirring it till it is enough, as is directed above: ice it.

Beauvilliers, The Art of French Cookery

GRILLED CREAM OF ORANGE FLOWERS. Creme grillee a la Fleur d'Orange. Follow exactly the same directions as in the preceding articles, in diminishing only the quantity of sugar; reserving a part of the half pound of sugar to bring it to the *caramel,* to give the cream the colour and taste of the *grille*.

Ibidem

ORANGE FLOWER SYRUP. Sirop de Fleur d'Orange. For three quarters of a pound of orange flowers fresh picked, take four pounds of clarified sugar *au perle,* throw in the flowers, and give them a strong boil; take them off the fire, and leave them to infuse two hours; put the syrup again on the fire, and give it a dozen of boils; have a search put over a dish, and pour it in to take out the flowers; put it again on the fire to finish, and bring it to its proper degree; let it cool in a basin; bottle it. Not to lose the orange flowers put them in sifted sugar, rub them well, and dry them in a stove.

Ibidem

FRANGIPANNI TART. Pound eight macaroons, pour sufficient boiling milk upon them to make them into a light batter; strain and beat six eggs, add them to the macaroons; sweeten it, and put it into a saucepan; stir it over the fire until it becomes of the requisite thickness. Put in four ounces of cream or fresh butter, and a tablespoonful of orange-flower water. Line the rim of a tart-dish with a puff-paste, lay in the frangipanni, put on a top crust, and bake for twenty minutes or half an hour, according to the heat of the oven.

Everybody's Pudding Book

ORANGE FLOWER WATER. Take four pounds of unpicked Orange Flowers, bruise them in a marble mortar, and pour on them nine quarts of clear Water. Distil in a cold still, and draw off five or six quarts, which will be exquisitely fragrant. If you are desirous of having it still higher flavoured, draw off at first seven quarts, unlute the still, and throw away the residue; empty back the water already distilled, and add to it two pounds of Orange Flowers bruised. Again luting the Still, repeat the distillation, and draw off five or six quarts. Then top, being careful not to draw off too much water, lest the Flowers should become dry and burn-to.

Orange Flower

The Toilet of Flora

ORANGE FLOWER BUTTER. Mix orange flower water with sweet butter and serve on toast with tea. If you don't have orange-flower water use some frozen orange juice.

HUILE DE VENUS. Six ounces of wild carrot flowers (Queen Anne's Lace), ten pints of white wine. Distil. Add ten pints of syrup of capillaire. If desired color with cochineal.

Syrup of Capillaire. Add sixteen pints of water to twenty-four pounds of white granulated sugar. Boil to a syrup and clarify with egg whites (3 or 4), scum and boil again, then add one pint of warm orange-flower water.

MacKenzie's 5,000 Receipts

OLD AFRICAN RECIPE. Take 2 cups of sugar and a cup of water and make a syrup. Then add pine kernels or almonds and grated lemon and a half cup of orange blossoms. Pour into a shallow pan and cut into squares.

The custom of wearing orange blossoms on the bridal dress comes to us from the Saracens.

ORANGE-BLOSSOM HONEY JELLY. Mix three cups of orange-blossom honey with 1 cup water and 1 tablespoon lemon juice. After it has reached the boiling point add a half cup of pectin, stirring constantly. Add 1 tablespoon orange-flower water and seal in sterilized jelly glasses.

EASTER WHEAT PIE. (Pastiera di Grano)

Orange Flower

❧ Pastry:
1 cup flour
2 egg yolks
4 tb. milk
½ c. powdered sugar
½ teaspoon vanilla or lemon flavor
¼ lb. butter

Sift flour, form pocket, add egg yolks and butter, blend with fork. Add sugar, flavoring and enough milk to hold mixture together. Roll out on lightly floured board from center to edges until ½ inch thick. Fit in pie pan. Fill. Criss cross top with pastry strips. Bake in moderate oven 1½ hours.

❧ Filling:

1½ lbs. ricotta, well drained
1 lb. cooked wheat (soak overnight in water, then boil until tender, about 3 hours. Add water as it boils away.)
2 cups sugar
3 egg yolks
3 egg whites
1 cup boiled milk
½ cup finely chopped citron, orange peel and coconut
1½ tablespoon orange flower water

Add sugar and egg yolks to ricotta, blend. Add beaten egg whites and all other ingredients. Blend thoroughly.

Joseph R. Anderson, Librarian (NYPL)

PALM BEACH STORY. Take one banana sliced crosswise, 1 cup of orange sections, 2 large peaches-diced, 1 cup diced pineapple, 1 cup strawberries and marinate in 2 ounces of cointreau and 2 ounces of kirsch, a tablespoon of orange-blossom water, 1 cup of sugar, ½ teaspoon vanilla and a dozen orange blossoms. Put in the refrigerator for a couple of hours. Have serving dishes chilled (this will make four to six portions), in each dish place some of the fruit mixture and have ready raspberry, lime, and orange sherbets. Place a small scoop of each on each serving and finish by placing three or four orange blossoms and crystallized violets on top of the sherbets.

ORCHIDS ~~~~~~~~~~~~~~~~~~~~~~~~~~~~~~~

THE ORCHID

In the deep forest it stands silent, guarding its chastity,
Trusting the light breezes to scatter its fragrance far and wide.
It does not refuse to bloom beside my mossy steps;
When plucked it does not hanker for a vase of gold.
Singly superior, it may serve as company to a book of odes;
Simply and dainty, it deserves a place in the bed chamber.
Don't smile. In my house are no happy children,
My few sprays near the steps in the courtyard look bright.

> *Liu K'o-chuang, Sung Dynasty*
> *Koehn, Fragrance from a Chinese Garden*

It symbolizes the Perfect Man. The exquisite scent is considered the Ancestor of Fragrances.

The I CHING says that if two people are of one mind its sharpness can cut metal, and its speech is as fragrant as the Orchid. Such friendship is called Gold Orchid.

> *Ibidem*

ORCHID COCKTAIL. Take an ounce and a half of your favorite gin, a teaspoon of lemon juice, a pony of cognac and half-pony of Creme de Violette. Shake and strain into a chilled cocktail glass. For an added touch the rim of the glass could be dipped into powdered sugar. Consume through lilac-colored cellophane straws. Different.

"I walked down the narrow track, between massy bowers of honeysuckle. Suddenly my eye was caught by a tall slender plant: a curious bearded spike of purplish-green blossom, standing up boldly above the tussocky grasses. I looked more closely; and, with an extraordinary spasm of excitement, recognized it for what it was.

It was the Lizard Orchid: that legendary flower, most celebrated of English 'rarities,' which I had sought for, year after year, on the Kentish chalk-lands— but without success. Once I had seen it ... but I had never seen it growing. And here, raising its fantastic head among the grasses, rooted and autochthonous as any other Tuscan weed—here was the half-mythical object of all my years of fruitless search; here was the dream made flesh at last, the myth incarnate.

∾ I searched among the bushes, and other spikes revealed themselves . . . once again, I was surrounded: but this time by presences which offered themselves, rooted and without power to resist, to my desires.

∾ I picked a spike; to PICK *a Lizard Orchid — the action had about it something unholy, something rather blasphemous . . . I picked several more; examining with a wondering delight the long, slender lips, two inches long, cleft at the tip like serpent's tongues, unfurling themselves in delicate spirals from the opening buds . . . Here, on this Tuscan hillside, it was no hawthorn or mullein that raised its august form among the grasses; it was, beyond any possibility of doubt,* HIMANTOGLOSSUM HIRCINUM, *the Lizard Orchid.*

∾ I had found the Lizard Orchid.

Orchids

Jocelyn Brooke, A Mine of Serpents

During the eighteenth century when orchid eating was very popular partly because of its nutrition and partly because of its aphrodisical qualities, the roots were made into what was called *salop*. Dr. Fernald says that although they are full of nutrition they are very rare and only under pressure of extreme hunger would it be justifiable to eat them, and that even at the present time in remote districts of the United States and Canada the roots have a large reputation as nerve-tonics and heal-alls.

BOILED SALOP. Take a teaspoon of powdered orchid roots and boil in a pint of water. Boil until it jellies and add a bit of wine, sugar and lemon juice or grated lemon rind.

HOW TO PREPARE ORCHID ROOTS. Wash fresh roots and rub the skin off with nylon net cloth. Spread the roots out on a pie plate and bake about ten minutes, by that time they have the transparency of bones. They can be left in the warm oven to harden or you can take them and leave them in the air for a few days. At that time you can make powder as you need it.

In mythological times it was believed that the orchid flower was the food of the satyrs.

"The full and plump Roots of the Satyrion or Orchis . . . are of mighty effecacy to provoke to Venery, which they that have Bulbous Roots do by Signature, but the lank or shrivelled mortifies lust, so that here is a Remedy both to help Nature if it be deficient, and to restrain it if it be too luxuriant."

William Coles

Moths Love orchids.

The roots of the Lizard Orchis or Goat-stones boiled in milk and seasoned with white pepper were particularly efficient. The plant is extremely rare today.

Orchids *Orchids are androgynous flowers, that is, the male and female characteristics are in the same plant.*

"Orchids grew all over the grey lichen-covered bark; they hung from the trailing lianas, sprouted from holes in the tree trunks near the ground or high up in the branches. They were of every conceivable shape and colour. It was quite incredible.

The golden sunbeams falling in shafts turned this orchid garden into a fairyland. The scent of the flowers was overpowering. We soon began to feel giddy, for the heady perfume induced a kind of intoxication . . . I simply could not conceive how such a place existed. Here a tree, imprisoned in a network of lianas would be covered with cascades of brilliant blossoms. Another, was ablaze with yellow orchids, while a third gleamed like a torch with clusters of scarlet flowers. Violet cattleyas adorned the withered branches. Epidendiums and odontoglossums of all colours: green, white, rose pink, spotted and striped; every group and family was represented. The lianas formed elegant arches and beneath them nestled more scarlet blossoms . . . I do not know how many days we camped outside our orchid bonanza. Each day we made three trips and returned each time with a splendid harvest of exotic flowers. Each night I fell asleep with the word orchids on my lips."

Ernst Lohndorff, The Forest of Fear

Louis Sobol, popular columnist for the New York Journal-American says, "I am reminded of a dinner millionaire realtor Robert Simon and his wife, the writer, tossed for the Einsteins some years ago. Mrs. Simon, for an added touch, had little orchids placed at each setting. Mrs. Einstein hesitated for a second or two and then, to the consternation of the hostess and other guests, began to eat the orchids. Whereupon, one by one, all the other guests began nibbling at the orchids, too!

ORCHID SANDWICH. Use white bread, lightly toasted and cover with caviar, layer with orchid petals.

PANSIES 〰〰〰〰〰〰〰〰〰〰〰〰〰〰〰〰

Pansies! Pansies! How I love you, pansies!
Jaunty-faced, laughing-lipped and dewy-eyed with glee. . .
                    James Whitcomb Riley

The Pansy has so many beautiful names: Love-in-Idleness, Herb Constancy; Herb Trinitatis; Call-me-to-you; Jack-jump-up-and-kiss-me; Little-My-fancy; Pink-of-my-John; Heart's Ease; Loving-thoughts; Stepfathers and Stepmothers; Three-faces-under-a-hood; Kit-run-in-the-fields; and the ancient name of Banewort.

And these names show all that they were to man: all his gratitude, his studious fondness, all that he owed them, all that they gave him are there contained, like a secular aroma in hollow pearls. And so they bear names of queens, shepherdesses, virgins, princesses, sylphs and fairies, which flow from the lips like a caress, a lightning-flash, a kiss, a murmur of love.
                    —Field Flowers by Maurice Maeterlinck
                    Dodd Mead (1904)

PANSY WINE. Good for addling wits.

4	quarts pansies
4	gallons water
8	pounds sugar
1	ounce powdered ginger
1	dozen lemons
1	dozen oranges
1	dozen apples
2	packages, yeast

Dry the pansies for three or four days in the sun, then put a layer in your crock, cover and sugar and use a pinch of the ginger, continue until crock is full . . . or until all pansies and sugar (and ginger) have been used. Let stand for three days and mash every day with a wooden spoon, then pare and slice the oranges and lemons; peel and slice the apples and add, plus the water which has been heated. Dissolve the yeast and add. Cover and let it set for about two weeks (when fermentation is stopped). At that time strain into glass jars and add a quart of brandy. Let it stand for two or three weeks, bottle and cork. Hide it somewhere as it should be a year old before drinking.

Pansies, eyes that laugh, bear beauty's prize
From violets, eyes that dream.
                    Robert Browning

The Pansy symbolizes Loving Thoughts.

PANSY FLOWER SYRUP. Take about two cups of pansyflowers and cover with water and let simmer for two or three hours. The vessel should be very tightly covered. Strain and add twice as much sugar as liquid. To make it stronger add more pansies.

Pansies

PANSY SALAD. I was once served a lemon gelatine salad, in which a purple pansy had been placed, face down of course, so it would be right-side up when unmolded. It was not only a delight to the eye but to the palate.

PANSY CRYSTALS. 1 cup pansy petals
1 oz. gum arabic
1 cup water
1 tablespoon corn syrup
1 cup sugar

Dry petals. Dissolve gum arabic in ½ cup hot water and cool. Carefully coat the pansy petals with this mixture. Thread them on a string and hang up to dry, not touching each other. Mix the corn syrup and sugar in ½ cup water and cook to a soft ball. Dip petals into syrup and dry. Sprinkle with finely granulated sugar.

PASSIONFLOWER

This is the famous plant sung by poets and celebrated by orators. The plant reasoned about by philosophers, with the utmost subtlety, praised by physicians for its marvellous value. Sought for eagerly by the sick, wondered at by the theologians, and venerated by all pious Christians.

—Aldinus, Physician to Cardinal Farnese (c. 1600)

PASSION FRUIT SOUP. Very popular in South America and used both for beverages and soups. The yellow pulp is very aromatic and contains a meld of flavors —combining the peach, the apricot, the pineapple, the guava, and banana, also a hint of lime juice. The South Americans use it in cocktails, punches, fruit desserts, fruit cups, and as a sauce for icecream or other frozen dessert.

The early explorers, those intrepid Frenchmen, Spanish, and Italians immediately declared it to be symbolic of the Passion of Christ. According to them it bears the emblem of the Crucifixion: the stamen represents the cross; corona, the crown of thorns; five anthers, the five sounds; three stigmas, the three nails which pierced hands and feet. The style represents the sponge which moistened His lips; petals represent the twelve disciples, (less Thomas and Judas); the bracts represent the resurrection on the third day; and the stalk, the Gospel.

Passionflower   MAYPOP SYRUP. Take a deep jar and fill it alternately with flowers and sugar. Add two tablespoons water, cover and place in boiling water for five hours. Strain and bottle. During the boiling process add the pulp of several fruits.

PEACH BLOSSOMS ~~~~~~~~~~~~~~~~~~~~~~~~~~~~~~

Enjoying The Peach Blossoms From A Boat
In the second moon Peaches bloom along the Flowery Road
Like red clouds reflected in ripples or a mountain wrapped
   in brocade.
I begged the East wind to be kind to them,
Never blow a petal into this human world.
            Lu Yu, Sung Dynasty

The peach blossom is an emblem of matrimony, its fruit is a symbol of longevity.

TO MAKE SYRUP OF PEACH-BLOSSOMS. Infuse peach-blossoms in hot water, as much as will handsomely cover them; let them stand in balneo, or in sand, for twenty-four hours covered close; then strain out the flowers from the liquor, and put in fresh flowers; let them stand to infuse as before, then strain them out, and to the liquor put fresh peach blossoms the third time, and (if you please) a fourth time; then to every pound of your infusion add two pounds of double refined sugar; and, setting it in sand, or balneo, make a syrup, which keep for use.

Mrs. Glasse, The Art of Cookery made Plain and Easy, 1803

CONSERVES. The flowers of Water Lilies, red Poppies, Peony, Peach, Primroses, Roses ... Violets, with all these are conserves made with their treble proportion of white sugar: yet note, that all of them must not be mixed alike, some of them must be cut, beaten, and gently boiled, some neither cut, beaten nor boiled, and some admit but one of them, which every artist in his trade may find out by this premonition and avoid error.

Nicholas Culpepper, The Complete Herbal and English
Physician Enlarged, London, 1653

PEACH BLOSSOM TEA. Use ½ ounce fresh flowers to the cup.

PEACH BLOSSOM VINEGAR. Infuse an ounce of the dried flowers in one pint of vinegar, cover tightly and infuse in the sun for fifteen days.

Peach Blossom   PEACH CORDIAL BUTTER. Mix one tablespoonful peach liquer into a quarter pound of butter, or to taste. Very good for fruit sandwiches.

PEACH AND OTHER FLOWER SUNDAES. Put vanilla ice cream into a cut glass bowl, and place your flower syrups around it in crystal bowls, and let each guest use his imagination.

"The art of treating plants, their flowers, roots and fruits to preserve them and to extract from them their elements, sugars, liquors, oils, and perfumes, dates back to the very cradle of civilization."

Careme, 1858

PEONY

In Praise of the Peony
Embroidered curtains embrace the King of Flowers,
Its gorgeous hues challenge the beauty of sunshine.
All its branches take colour from the sun,
Every petal is filled with heavenly fragrance.
It embedded its roots in a plot of leisure land,
Filled with purity it follows spring's late flowers.
Have pity for it! The others are in the Spring Hall,
With music and dance, lending their beauty to a jade banquet.
Sui Shih, Ming Dynasty

When wet it is like a nest of exquisite brocade,
Fragments of clouds on rich coifs of fairy hair.
Sung Ch'i, Sung Dynasty

Known as the King of Flowers or the Flower of Riches and Honour. The Peony is the emblem of Love and Affection and of Brightness and Masculinity.

It is considered an omen of Good Fortune.

PEONY FLOWER SYRUP. Take a pound of peony flowers put them in three pints of hot water and let set overnight. Then boil and strain the flowers out, if not strong enough add more flowers and let it set again overnight, then add three pounds of sugar and boil to a syrup.

Peony

PEONY WATER. Take 2 pounds of peony flowers and infuse in wine for 24 hours. Take the flowers out and distil them with two pints of water, sweetening to taste with sugar or honey.

PEONY KERNELS are eaten as a condiment and used in cooking to decorate creams in the same way as sliced almonds.

Peony Water was a favorite drink in the seventeenth and eighteenth centuries.

"I have peper and piones" quod she, "and a pound of garlic . . ." (William Langland, Piers Plowman, 14th Century) said Betsy Brewstere when she entreats Glutton to come in and try her ale, but Glutton can't be enticed until he knows what the seasoning is.

Peony flowers are used in China to scent the higher grades of tea.

The Day Lily can make you forget your sorrows, but the beauty and fragrance of the Peony will sober you.

Koehn, Fragrance from a Chinese Garden

The "Pionie" is one of the flowers which Markham recommends for preserving.

"Stick the cream with Paeony kernels".

Mrs. Glasse's Cookery, 1797

In 1387 when the Duke of Lancaster entertained Richard II, a hundred dozen peony roots was on the grocery list. The Earl of Devonshire in 1389 had "peionys" served at his wedding breakfast.

A SAUCE FOR PEIOUNS. Take percely, oynouns, garleke, and salt and mynce smal the percely and the oynouns and grynde the garleke, and temper it with vynegre y-now: and mynce the rostid peiouns and cast the sauce thereon abouet, and serve it forth.

Pliny says the peony is the oldest of all plants and Theophrastus described it in his "Enquiry into Plants" written in 320 B.C.

In mediaeval England the seeds of the male peony were used as a charm against witchcraft.

PLUM BLOSSOMS ❦❦❦❦❦❦❦❦❦❦❦❦❦

Wind and Moon are its spirit, Pearl and jade its bone;
Ice and Snow its hair-pin and ear-rings, Ch'iung-yao
Jade its pendants.
                    Wang Yu-ch'eng, Sung Dynasty

"He trimmed his brush with the utmost care, and wrote on the exquisite white paper: 'No deep drift bars my path, but with their whirling these thin parched snowflakes have bewitched my dizzy brain'. This he tied to a sprig of plum blossom, and sending for one of his servants, bade him take it not across the garden, but by way of the western gallery.
                    Lady Murasaki (translated by Arthur Waley)

PLUM FLOWER DUMPLINGS. The flowers of the white Plum and Sandlewood are powdered and mixed with water. When the water has absorbed the fragrance, the powder is removed. Flour is then mixed with the water to make a dough from which thin dumplings in the shape of a five-petaled Plum flower are cut. These are dropped in boiling chicken-broth. Should you be lucky enough to eat this, you will never forget the Plum flower.
                    Shan Chia Ch'ing Kung

PLUM BLOSSOM TEA. The same book (Shan Chia Ch'ing Kung) bids you gather the buds of the Plum blossom with a bamboo knife. To keep them from opening, keep them in wax and place them in covered jars. During the hot summer take some, drop them into a cup of boiling water where the buds will open and the water absorb their fragrance. This makes a most delicious and refreshing beverage.
                    Alfred Koehn, Fragrance from a Chinese Garden
                    Published At the Lotus Court, Peking, China, 1944

TO PICKLE PLUMB-BUDS. Take Salt and Water; boil it together; then put in your Plumb-buds, and boil them not tender, then strain them from the water, and let them be cold; then take what quantity you think fit of White-wine Vinegar, and boil it with two blades of Mace, and a little whole Pepper, then put them into the Pickle, and let them stand nine Days, then scald them in a brass Kettle, six times, till they are as green as Grass; take care they are not soft; tye them down with Leather: The same way pickle Elder-buds, and they are very pretty.
                    Henry Howard, England's Newest Way in All
                    Sorts of Cookery, London, 1717
                    (Cook to His Grace the Duke of Ormond, and since
                    to the Earl of Salisbury, and Earl of Winchelsea.)

POPPY ぐゃゃゃゃゃゃゃゃゃゃゃゃゃゃゃゃゃゃゃゃゃゃゃゃ

And poppy will erect her tufted head;
And earth be with a thousand beauties spread;
In this one flow'r her wealthy pride she shows,
In this one flow'r which she to Ceres owes;
Some silver-white, some dy'd with scarlet stains
Their lofty heads unite t' enrich the plains;
The seeds when pressed afford a juice,
Pow'rful in med'cine famous and of sov'reign use
Or bind the stubborn cough, and ease the lab'ring breast.
                        Rapin

Beneath the grey haze of the olives, the poppies lay in drifts of arterial scarlet, in the copses the crickets had begun their arid, interminable scraping, and the cuckoo changed his tune.
                Jocelyn Brooks, A Mine of Serpents

An ancient belief was that the picking of poppies was apt to cause a thunder-storm.

The slices of bread and butter which they give you with your tea are as thin as poppy leaves. But there is another kind of bread and butter usually eaten with tea, which is toasted by the fire, and is incomparably good. This is called 'toast'."
                Diary of Charles P. Moritz of Berlin during
                his travels in England, 1798

To Make Poppy Brandy. Take 6 quarts brandy, put into it a peck of pict poppy flowers; let them infuse together one night: the next morning stur it & take rasins of the Sun, figgs, of each 6 ounce sliced, 3 ounces of dats stoned and sliced, Corander and carraway seeds, mace, nutmegs, of each 9 drams, Anaseeds 3 drams Cloves 6 drams, an ounce of Liquiris sliced; bruse your spices and seeds and put all theas ingredience into a Canvis bag & hang in your pot but do not let the bag com to the bottom of your pot for the strenth of the thinngs will go better into the brandy. Let it infuse 5 or 6 days then run the brandy through cotton bag; put into every bottel a little sugar. When your brandy & spices are infusin be shuer to cover it close.

                Elizabeth Wainwright, The Receipt Book of a Lady of
                the Reign of Queen Anne, 1711

We usually think of the Poppy as a coarse flower; but it is the most transparent and delicate of all the blossoms of the field. The rest, nearly all of them, depend on the texture of their surface for colour. But the Poppy is painted GLASS; *it never glows so brightly as when the sun shines through it. Wherever it is seen, against the light or with the light, always it is a flame, and warms the wind like a blown ruby.*
          Ruskin, Proserpina (IV)

Poppy

POPPY SEED OIL. Poppy seed oil is another product used to some extent as a salad oil. Although this is obtained from the seeds of the Opium Poppy, neither the seeds nor the oil contain any opium, or indeed, anything of an injurious character. In some parts of Europe the seeds themselves are used as a filling for an agreeable form of pastry. Oil intended for use as a salad oil is obtained by pressure, without heat, and is afterwards filtered. It keeps remarkably well and has a characteristic and pleasant nutty taste. Inferior grades of poppy-seed oil should be avoided.

Poppy seeds have many uses, try these: Add to glazed carrots, scrambled eggs, cauliflower, fruit cake batter, and cream cheese spreads.

About nine hundred thousand seeds make a pound, so don't bother counting the seeds, just use them by the tablespoon. The best poppy seeds come from the Netherlands.

"The golden poppy is God's gold,
The gold that lifts, nor weighs us down."
          Joaquin Miller

"A poppy bud, packed into tight bundles by so hard and resolute a hand that the petals of the flower never afterwards lose the creases, is a type of the child. Nothing but the unfolding, which is as yet in the non-existing future, can explain the manner of the close folding of character.
       In both flower and child it looks much as though the process had been the reverse of what it was—as though a finished and open thing had been folded up in the bud—so plainly and certainly is the future implied, and the intention of compressing and folding close made manifest."
          Meynell, The Child of Tumult

In Virgil's time poppies were eaten and poppy-tea was once very popular.

Poppy

Poppy Syrup. Take the Heads of black Poppies freshly gathered six ounces, and of white ones, not thoroughly ripe, eight ounces, Water a gallon: boil them to the consumption of two quarts of the Liquid, and put therein Sugar a pound and half, or two pound, and boil them to a Syrup. This is excellent good to allay the Heat of the Head and other Parts.

William Salmon, The Family Dictionary, London 1705

Saltus in Imperial Purple speaks of dormice baked in honey and poppies.

The red poppy means "Evanescent Pleasure".

But pleasures are like Poppies spread
You seize the flower, its bloom is shed.
Robert Burns

Poppy Syrup. Take 4 oz. of dried poppy petals, and put them in a jar with a cover to it; Boil 2½ lbs. of water; pour it, boiling, on to the poppies, and let them steep therein for six hours, keeping the jar closed; Strain through a broth-napkin, and filter the liquid through a felt bag into a jar; add to it 3 lbs. 6 oz. of sugar; close the jar and melt the sugar *au brain-marie*. When cold, bottle the syrup, and keep it in a cool place.

Paris Pharmacopoeia, 1866

Red Poppy Cordial.
1 peck scarlet poppies
1 gallon brandy
1 pound sugar
2 pounds raisins
1 ounce liquorice, sliced
1 ounce sweet fennel seed
half ounce saffron
1 pint cowslip water
1 ounce coriander
¼ ounce ground ginger

Mix poppies with brandy and let set for forty-eight hours, then strain the poppies out, add other ingredients and let stand for two months, shaking every day. Strain and bottle.

PRIMROSE ❧❧❧❧❧❧❧❧❧❧❧❧❧❧❧

"How beautiful are the retired flowers! How would they lose their beauty were they to throng into the highway, crying out: 'Admire me, I am a violet! Dote upon me, I am a Primrose!'"
                          John Keats, Letter to Sir Joshua Reynolds, 1818

PRIMROSES. — That touch'd mine eyes like kisses cool.
          Coventry Patmore, The Rod, the Root, and
          the Flower, London, 1914

CANDIED PRIMROSE. Gather the primroses when dry, and pull the flowers from the green calyx. Make a syrup of sugar and water, and boil it until when a little is dropped into cold water it is crisp. Then put in the primroses for a minute. Take them out and dry them on a sieve. Leave them in a warm place to dry, then sprinkle them with powdered sugar. Gently open the flowers and sift any superfluous sugar from them, and keep them in a dry place.

TO CANDY ALL KIND OF FLOWERS IN WAYES OF THE SPANISH CANDY. Take double refined sugar, put it into a posnet with as much rose-water as will melt it and put into it the pappe of half a roasted apple, and a grain of musk, and then let it boyl till it come to a candy height, then put in your flowers being picked, and so let it boyl, then cast them on a fine plate, and cut inwayes with your knife, then you may spot it with gold and keep it.
                          Elizabeth Grey, Countess of Kent, A Choice Manual of
                          Secrets, 1653

TO DISH UP FRUITS AND PRESERVED FLOWERS. Take a large Dish, cover it with another of the same bigness, and lay the uppermost all over with Almond paste; inlaid with white, red, green, blue or white Marmalad in the Figures of Banks of Flowers. Then take branches of candy'd Flowers and stick them upright in the Paste in as handsome orders as you can, then erect little Bushes covered with Paste, and upon them fasten preserved Apples, Apricochs, Currants, Gooseberries, Peaches, Pears, Plums, etc., and for Leaves you may make use either of coloured Paste, Parchment or Horn. This will be very proper in winter.
                          William Rabisha, The Whole Body of Cookery Dissected,
                          1675

TO CANDY FLOWERS THE SPANISH FASHION. Take flowers of any Sort whatsoever and picke off the leaves from the flower and make a Sirrop of Sugar and put in the Blossoms of your flowers as many as will go into the Sirrop boyle them with stirring until it be turned to Sugar again set it off the fire and with the back of a spoon stir them and bruise the sugar from them and they will be canded and no Sugar seen upon them.

H. W. Lewer, A Book of Simples

Primrose DISRAELI SALAD. The primrose was Disraeli's favorite flower. He liked the young shoots gathered and soaked in salt water for a few minutes, then drained and boiled for about 10 to 15 minutes. Serve with sauce vinaigrette, decorated with the flowers.

Another way is to brown slightly in butter, eat hot served with sweetened orange juice.

The flowers of the evening primrose are known for their visible movements at dusk, at sunrise they shut again with a loud popping noise. Both roots and leaves are edible.

PRIMROSE VINEGAR. Take thirty quarts of cold water, twelve pounds of brown sugar, a peck of primroses, and a cake of yeast. Boil for ten minutes, let it stand for a few days, then age in a cask for a year.

PRIMROSE POTTAGE. Take half pound of rice flour, two ounces of almonds, half an ounce of honey and saffron. Add to the pounded almonds primrose flowers and boil the whole. Serve with primrose petals in the pottage.

Early English Text Society, 15th Century
Cookery Book

PRIMEROLILE. To make primerolle in pasthe take blanched almonds and flour of primerolle grind it and temper it with swet wyne and good brothe drawinge into the thik mylk put it into a pot with sugar salt and saffron that it have colour like primerolle and boil it that it be stondinge and alay it with flour of rise and serve it as a standinge potage and straw thereon flour of primerolle above and ye may diaper it with rape rialle in dressinge of some other sewe.

A Noble Boke off Cookry ffor a Prince Houssolde or
any other estately Houssolde, 1470

(This is the original of the recipe for "Primrose Pottage.)

Pale primroses
That die unmarried, 'ere they can behold
Bright Phoebus in his strength.
Shakespeare, Winter's Tale

PRIMROSE PUDDING. Dry cherries, pistachios, almonds, etc.; fine white bread-crumbs ½ lb., castor sugar 1 tablespoon; boiling milk 1 teacupful (or ¼ pint); suet, finely chopped 4 oz.; primrose petals 1 pint, eggs 3, champagne sauce.

1. Butter a mould well and decorate it with the cherries, nuts, et.
2. Nip off the white at the base of the primrose petals.
3. Put the breadcrumbs into a basin, stir in the sugar and pour the boiling milk over the mixture.
4. Stir in the suet and primrose petals.
5. Whisk up the eggs to a very light froth and mix a little at a time.
6. Pour the mixture carefully into the mould. Cover with well buttered brown paper and steam for 1¼ hours.
7. Serve with champagne or some other wine sauce.

This could also become a primrose tart. A boiled custard flavored with primroses is delightful.

PRIMROSE WINE. Take two gallons of primrose blossoms (minus calyxes), 8 pounds sugar, 2 teaspoons powdered ginger, a half-dozen cloves, 2 pounds raisins (cut in half), 3 lemons, 2 packages yeast, 3 gallons water, a cup of brandy, and a package of unflavored gelatin. Put flowers into a crock and boil together with sugar, ginger, and cloves. Pour over flowers and stir. Then add raisins and thinly sliced lemons. Cover the crock and let set for a week, then strain into a wooden keg and add the yeast. After fermentation has ceased clear it with gelatin, close it tight and keep for a year before bottling, and then another six months should pass before drinking.

Primrose

RATTAN

In gala robes she comes down from her chamber
Into her courtyard, enclosure of spring . . .
When she tries from the centry to count the flowers,
On her hairpin of jade a dragon-fly poises.

> Liu Yu-hsi
> (Tr. by Witter Bynner, The Jade Mountain
> Knopf, 1929)

In China, where flowers are honored in many ways and with many festivals, Faah Seen, the Taoist Goddess of Flowers, is honored on the twelfth day of the Second Moon—the "birthday" of flowers in general. The festival is called

Faah Jiu—Flower Dawn—women and children start the day by decorating the trees and shrubbery with ribbons and paper flowers; then they gather together in prayer and ask for abundance. Intricate headdresses are decorated with real flowers.

Rattan

RATTAN CAKES. Tung law bang. Take the flowers (kraunhia floribundia), which are butterfly shaped and are either purple or white and mix with suet and flour. These cakes are unleavened, pourous, and taste very good.

RHODODENDRON

The valley of the Doon lay stretched before me, and the hills around me. There is a Rhododendron tree on this estate that bears white flowers — it is a great rarity and highly prized. The Hill men are fond of sucking the juice from the petals, which it is said to possess an intoxicating quality.

Parkes, The Wandering of a Pilgrim

Its symbolical meaning is danger, warning.

Dr. Fernald in "Edible Wild Plants of Eastern North America" speaks of Rhododendron lapponicum (Lapland Rosebay) advocates the leaves and flowering tops infused and drunk as tea.

RHODODENDRON JELLY. Clean and pick out the stamens of the flowers (say about 4 lbs.) and place on the fire with 8 small tumblers water. Boil this till all the juice is extracted from the petals, then strain in a course strainer. Mix with the juice equal parts white sugar (i. e. 4 lbs.) and the juice of a large lemon, and cook till it becomes the consistency of jelly. An excellent substitute for red currant jelly.

L. V., Indian Chutneys, Pickles & Preserves
Published by Thacker, Spink & Company, 1914

ROSELLE

The Roselle or Florida cranberry is a tropical plant, native to India, though it is cultivated in Australia extensively. It was brought to the West Indies sometime before 1855 where it is known as "red sorrell" or Jamaica sorrell. In California it is known as the "Lemonade Bush." Throughout the South it is known as "Jelly Okra." The bushes are covered with vivid wine-red flowers, and their waxen petals make delicious sauces, jams, chutneys and jellies.

ROSELLE JELLY. Remove the petals of the flower from the seed; then mince finely by running through the meat grinder. To every cup of minced petals add three cups of water. Boil quickly as the color is much better if it does not stand around. After boiling five minutes it will be ready to strain. Strain and make as any other jelly. In flavor and appearance this jelly cannot be surpassed.

Roselle

The Khaki Kook Book by Mary Kennedy Core (1917)

ROSELLE SAUCE. Remove petals from the seed, and for every cup of petals take two cups of water. Stew gently for a few minutes, then add a cup of sugar for every cup of fruit. These two things must be remembered if one wishes to get the best results from the fruit. It must be well diluted and it must be cooked quickly, as it is apt to lose its bright color if it stands around.

Ibidem

The Florida Office of Home Demonstration Work, Agricultural Extension Service, Tallahassee, has sent me a pamphlet in which it states that it grows up to 8 feet in height with upright red stems; and that calyxes are used for juice, sauce, jelly and wine, and twelve excellent recipes.

There is also a bulletin which was published in January, 1932 by the Agricultural and Natural Resources, Bureau of Science, Manila, Philippine Islands, in which there are fifty-nine recipes by Maria Y. Orosa. They are divided into eighteen categories: jelly, jam, butter, preserve, conserve, marmalade, paste, chutney, pickle, catchup, sauce, juice, syrup, wine vinegar, nata, punch, and cocktails. She also advises using only porcelain or aluminum pans, wooden spoons, and only stainless knives for cutting.

In the Philippines the young leaves are used as a substitute for spinach, or cooked with fish or meat for making "sinigang" (Filipino dish cooked with acid fruit or acid leaves). From her collection I chose "Nata" as it was something I had never heard of and thought that my readers would like to share something new with me.

ROSELLE NATA. While the acid or acetic fermentation is taking place, a pinkish gelatinous film grows on top. In about 3 weeks the film is from $\frac{1}{2}$ to $\frac{3}{4}$ inch thick. Collect this "nata" and soak in plenty of water. Change the water at least four times a day. Continue the operation until the odor of the vinegar can no longer be detected. Slice to desired pieces and blanch in boiling water. Rinse and drain. Make a syrup of 1 part sugar and 1 part water. Boil slowly in this solution 30 minutes. Drain and pack the pieces in preserving jars. Strain the syrup left after boiling the nata in it, and to every cupful add ¼ cupful of roselle syrup. Bring to a boil and fill the jars containing the nata, with this syrup. Half seal the jars; sterilize for 30 minutes and seal completely. Cool in an inverted position. Label and store in a cool, dry place.

Roselle

ROSELLE PRESERVES: Roselle petals and honey make a delicious preserve.

1 pound flowers
1 pound honey
1 pound water

Cook all together until petals are soft. Remove petals and boil down, add petals and seal in jelly glasses.

ROSELLE TARTS: Prepare petals as you would fruit, with sugar, and use for a tart or pie filling. Top with whipped cream.

ROSEMARY

"O dewy flowers that open to the sun . . .
What knowest thou of flowers, except, belike,
To garnish meats with? hath not our good King
Who lent me thee, the flower of kitchendom,
A foolish love for flowers? what stick ye round
The pasty? wherewithal deck the boar's head?
        Flowers? nay, the boar hath rosemaries and bay."
        Tennyson, Gareth and Lynette, (King Arthur
        had sent to Castle Perilous the kitchen knave
        instead of Lancelot as her champion).

"There's Rosemary, that's for remembrance,
I pray you love, remember,
        Shakespeare, Hamlet

ORANGES OR TANGERINES WITH ROSEMARY. Separate a half dozen oranges or tangerines into segments and add 1 cup sugar, 2 cups water, 1 tablespoon rosemary and 1 teaspoon vanilla flavoring and cook together gently until it reaches the light syrup stage. These should be served cold with whipped cream.

Rosemary

WHITE METHEGLIN. Take of Sweet-bryar a great handful; of Violet-flowers, Sweet marjoram, Strawberry leaves, Violet leaves, and one handful, Agrimony, Bugloss, Borrage, and half a handful Rosemary; four branches, Gillyflowers (the Yellow wall-flowers with great tops), Anniseeds, Fennel, and Caraway, of each a spoonful, two large Mace. Boil all these in twelve gallons of water for the space of an hour; then strain it, and let it stand until it be Milk-warm. Then put in as much honey as will carry an Egge to the breadth of sixpence at least; then boil it again, and scum it clean; then let it stand, until it be cold; then put a pint of Ale-barm into it, and ripen it as you do Beer, and tun it. Then hand in the midst of the vessel a little bag with a Nutmeg quartered, a Race of Ginger sliced, a little Cinnamon, and mace whole, and three grains of Musk in a cloth put into the bag amongst the rest of the Spices. Put a stone in the bag, to keep it in the midst of the Liquor. This quantity took up three gallons of honey; therefore be sure to have four in readiness.

The Closet of Sir Kenelm Digby Opened, 1699

ROSEMARY TEA. Pour one pint of boiling water on a heaping tablespoonful of young tips.

ROSEMARY WINE. Infuse a bunch of rosemary tips (about six inches long) in sound white wine for a few days, when the wine will be fit to use.

ROSEMARY HONEY. Infuse rosemary flowers with pure honey, which will be like the celebrated honey of Narbonne, so very good because of the rosemary flowers in that vicinity which invite the bees.

TO MAKE A DYSCHEFULL OF SNOWE. Take a pottell of swete thycke creame and the whytes of eyghte egges, and beate them altogether wyth a spone, then putte them in youre creame and a saucerfull of Rosewater, and a dyshe full of Suger wyth all, then take a stycke and make it cleane, and then cutte it in the ende foure sware, and therewith beate all the aforesayde thynges together, and ever as it ryseth take it of and put it into a Collaunder, this done take one apple and set it in the myddes of it, and a thicke bushe of Rosemary, and set it in the myddes of the platter, then cast your Snowe uppon the Rosemary and fyll your platter therewith. And yf you have wafers caste some in wyth all and thus serve them forthe.

A Proper Newe Booke of Cokerye, 1575

ROSEMARY IN SNOW. (Second modernization of above recipe.) Take a quart of thick cream, and five or six eggs, a saucerful of powdered sugar and an equal amount of Rosewater, (an infusion of one leaf of Rose Geranium steeped in one-half cup of boiling water, substitutes nicely for the difficult-to-purchase, Rosewater). Beat them all together until the egg whites rise in peaks. Take a loaf of white bread, cut away the crust, and set it in a silver platter with a great Rosemary bush set in the middle of it. Then lightly pile the snow with a spoon on the Rosemary branches and serve it at once.

Rosemary

> Vol I 1947—American Herb Grower Magazine,
> now called The Herb Grower Magazine,
> published at Falls Village, Conn.

(This same recipe had also been modernized in 1653, A Book of Fruits and Flowers.)

Dark spiked rosemary and myrrh,
Lean stalk'd purple lavender;
Hides within her bosom, too,
All her sorrows, bitter rue.

> *Walter De La Mare*

DRESSING FOR A TROUT. A handful of sliced Horseradish root, with a handsome little faggot of Rosemary, Thyme, and Winter Savoury is recommended in the directions for dressing a trout, in Cotton's sequel to Izaak Walton's Compleat Angler, 1676.

Another dressing for fish can be made of rosemary fried in a little butter with a tablespoonful of flour, two cups of stock (which can be made with bouillon cubes), lemon juice and anchovy sauce, mix and boil from five to ten minutes and pour over fish.

TO MAKE ROSEMARY WATER. Take the rosemary and the flowers in the middest of May, before sunne arise, and strippe the leaves and the flowers from the stalke, take four or five elecampane roots and a handful or two of sage, then beate the rosemary, the sage and the rootes together, till they be very small, and take three ounces of cloves, three ounces of mace, one and a half pounds of aniseed and beat these spices every one by itself. Then take all the hearbes and spices and put therein foure or five gallons of good white wine, then put in all these hearbes and spices and wine into an earthen pot, and put the same pot in the ground the space of sixteen days, then take it up and still in a Still with a very soft fire.

> The Good Housewife's Jewell, 1585

To Make Conserve Of Rosemary Flowers. Take two Pound of Rosemary-flowers, the same weight of fine Sugar, pwnd them well in a Stone-Mortar; then put the Conserve into well-glaz'd Gallipots. It will keep a Year or two.
Sir Hugh Platt, Delights for Ladies

Rosemary

Hungary-Water. From Mrs. DuPont of Lyons; which is the same, which has been famous, about Montpelier. Take to every gallon of Brandy, or clean Spirits, one handful of Rosemary, one handful of Lavender. I suppose the handfuls to be about a Foot long a-piece; and these Herbs must be cut in Pieces about an Inch long. Put these to infuse in the Spirits, and with them, about one handful of Myrtle, cut as before. When this has stood three Days, distil it, and you will have the finest Hungary-Water that can be. It has been said that Rosemary-flowers are better than the Stalks; but they give a faintness to the Water, and should not be used, because they have a quite different smell from the Rosemary, nor should the Flowers of Myrtle be used in lieu of the Myrtle, for they have a scent ungrateful, and not at all like the Myrtle.
R. Bradley, The Country Housewife and Lady's Director, 1732

(A hermit gave this recipe to Queen Elizabeth of Hungary.)

"As for rosemarie I lette it runne all over my garden walls, not onlie because my bees love it, but because it is the herb sacred to remembrance and to friendship, whence a sprig of it hath a dumb language."
Sir Thomas More

The Countess of Hainault to her daughter, Queen Philippa of England, "Rosemary passeth not in highte the highte of Criste whill he was man in erthe," she also said that when the plant reaches thirty-three years in age it will not increase in height but in breadth.

A Spanish legend says that the flowers were originally white, but that since the Virgin Mary threw her robe over them, they have preserved the memory of her having thus honoured them by turning the colour she wore

Salat. Take parsel, sauge, garlic, chibollas (young onions), leek, borage, myntis, porrectes (French porrette), fennel, and ton cresses, rew, rosemarye, purslayne, lave, and waisshe hem clein; pike him, pluck hem small with thyn (thine) honde, and myng (mix) them well with rawe oils. Lay on vinegar and salt, and serve forth   The Form of Cury (A manuscript compiled about 1390 by the Master cooks of King Richard II).

"Chiefly of the Aromatick Esculents and Plants are preferable, as generally endowed with the Vertues of their Simples, in a more intense degree; and may therefore be eaten alone in their proper Vehicles, or Composition with other Salleting sprinkled among them; But give a more palatable Relish, being Infused in Vinegar; Especially those of the Clove Gillyflower, Elder, Orange, Cowslip, Rosemary, Arch-Angel (dead nettle), Sage, Nasturtium Indicum, etc."

Evelyn

Rosemary

CONSERVE OF ROSEMARY FLOWERS AFTER THE ITALIAN METHOD. Take new Rosemary flowers one pound, of white sugar one pound, so beat them together in a marble mortar with a wooden pestle, keep it in a gallypot or vessel of earth well glassed or in one of hard stone. It may be preserved for one year or two.

It comforteth the heart, the stomach, the brain, and all the nervous parts of the body.

A Queen's Delight, 1695

For the sickly take this wort rosemary, wonderfully thou healest him.
Leech Book of Bald, (circa A. D. 900)

SIR WILLIAM PASTON'S MEATHE. Take ten gallons of spring water, and put therein ten pints of the best honey. Let this boil half an hour, and scum it very well; then put in a handful of Rosemary, and as much Bay leaves; with a little lemon peel. Boil this half an hour longer, then take it off the fire, and put it in a clean Tub; and when it is cool, work it up with yeast, as you do Beer. When it is wrought, put it into your vessel, and stop it very close. Within three days you may Bottle it, and in ten days after it will be fit to drink.

The Closet of Sir Kenelm Digby Opened, 1699

ROSEMARY BUTTER. Take one stick of butter, and fresh flower petals after they have been washed and dried, allow butter to soften, mix with petals, and place in tightly covered jar.

"Rosemary mighteth the boones and causeth goode and gladeth and lighteth alle men that use it. The leves layde under the heade whanne a man slepes, it doth away evell spirites and suffereth not to dreeme fowle dremes ne to be afeade. But he must be out of deedely synne for it is an holy tree. Lavender and Rosemary is as woman to man and White Rose to Reede. It is an holy tree and with ffolke that been just and rightfully gladlye it groweth and thryveth.
On the virtues of Rosemary sent by the Countess of Hainault
to her daughter, Queen Philippa of England.

"O Thou great shepheard, Lobbin, how great is thy griefe?
Where bene the nosegays that she dight for thee?
The colored chaplets wrought with a chiefe
The knotted rush-rings and gilt rosmarie?
Spenser, Shepheard's Calendar (November)

Rosemary

ROSEMARY WATER. Take the flowers of rosemary and boyle them in fayre water and drink that water for it is much worth against all manner of evils in the body. Take the flowers thereof and make powder thereof and binde it to thy right arme in a linnen cloath and it shale make thee lighte and merie.
Rycharde Banckes's Herball, 1525

ROSEMARY VINEGAR. Take two heaping teaspoons of the dried flowers and mix with one pint of vinegar, cover tightly and let it stand for two weeks. Shake well once a day. Taste at the end of two weeks, and if the flavor is not strong enough, strain out the petals and replace with fresh ones. Let stand and cork tightly.

(Any flower vinegar can be made the same way.)

ROSEMARY TEA SHERBERT. Prepare two cups of rosemary tea; mix a half cup of sugar and a half cup of water, let it come to a boil, add a tablespoonful of lemon juice and a half cup of orange juice, mix with the tea and freeze. Serve in sherbet glasses.

Bread baked in an oven in which a few faggots of rosemary have been burned is delicious. Elliot Paul in his "Life and Death of a Spanish Town" describes early morning there where the fires were kindled daily with twigs of Rosemary brought from the hills. The fragrance of the blue smoke is enchanting.

Candied rosemary flowers were very popular in Tudor times.

"The flowers of Rosemary," says an old author, "made up into plates (lozenges, or tablets), with sugar, and eaten, comfort the heart, and make it merry, quicken the spirits, and cause them to be lively."

In the early eighteenth century rosemary preserves were used to dress beef.

Charles Lamb, in his story, Rosamund Gray (1798), old blind Margaret had "a cookery book, with a few dry sprigs of Rosemary and Lavender, stuck here and there between the leaves."

TO MAKE HYPOCRAS. Take four gallons of Claret Wine, eight ounces of Cinamon, and Oranges, of Ginger, Cloves and Nutmegs a small quantity, Sugar six pound, three sprigs of Rosemary, bruise all the spices somewhat small, and so put them into the Wine, and keep them close stopped, and often shaked together a day or two, then let it run through a jelly bag twice or three times with a quart of new milk.

The Queen's Closet Opened, 1655

To Candy Branches In Their Colour And Smell. Take two ounces of gumme Arabecke, steep it in a quarter of a pint of rose-water, then take the branches of rosemary and dip them in the Gumme water, then take white sugar-candie, break it in small pieces like Sparkes of Diamonds, then take your branches of rosemary and shake it out of the water, but dry it not, then roule it in the sugar-candie, and so farre as your rosemary is wette the candie will sticke upon it, and then lay it upon white papers in the sunne, now and then turning them, and when they be through dry, put them in boxes for your use.

John Murrell, A Delightful Daily Exercise
for Ladies and Gentlemen, 1621

Rosemary

Rosemary is good for many things: it will make the hair grow, it is a nerve tonic and stomachic, will cure vertigo, strengthens sight and memory, and is a cordial for the heart.

Rosemary Punch. 2 tablespoons crushed rosemary leaves
3 tablespoons sugar
¼ teaspoon salt
½ cup water
2 cups apricot nectar
1 quart ginger ale
1 cup frozen lime juice

Simmer rosemary leaves, sugar, and salt in the water for 2 minutes. Cool and strain. Combine nectar, ale and lime juice, add rosemary syrup. Serve in tall, chilled glasses over shaved ice and garnish with twists of lime rind.

Spirit Of Rosemary. Gather a Pound and a half of the fresh tops of Rosemary, cut them into a Gallon of clean and fine Melasses Spirit, and let them stand all Night, next Day distill off five pints with a gentle Heat: this is of the nature of Hungary-Water, but not being so strong as that is usually made, it is better for taking inwardly.   Elizabeth Cleland, Receipt Book, 1759

Rosemary Sugar. Clean and dry well several sprigs of rosemary. Place them in a tightly-covered jar and cover with 1 lb. of sugar. Shake well and leave for 24 hours. Shake well again and stand for several days. Remove rosemary sprigs—and the sugar is ready for use with milk puddings and egg custards.

ROSES ～～～～～～～～～～～～～～～～～～～～～～

Dedicated to the Garden Club of Guadalajara,
  Jalisco, Mexico, of which I was a member.

Roses that have never been acquainted
With roses in bowls,
Those old, imperishable roses painted
On silk and paper scrolls.

Wytter Bynner, Take Away the Darkness

"The Plant of Roses, though it be a shrub full of prickes, yet it hath beene more fit and convenient to have placed it with the most glorious flowers of the world than to inserte the same here among base and thornie shrubs; for the rose doth deserve the chiefest and most principall place among all flowers whatsoever being not only esteemed in his beautie, vertue and his fragrance and odoriferous smell, but also because it is the honor and ornament of our English scepter . . . The distilled water of roses is good for the strengthening of the heart and refreshing of the spirits and likewise in all things that require a gentle cooling. The same being put in iunketting dishes, cakes, sawces and many other pleasant things, giveth a fine and delectable taste. It bringeth sleepe which also the fresh roses themselves promote through their sweet and pleasant smell."

John Gerard, The Herball — 1597

ROSE HONEY. "Rose shreede smalle and sod in hony makyth that hony medycynable wyth gode smelle: And this comfortyeth and clenseth and defyeth gleymy humours."

Barthelomaeus Anglicus,
De Proprietatibus Rerum, about the
middle of the 13th century

ROSE CREAM. Crema de Rose. "Into a quart of spirits of wine, put twelve drops of oil of roses and three of oil of nutmeg; shake it well and add a quart of syrup, with a sufficient quantity of the pink tincture to produce a rose colour."

Indian Domestic Economy and Receipt Book,
Christian Knowledge Society Press, Madras, 1853.

ROSE HIP JAM.
- 1 orange
- 1 lemon
- 1 cup water
- 1½ to 2 cups sugar
- 1½ cups prepared rose hips
- 2 ounces finely minced preserved ginger

Thinly peel the orange and lemon and boil peel in water 5 minutes. Add sugar and stir until dissolved, then add prepared rose hips with the juice of the orange and lemon; boil covered for 15 minutes. Then uncover and boil until the hips are clear and transparent and syrup is thick. Add ginger and pour into hot sterilized glasses and seal.

Roses

ROSE HIP JELLY. Rose hips
　　　　　　　　　Water
　　　　　　　　　Sugar

Wash hips, and to 1 pound hips add 1 cup water and boil until fruit is soft. Put through a fine sieve to remove seeds. Measure and heat liquid; when simmering add an equal amount of sugar and boil quickly to jelly stage. Pour into hot sterilized glasses and seal when cool.

SWEET BRIAR ROSE HIP JAM.　　2 cups hips, before seeding
　　　　　　　　　　　　　1½ cups sugar
　　　　　　　　　　　　　　1 cup water
　　　　　　　　　　　　　　2 tablespoons lemon juice

Prepare hips and measure 1 cup. Boil sugar and water 4 minutes, add hips and lemon juice and boil, covered, 15 minutes, uncover and boil 5 minutes more. The berries should be clear and transparent and syrup thick. When done, pour into hot sterilized glasses and seal.

ROSE SOUFFLE CAKES. Pick a handful of rose leaves, and give them a boil in syrup made of a pound of sugar. Have ready an icing made of two ounces of sugar, and the white of an egg well beat up and tinged with cochineal. Stir a spoonful of this into the syrup till it rises; fill the small moulds and bake.
　　　　　　　　　Mrs. Margaret Dods, The Cook and Housewife's
　　　　　　　　　Manual, Edinburgh, 1828

"Remnants of packthread and cakes of roses
Were thinly scatter'd to make up a show."
　　　　　　　　　Romeo and Juliet. Act V, Scene I

"What's in a name? that which we call a rose
By any other name would smell as sweet."
　　　　　　　　　Romeo and Juliet. Act II, Scene I

RED ROSES
A cool red rose and a pink cut pink, a collapse and a sold hole, a little less hot.
　　　　　　　Gertrude Stein, Tender Buttons

ROSE CREAM CAKE.   2 cups sugar
                    1 scant cup butter
                    1 cup milk
                    3½ cups flour
                    whites of 8 eggs

Roses

Sift the flour 5 times, 2 large teaspoons of baking powder well mixed through the flour. Bake in 3 layers, coloring the middle layer pink with fruit extract. Boiled icing, flavored with extract of rose.

Mrs. E. W. Ensign, The Club Woman's
Cook Book by The Ramblers Club,
Minneapolis 1911

ROSE CHOCOLATE CREAMS.   Fondant
                          Damask rose color paste
                          ½ to 1 teaspoonful rose extract
                          ½ lb. Baker's "Dot" chocolate

Put a part or the whole of the fondant into a double boiler over boiling water. With the point of a toothpick take up a little of the color paste and add to the fondant; add the extract and stir until the mixture is hot, thin, and evenly tinted. With two teaspoons drop the mixture into impressions made in starch; it should be hot and thin enough to run level on top. When the shapes are cold, remove from the starch, brush carefully and coat with "Dot" chocolate.

Walter Baker & Company, Ltd.
Pamphlet of 1911

Crystallized rose petals harmonize with peaches, try them with a peach gateau. Peaches flavored with rose extract are a delightful treat.

POWDER OF ROSES: "If the aforesayde poulder be put in a lampe and after be kindled all men shall appear blacke as the deuell. And if the aforesaid poulder be mixed with oyle of the olyue tree and with quycke brymstone and the house annointed wyth it, the Sunne shyning, it shall appeare all inflamed."

Albertus Magnus, The Boke of Secretes
circa 1200

Roses

SAN JOSE PUDDING. 2½ heaping tablespoons Cox powdered gelatine
1½ cups boiling water
1 cup cream
1 cup whipping cream
4 tablespoons sugar
2 tablespoons sherry wine
2 ozs. glace fruits
2 ozs. maraschino cherries
2 ozs. pecan meats
Candied rose petals

Dissolve gelatin with water and add cream and sugar. When cook, add wine and fold in whipped cream. Set on ice, when beginning to set, add fruits, cherries, and nuts cut in small pieces. Chill, serve in dainty glasses, with garnishment of candied rose petals.

Cox pamphlet, 1909

JELLY ROSETTES. Line some patty pans daintily with pastry, fill with uncooked rice and bake. When ready and cold fill with chopped lemon jelly. Put a rose of whipped sweetened cream on top, using forcing bag and rose tube, decorate with candied rose petals and chopped pistachio nuts. (The lemon jelly is flavored with cinnamon, cloves, coriander seeds and a bay leaf.)

Cox's Gelatine Cookery, Edinburgh, 1909

ROSE CREAM STICK. Boil three pounds of granulated sugar with half a pint of water; let it dissolve slowly on a cool part of the range; then add a large tablespoonful of vinegar and a teaspoonful of gum arabic dissolved in very little water. Boil till it is brittle, remove from fire and flavor with rose extract. All work must be quick. Rub the hands with sweet oil or butter and pull vigorously till the candy is white, then add a few drops of rose coloring. Twist or braid or pull into thin strips and cut it off.

ROSE PUFF RINGS. Prepare puff paste from any good recipe. Take pieces and form into inch or inch and a half circles about half inch thick. Place on a lightly floured baking pan about an inch apart and bake in a 400 degree oven until light brown. Remove from oven and let cool. On each circle spread rose petal conserve and add a topping of sweetened whipped cream. The whipped cream can be colored with a bit of red food coloring and the flavor can be deepened with a drop of oil of roses.

Roses

The rose of gardens is planted and sette and tylthed as a vyne. And if it is for-gendred and not shred and pared and not clensed of superfluyte: then it gooth out of kynde and chaungeth in to a wylde rose. And by oft chaunging and tylthing the wylde rose ben dyuers in multitude of floures: smelle and colour: and also in vertue. For the leves of the wylde rose ben fewe and brode and whytyssh: meddlyd with lytyll rednesse and smellyth not so wel as the tame rose, nother is so vertuous in medicyn. The tame rose hath many leuys sette ny togyder: and ben a., red, other almost white: wy wonder good smell . . . And the more they ben brused and broken: the vertuouser they ben and the better smellynge. And springeth out of a thorne that is harde and rough: netheles the Rose folowyth not the kynde of the thorne: But she arayeth her thorn wyth fayr colour and good smell. Whan ye rose begynneth to sprynge it is closed in a knoppe wyth grenes: and that knoppe is grene. And whane it swellyth thenne spryngeth out harde leuys and sharpe . . . And whane they ben full growen they sprede theymselues ayenst the soone rysynge. And for they ben tendre and feble to holde togyder in the begynnynge; theyfore about those smale grene leuys ben nyghe the red and tendre leuys . . . and ben sette all aboute. And in the mydill thereof is seen the sede small and yellow wyth full gode smell.

Among 'all floures of the worlde the floure of the rose is cheyf and beeryth ye pryse. And by cause of vertues and swete smelle and savour. For by fayrnesse they fede the syghte: and playseth the smelle by odour, the touche by softe hand-lynge. And wythstondeth and socouryth by vertue ayenst many syknesses and euylles."

> *Bartholomaeus Anglicus, De Proprietatibus Rerum, about the middle of the 13th century.*

❧ *On being asked what keeps him young, Enos Slaughter, youngest 41-year-old man in the major leagues replied, "Rose hip tea. I drink that. Got lots of vitamin C in it."*

❧ *And, what's rose hip tea? "Why," said Slaughter, surprised that anyone didn't know about rose hip tea, "why that's made from the rose bush. Lots of vitamin C. 'Course, you need the other ones too."*

> *New York Post, Monday, August 5, 1957*

RUBAIYAT OF OMAR KHAYYAM

I sometimes think that never blows so red
The rose as where some buried Caesar bled;
*   That every Hyacinth the Garden wears*
Dropt in her Lap from some once Lovely Head.

> *Edward Fitzgerald*

Rose Fritters. Dip petals in brandy, then into batter, fry in deep fat. Serve dusted with sugar.

Spirit Of Roses. Take of Damask, or Red Roses, being fresh, as many as you please, infuse them in as much warm water as is sufficient for the space of twenty four houres: Then strain, and press them, and repeat the infusion severall times with pressing, untill the liquor become fully impregnated, which then must *Roses* be distilled in an Alembick with a refrigerator, let the Spirit which swims on the Water be separated, and the water kept for a new infusion.

This kind of Spirit may be made by bruising the Roses with Salt, or laying a lave of Roses, and another of Salt, and so keeping them half a year or more, which then must be distilled in as much Common water, or Rosewater as is sufficient. John French, The Art of Distillation, 1652

Gather ye rose-buds while ye may,
Old Time is still a-flying.
Robert Herrick

Candied Rose Petals. There are many recipes for candied rose petals. Here is one: Take a cup of rose petals, 1 cup powdered sugar and 1 cup of granulated sugar. Soak the petals in cold water. Drain and pat dry with a soft towel. Cook the powdered sugar for ten minutes, letting it boil for five minutes. Add petals and cover each petal with the syrup. Remove one at a time and place on waxed paper. When dry sprinkle lightly with the granulated sugar.

Rose Nectar. Have a cup of rose petals and build up in layers with powdered sugar in a suitable bowl. Cover and let it set for three days. Boil 1 cup water and add 2 cups of alcohol and a teaspoon of glycerine. Put petals into a jar and cover with liquid mixture. Let it set for a week, then strain into bottles. Cork tightly.

Rose Petal Honey, Which Was A Favorite Of Martha Washington. Take two pints of honey and bring to a boil, adding a pint of rose petals. Let it stand for a few hours, heat again, strain into honey pots.

Rose Hips With Tomato Juice. Make about a cup of rose hip puree and season tomato juice with lemon juice, chopped parsley, salt and pepper, and Worcestershire sauce. Mix puree and tomato juice, chill and serve with triscuits . . . or sesame seed crackers, or any kind YOU prefer.

"What a pother have authors made with Roses! What a racket have they kept! I shall add, red Roses are under Jupiter, Damask under Venus, white under the Moon, and Provence under the King of France. The white and red Roses are cooling and drying, and yet the white is taken to exceed the red in both the properties, but is seldom used inwardly in any medicine. . . . To write at large of every one of these would make my book smell too big.

Nicholas Culpeper,The Complete Herbal, 1653

Roses

ROSE MOUSSE. Beat a half dozen egg whites until they stand in peaks and gradually add rosepetal jam. Pour into a souffle dish, add a couple of ounces of rose brandy and set in hot oven for about five minutes.

ROSE PETAL PARFAIT. Take half a cup of rose petal jam and add three ounces of rose brandy. Add to a pint of whipped cream, serve in parfait glasses with petit fours.

ANOTHER DESSERT. Take red rose petals, sprinkle with powdered sugar and pound in a mortar. Mix with softened vanilla ice cream and decorate with crystallized rose petals.

ROSE PETAL JAM. Take about twenty-five or thirty large red cabbage (if possible) roses and cut off the white ends. Make a syrup of three pounds of sugar and two pints of water. Then add the juice of half a lemon and the rose petals. Boil until the roses crystallizes, stirring frequently with a wooden spoon. Turkish cooks keep this for years.

ROSE WATER. Fill a vessel with red rose petals and cover with water. Keep water just at the boiling point, but do not boil. After an hour remove the petals and add more petals. Repeat this until it has the proper strength, then bottle.

ROSE SYRUP. Take a pint of warm rose water and dissolve two pounds of fine granulated sugar in it. A Turkish recipe recommends adding a few poppy petals and a tablespoon of lemon juice, but it is not necessary to add these ingredients. Some purists like just the roses and sugar. Bottle and keep in refrigerator.

ROSE LIQUEUR BRANDY. Take about two cups of heavily scented rose petals and add to a quart of cognac. Let stand for a month then make a syrup of two cups of sugar and three cups of water. Boil and add two cups of rose petals, and at the end of an hour strain and mix with the cognac which has also been strained, and bottle.

COUNT DE MAUDUIT'S RECIPE FOR HAPPINESS
In a large silver urn,
Pour six cups of Kindness,
Five cups of Tenderness,
Four cups of Affection,
Three cups of Understanding,
Two cups of Good Nature,
One whole cup of Truth,

Roses   *One half cup of Smiles,*
One teaspoonful of Tears.
Stir well and add:
One generous dash of Naughtiness,
Two of Sympathy,
Three of Wisdom,
And a good helping from the "Filtro d'amore".
Mix all these ingredients well together,
Then sprinkle with Spice of Life,
And finally strew with Red Roses.

FOR TO MAKE ROSEE. Tak the flowris of Rosys and wasch hem wel in water and after bray hem wel in a morter and than tak Almondys and temper hem and seth hem and after tak flesch of capons or of hennys and hac yt smale and than bray hem wel in a morter and than do yt in the Rose so that the flesch acorde wyth the mylk and so that the mete be charchaunt and after do yt to the fyre to boyle and do thereto sugur and safron that yt be wel ycolowrd and rosy of levys and of the forseyde flowrys and serve yt forth.

> The Forme of Cury, A Roll of Ancient English Cookery—Compiled about A.D. 1390 by the Master-Cooks of King Richard II

ROSES. Take thyk mylke as to fore welled. cast to fug a gode porcion pyn. Dates ymynced. canel. & powdo gyng and seep it, and alye it with flos of white Rosis, and flo of rys, cole it, salt it & messe it forth. If wilt in stede of Almande mylke, take swete crem of kyne.

> The Forme of Cury

The French call the eglantine or wild rose jam, "Confiture de Cynorrhodons."

ROSE VINEGAR. Take dried rose petals and put them in small crocks and cover with vinegar. Set in a warm place for a day or so, and as you use the vinegar replace with additional dried roses and vinegar.

Rose Shrub. Take one and a half pounds of fresh rose petals, add three cups of water and boil up. Remove from heat and when cool, strain. Then add two and half pounds of sugar, and the beaten white of an egg, boil, skim, strain and bottle.

Rose Compote. Cook as for Rose Shrub, but add a tablespoon of lemon juice and a few drops of oil of roses. Mix well and pour into jars.

Roses

Cooks in our grandmother's time, and before, placed rose petals, sometimes crystallized, in a cherry pie. They may be placed on the bottom before the cherry mixture is poured, or on top before placing the top pastry.

Rose Cake. Take a box of white cake mix and add a tablespoon of rose water and two tablespoons ground almonds. Color one half of the mixture pink if desired, and pour into muffin tins. Ice one half of cup cakes with green icing and the other with pink and decorate each cake with a crystalized rose petal.

Small Rose Candy. (Petit Candi a la Rose) Praline two handsful of rose leaves in clarified sugar, boiling them to the *souffle'*, then take them off the fire, and work them till the sugar grains; search them in an open hair search to get out the superfluous sugar; rub the flowers with the hands, and put them into the stove to dry; prepare sugar as for other candies, and put it into a mould; the sugar for the mould ought to be coloured a little with cochineal: cover as directed above with the rose leaves.

> A.B. Beauvilliers, The Art of French Cookery,
> London 1827

GO LOVELY ROSE
The rosebush sales are under way
*   And ramblers, rooted well in sod,*
Will be available till May
*   At local stores in league with God.*
> *Margaret Fishback, One to a Customer*

My love is like a red, red rose
That's newly sprung in June:
My love is like the melodie
That's sweetly play'd in tune.
> *Robert Burns*

Herself a rose, who bore the Rose,
She bore the Rose and felt its thorn.
All loveliness new-born,
Took on her bosom its repose,
And slept and woke their night and morn.
                    Christina Rossetti

Roses   *The rose was plucked on Midsummer Eve, and if it had not faded by the beginning of the next month, the maidens knew their lovers were faithful.*

POTTED ROSES. This is what I call Potted Roses, and it is thus prepared: I first pound some of the most fragrant Roses in a mortar; then I take the brains of birds and pigs well boiled, and stripped of every particle of meat. I then add the yolks of some eggs, some oil, a little cordial, some pepper and some wine: after having beaten and mixed it well together I throw it in a new pot and place it over a slow but steady fire.
                    Cook for the King of Sicily

(He also said that when the pot was uncovered the delicious fragrance overcame the guests with delight.)

Pastes ot various flowers can be made boiled down with Rose-water.

Jemelloes were made of sugar, caraway seeds, and Rose-water.

Rose plate was excellent for banqueting.

Gingerbread was flavored with Rose-water and gilded and was considered very elegant.

ROSA SOLIS. Potent drink of Elizabethan days, strong with aqua vitae and pungent with Orange flower water and cinnamon extract, it was beloved of roysterers, scourers, and Mohocks, such rakehells as Captain Ferrers, who, crazed with this liquor, leaped dare-devil from a high second-story balcony, "The desperatest frolic I did ever see," wrote Pepys.

Many Persian volumes of poems were scented with Attar of Roses, copies of the poems of Jami in the Oxford Library, even after four centuries are fragrant with the original Rose perfumes.

WINE ROSAT. A weight of 40 denirs (five ounces of Rose leaves) well stamped, put them into a linen cloth together with a little weight that they may settle downwards and not float about. Let them hang thus in 20 sextars (three gallons) and 2 Wine Quarts of Must. Keep the vessel close stopted for 3 Months, then open it and strain the said floures into the Liquor.

Pliny

Roses

LOZENGES OF RED ROSES. Boyl your Sugar to sugar again, then put in your red Roses, being finely beaten and mayd moist with the juice of a lemon. Let it not boyl after the Roses are in, but pour it upon a Pye plate and cut it into what form you please.

Cook for Queen Henrietta Maria, The Queen's Closet Opened, 1656

ROSE fossils have been discovered, millions of years old, back to the Oligocene period.

The Hanging Gardens of Babylon had more than three hundred thousand roses.

The custom of bestowing the Golden Rose once a year by the Pope began in 1049. It is a mark of great approval, but often no one is considered worthy. Pope Leo gave the Golden Rose seven times in his reign, and each time to women.

ROSE PETAL PARAFAIT. Fill each parfait glass with layers of washed red rose petals, finely chopped dates, sliced bananas, rose-petal jam (or other jam). Pour 2 tablespoons orange juice into each glass. Top with large portion of whipped cream; garnish with chopped rose petals, orange slice.

PICKLED ROSEBUDS. Pick and wash well 35 or 40 baby rosebuds. Place rosebuds in 1 quart jar. Combine ½ cup sugar and 2 cups white wine vinegar; pour over rosebuds. Seal with paraffin and store in warm, dark place for about one month. Buds may be used in salads or with sandwiches.

Freeze rose petals or rosebuds in ice cubes.

Rose petals added to pancakes, muffins, custards and puddings add intrigue.

BURNT ALMONDS FLAVOURED WITH ROSE WATER. Prepare and sugar the almonds as directed for Burnt Almonds, but flavour with Rose water, add a few drops of chochineal, a very little will be sufficient as the sugar should be of a pale rose colour only.

Jules Gouffe, Book of Preserves

Roses

ROSE DROPS. MIX some coarsely sifted sugar to a stiff paste with some Rose Water: add a few drops of prepared cochineal to give it a pink tinge. Put part of the paste in a *pastille* sugar boiler, and stir it over the fire until it boils, then hold the sugar boiler in the left hand, inclining it over a baking sheet, and, with a wire held in the right hand, cut off the drops as they fall from the spout, they will then fall in even-sized drops on to the baking sheet. Put the drops to dry in the hot-closet for twenty minutes, and put them on a sieve to cool.

Ibidem

ROSE BLOSSOM JELLY. Pick 10 oz. of cabbage rose petals, steep them in a syrup as directed above, strain the syrup through a jelly-bag, mix it with 2¼ oz. of clarified gelatine, add a tablespoonful of Maraschino and a few drops of prepared cochineal to give the jelly a pale rose tint. Finish and serve.

Observation: For this, like all coloured jellies, untinned-copper utensils and silver spoons should alone be used for the preparation of both syrup and gelatine, or the colour and limpidity of the jellies would be spoiled, and their pleasing appearance destroyed.

Jules Gouffe, Royal Book of Pastry and Confectionary

ROSE BAVAROIS CREAM. Pick some cabbage roses so as to get 3 ozs. of the petals; boil 1 quart of cream, throw the rose leaves in it, and let them remain thus for two hours. Break 8 yolks of egg in a stewpan, mix in 10 oz. of pounded sugar and the cream and rose leaves, and stir over the fire, without boiling, till the custard coats the spoon; add 2 oz. of drained gelatine, previously steeped in cold water; strain the whole through a pointed strainer into a basin, put the basin on ice, stir until the contents begin to set, then mix in lightly 1 quart of well-whipped double cream. Set in ice and after two hours, turn the cream out of mold and serve.

Gouffe, Royal Book of Pastry and Confectionary

Under the bluffs that overhung the marsh he came upon thickets of wild roses with flaming buds, just beginning to open. When they had opened their petals were stained with that burning rose-colour which is always gone by noon — a dye made of sunlight and morning and moisture, so intense that it cannot possibly last — must fade, like ecstasy.

Willa Cather

Roses

Pliny recommended the dog rose for the cure of hydrophobia, hence its name, Rosa Canina.

But the roses — they were loveliest of all . . . In the early morning, washed in the dew, they felt so soft, so pure, I could not help wondering if they did not resemble the asphodels of God's garden.

Helen Keller, *The Story of My Life*

A lecture of much moralitie might be read upon the Rose, the parts delivered by many authors both Greekes and Latines, all of which to insert in this place is not my minde, onely I will recite a few of many to give you a taste of the plenty and excellencie. . . .
The miserably infatuated Turkes will not suffer a Rose leafe to lye upon the ground, or any to tread on them in honour of their Mahomet, from whose sweat they are perswaded the Rose sprang up; somewhat like unto the old Pagans, who held the Rose which formerly was white to become red from the blood of Venus *falling thereon from her foote hurt by a thorne, as shee ran among the bushes to help her* Adonis. Philostratus *dedicateth the Rose to* Cupid *whom it doth represent in every part. It is fresh young and delicate as Cupid, it is crowned with gold yellow haires, it beareth thornes as darts and leaves as wings, the Crimson beautie of the flowers as his glory and dignitie, neither the Rose nor Cupid keepeth any time, and besides this he calleth the Rose the light of the earth, the faire bushie toppe of the spring, the fire of love, the lightning of the land.*

John Parkinson, *Theatrum Botanicum, 1640*

ROSE-WINE. To make wine of roses: take drie roses of the mountaines, anise, and honie, of euerie one alike, and a little saffron, binde them together and put them in wine. You may see a larger discourse of wines in the fifth Book of Dioscorides.

Charles Estienne, Maison Rustique or The Countery Farm,
London, 1606

ROSE BRANDY. Gather heavily-scented rose petals. Handle gently. Place in a bowl or pitcher and cover with brandy; next day take out the leaves and replace with fresh ones, continuing the process until the brandy is sufficiently flavored. Keep closely covered while in process and bottle when ready. Excellent for cakes.

Roses

ROSE HIP SOUP	½ pound dried rose hips
(HAGEBUTTEM SOUP)	3 pints water
	2 oz. potato flour
	3 to 4 tablespoons Madeira (or sherry)
	A dozen blanched almonds (shredded)
	1 teaspoon lemon juice
	1 tablespoon sugar

Wash the hips, soak them some hours in water and then let simmer till quite soft, and then force through a strainer or sieve. Boil up again and add the other ingredients and serve with little dumplings or put a spoonful of whipped cream on top of each cup.

An adaptation based on a recipe by Ella Oswald
German Cookery for the American Home, New York 1907

QUEEN HENRIETTA MARIA'S ROSE DRINK. Put a half cup of rose petals in a cup of boiling water and simmer for ten minutes. Strain and add honey to taste. The queen liked it when cool.

As a variation add one fourth cup of orange flower water to rose petal jam.

TO MAKE A CAKE WITH ROSE WATER, THE WAY OF THE ROYAL PRINCESS, THE LADY ELIZABETH, DAUGHTER TO KING CHARLES THE FIRST. Take halfe a pecke of flowre, half a pinte of rose water, a pint of ale yeast, a pint of creme. A pound and a half of butter six egges (leave out the whites) four pounds of currants, one half pound of sugar, one nutmeg and a little salt. Work it very well and let it stand half an hour by the fire and then work it again and then make it up and let it stand an hour and a halfe in the oven, let not your oven be too hot.

W. M. Cook to Queen Henrietta Maria, The Queen's
Closet Opened

CONSERVE OF ROSES, VIOLETS, COWSLIPS, OR MARIGOLDS. Take red rose-buds, clip all the white, either bruised or withered from them; then add to every pound of roses three pounds of sugar, stamp the roses very small, putting to them a little juice of lemons or rose water as they become dry; when you think your roses small enough then put your sugar to them so beat them together till they be well mingled, then put it up in gallipots or glasses.

Roses

  In this manner is made the conserve of flowers of violets, which both cool and open in a burning fever or ague, being dissolved in almond milk and so taken; and excellent good for any inflammation in children.

  Thus you may also make conserve of cowslips, which strengthens the brain and is a preservative against madness, it helps the memory, assuaget the pain of the head and helpeth most infirmities thereof.

  In like manner you may also make conserve of marigolds which taken fasting in the morning is very good against melancholy.

Mrs. Woolley, The Gentlewoman's Companion, 1673

TO MAKE ROSE-DROPS. The roses and sugar must be beat separately into a very fine powder, and both sifted; to a pound of sugar an ounce of red roses, they must be mixed together, and then wet with as much juice of Lemon as will make it into a stiff paste; set it on a slow fire in a silver porringer, and stir it well; and when it is scalding hot quite through take it off and drop in small portions on a paper; set them near the fire, the next day they will come off.

E. Smith, The Complete Housewife, 1736

SUGAR OF ROSES IN VARIOUS FIGURES. Clip off the white of rose-buds and dry them in the sun. Having finely pounded an ounce of them, take a pound of loaf sugar. Wet the sugar in rose water, and boil to a candy height. Put in your powder of roses and the juice of lemon. Mix all well together, put it on a pie plate, and put it into lozenges, or make it into any figure you fancy, such as men, women or birds. If you want ornaments for your dessert, you may gild or colour them to your liking.

John Farley, Principal Cook at the London Tavern 1804
The London Art of Cookery

CONSERVE OF ROSES. Take buds of red Roses somewhat they be ready to spread; cut the red part of the leaves from the white, and beate and grinde them in a stone mortar with a pestle of wood and to every ounce of roses, put three ounces of sugar in the grinding (after the leaves are well beaten) and grinde them together till they be perfectly incorporated, then put in a glasse made of purpose, or else into an earthen pot, stop it close and so keepe it. Thus you may make conserves of all kindes of flowers commonly used for conserves.

> John Partridge, Treasurey of Hidden Secrets and
> Commodious Conceits, 1586

Roses

SUGAR OF ROSES. Take the deepest-coloured red Roses, pick them, cut off the white buttons and dry your red leaves in an oven, till they be as dry as possible: then beat them to powder and searse them, then take halfe a pound of sugar beaten fine, put it into your pan with as much fair water as will wet it, then set it in a chafing dish of coals and let it boyle till it be sugar again; then put as much powder of the Roses as will make it look very red, stir them well together, and when it is thoroughly cold, put in boxes.

> Sir Hugh Platt, Delightes for Ladies, 1594

PICKLED ROSEBUDS. Pick rosebuds and put them in an earthern pipkin, with white wine vinegar and sugar and so you may use cowslips, violets or rosemary flowers.

> Murrell's Two Books of Cookeries & Carving, 1560

TART OF HIPS. Take hips, cut them and take out the seeds very clean, then wash them and season them with sugar, cinnamon and ginger, close the tart, bake it, scrape on sugar and serve it in.

> The Art and Mystery of Cookery Approved by the
> Fifty-five Years Experience and Industry of
> Robert May, 1671

Like the rose, Mighty like the rose, A rose is a rose is an onion.

> *Ernest Hemingway, For Whom the Bell Tolls*

✍ *Meant Sarcastic*
We know, of course, that for our sins
We buy our peaches packed in tins;
And there's another modern vice
Of eating apples off the ice;
But wouldn't it be simply grand
If all our roses could be canned?

> *Reginald Arkell, Green Fingers*

Often is the nettle nearest to the rose.
                    Ovid, Remediorum Amoris

A rose is a rose is a rose is a rose.
            Gertrude Stein, Geography and Plays (Sacred Emily, 1922)

Roses

Use Rose Vinegar in fruit salad dressings. Very epicurean.

Melon balls are improved with a garnish of rose petals.

Nero was particularly fond of rose pudding.

Add strawberry juice to your rose jelly ingredients.

Petals of red Roses are found to contain a volatile oil, colouring matter, tannin, gallic acid, fatty elements, albumen, soluble potash salts, insoluble calcareous salts, silica, and oxide of iron.
                    W. T. Fernie, Meals Medicinal

Rose-leaf jam was a favourite preserve with Queen Natalie of Servia. The French jam is made from pink roses, placed in a glass pot, which is then filled with pure sugar syrup; the petals merely curl up, but do not become crushed.

ROSE-PETAL AND CHERRY SALAD. Stone ripe, sweet, cherries, and in place of the stones put some sour milk (or cottage cheese); serve with tomatoes and lettuce and cherry vinegar; or if it is too much trouble to stuff the cherries with the cheese, make the latter into little balls and after the cherries have been tossed in cherry vinegar arrange on lettuce leaves; garnish with the cheese balls, and serve with rose-petals scattered over it. The spiced cherry vinegar is a great improvement on the maraschino flavouring, and quite distinctive.

ROSE WATER GELATIN. Heat a pint of milk and dissolve into 1 envelope of unflavored gelatin, then add half a cup of rose water and a scant half cup of sugar. To enhance the rose flavor the mold could be greased with a bit of salad oil combined with a drop or two of essence of roses.

Evliya Celebi, distinguished Turkish traveller and historian of the 17th Century says the patron saint of the cooks is Adam who served the soup known as Baba Corbasi (Daddy's Soup); the second, Abraham, and the third, the Prophet.

Rose Sandwich. Take thinly sliced pumpernickel bread with soft cream cheese, cover with red rose petals and sprinkle with cinnamon.
A variation. Use rye bread, spread with cream cheese, layer with pink rose petals.

Put three or four drops of essence of rose in the whipped cream for strawberries.

Roses

Very fashionable during the 17th Century were ices made with roses.

Athenaeus in the "Banquet of the Learned" has the scholarly host Laurentius give his recipe for what he terms the "Dish of Roses," prepared, he states, in such a way that you may not only have the ornament of a garland on your head, but also in yourself.

"'having pounded a quantity of the most fragrant roses in a mortar,' says Laurentius, 'I put in the brains of birds and pigs boiled and thoroughly cleansed of all the sinews, and also the yolks of eggs, and with them oil, and pickle-juice, and pepper and wine. And having pounded all these things carefully together, I put them into a new dish, applying a gentle and steady fire to them.' And while saying this he uncovered the dish, and diffused such a sweet perfume over the whole party that one of the guests present said with great truth:

'The winds perfumed, the balmy gale, convey
Through heav'n, through earth, and all the aerial way'—
so excessive was the fragrance which was diffused from the roses."

Truly a noble pot-pourri—meet for the gods of high Olympus. The pickle-juice, the pepper, and the wine denote the address of a master in disguising any possible taint of the pan, while the yolks of eggs and the oil would necessarily blend and assimilate with the attar of the rose-leaves. Thus does a great architect plan the construction of a cathedral, or a wizard of the brush adjust his pigments upon a canvas that is destined to become immortal.

George H. Ellwanger, Pleasures of the Table

Arabian Pan Cakes. Add a little honey to the batter, fry in almond oil and serve with syrup flavored with attar of roses.

Armitage, Fit for a King

Emperor Theodosius, who was a Spaniard by birth, had a perfume garden, all flowers were cut to distil the essences in which he lived, a scented mist. Even prisoners had first to be sprayed with rose water. On the road from Blanes toward Guadix he had milestones set, and on each plinth was carved a full blown rose.

Roses

ROSE COOKIES ENHANCED WITH CARAWAY SEEDS. Cream a half pound of butter and a half pound of sugar together and add a teaspoon of nutmeg, two tablespoons of caraway seeds and a quarter cupful of rosewater, then make a stiff dough with 4 cups of flour. Put in the refrigerator for several hours, or more, then roll out into cookies and bake on a well-buttered cookie sheet for about 10 minutes. Watch that they don't get too brown.

TO MAKE SWEET ROSE CAKES. Take a bushell of dammaske Roses dryd one day & 2 ounces of Cloves brused, 4 handfulls of Lavender tops when they first com out green.

Let them be a lettel dryd: put theas into a pott 24 hours covered Close with a quart of damask Rose. water; the next day still them in an ordinary still till they be pretty dry & in every quart hang four granes of musk.

(This one was marked by an X, which she used for recipes she considered especially good. Elizabeth Wainwright, The Receipt Book of a Lady of the Reign of Queen Anne, 1711

The Victorians were especially fond of rose petal sandwiches at tea time, dark red roses on thin slices of bread, with real country butter, or the famous English thick cream.

JAM MADE WITH THE BERRIES OF WILD DOG ROSES. Choose ripe large sound berries from a dog rose bush (Eglantine). They should be hard. Scrape each berry and cut off tip through opening, remove pulp with the aid of a bodkin or tiny spoon, being careful not to break berry. Tie a piece of linen round the bodkin or little spoon and wipe the inside to remove any pulp that may remain. There are fine hairs which must be removed. Drop berries into cold water and rinse several times shaking about to make sure that all little hairs are gone. Put into a saucepan, pour over boiling water, put on fire and as soon as the water boils again pour berries out on a sieve and pour cold water over them. Then put a clean cloth over the sieve and put each berry standing with the little hole underneath to drain well.

Prepare syrup. For every pound of berries use 3 lb. sugar and three-fourths cup water. Let it boil twice then put in berries and cook till tender. Remove scum which forms on jam. When tender pour into china bowl, tie a cloth and let stand for several days. Every now and then move the bowl about, so that the berries are well filled with the syrup. Pour into jars and close with air-tight stoppers or parchment paper. Keep in a dry place.

Princess Alexandre Gazarene, The Russian Cook Book, 1924

Rose jelly is very good with pork or game.

ROSE-WATER AND ROSE-VINEGAR OF THE COLOUR OF THE ROSE, AND OF THE COWSLIP AND VIOLET VINEGAR. If you would make your Rose-water and Rose-vinegar of a rubie colour then make choice of the crimson-velvet coloured leaves, clipping away the whites with a pair of sheares: and being thorow dryed, put a good large handfull of them into a pint of Damask or red Rose-water; stop your glasse well, and set it in the sunne, till you see that the leaves have lost their colour or for more expedition, you may performe this works *in balneo* in a few hours; and when you take out the old leaves you may put in fresh, till you find the colour to please you. Keepe this Rose-water in the glassess very well stopt; the fuller the better. What I have said of Rose-water, the same may also be intended of Rose-vinegar, violet, marigold and cowslip vinegar; but the whiter vinegar chuse for this purpose, thereof will be the brighter, and therefore distilled vinegar is best for this purpose.

Sir Hugh Platt, Delightes for Ladies, 1594

VINEGAR OF ROSES. In summer time when roses blow, gather them, ere they be full sized or blown out, and in dry weather plucke the leaves, let them lie halfe a daye upon a faire boored, then have a vessell with vinegar of one or two gallons (if you will make so much roset) put there in a great quantity of the said leaves, stop the vessel close after that ye have stirred them well together; let it stand a day and a night, then divide your vinegar and rose leaves together in two parts, put them in two great glasses, and put in rose-leaves enough; stop the glasses close, set them upon a shelfe under a wall side on the south side without your house where the sunne may come to them the most part of the day; let them stand there the whole summer long, and then straine the vinegar from the Roses, and keep the leaves and put in new leaves of halfe a daies gathering, the vinegar will have the more odour of the Rose.

✒ You may use instead of vinegar of wine, white, red, or claret, but the red rose is astringent, and the white is laxative. Also the Damask Rose is not so great a binder as the red Rose and the white looseth most of all: Hereof you may make Vinegar roset.

✒ Then also you may make vinegar of violets or of elderne flowers but you must first gather and use your flowers of elderne, as they shall be shewed hereafter, when we speake of making conserve of elderne flowers.

John Partridge, The Treasurie of Hidden Secrets
and Commodious Conceits, 1586

Roses

A White Leach. Take six table spoonfuls of Rose water, two drops of oil of Mace, two grains of Musk. Warm together sufficiently to melt four ounces of Ising-glass. When the Ising-glass is melted strain through a jelly bag. When cold cut in slices and serve with cream.

Recipe dated 1890

Roses

Rose Wafers. Put the yolks of four eggs, and three spoonfuls of Rose-water to a quart of flour, mingle them well, make them into a batter with cream and double-refined sugar, pour it on very thin, and bake it on Irons.

The Recipe Book of John Nott, Cook to the
Duke of Bolton, 1723

Rose Petal And Fruit Dessert. Mash three large ripe bananas with a cup of chopped dates and place on a bed of rose petals, which you have already previously arranged in the bottom of a glass dish. A cut-glass bowl would be suitable, if you have one. Cover the banana mixture with rose petal jam and put about two tablespoons of frozen orange juice concentrate over it. Serve with whipped cream and decorate with crystallized rose petals.

To Candy Rose Leaves As Natural As If They Grew On Trees. Take of your fairest Rose leaves, Red or Damask, and on a sunshine day sprinkle them with Rosewater, lay them on one by one on a fair paper, then take some double refined sugar beaten very fine, put it in a fine lawn searse when you have laid abroad all the rose leaves in the hottest of the sun, searse sugar thinly all over them and anon the sun will candie the sugar; then turn the leaves and searse sugar on the other side, and turn them often in the sun, sometimes sprinkling Rose-water and sometimes searsing sugar on them, until they be enough, and come to your liking and being thus done you may keep them.

William Rabisha, The Whole Body of Cookery
Dissected, 1675

MEXICO

FLOWERS ON THE MENU

Take petals of one dozen freshly cut white roses, cover with pint of water in saucepan. Add one cup sugar, one teaspoon lemon juice and boil five minutes. Boil second pint of water, add box of plain gelatine and mix with rose mixture. Cool. Pour into baked pie shell. Top with whipped cream or peach halves.

Roses

This fragrant pie filling is one of many floral concoctions served by old-fashioned Mexican housewives versed in the vanishing art of flower cookery. In some middle class provincial kitchens, flowers go into the making of soups, entrees, salads and beverages, as well as desserts. Sample floral menu, recently served at a dinner party in Morelia: a fragrant soup of yellow wild flowers called chipilins, squash flower pie, fried palm blossoms with boiled cactus buds, jelly made from a ruby-red species of hibiscus, rose-petal pie, orange blossom tea. For those who like worms with their flowers, there was an omelet* made with acacia blossoms and the tasty little white worms found only in the maguey plant.

Mexico's floral cuisine traces back to pre-Spanish days, when the Aztecs thriftily cooked and ate the flowers they had placed before the altars of the gods. Flower-eaters no longer, Mexican Indians in the backlands and city slums now live largely on corn meal, beans and chili, a low-vitamin diet that keeps many of them too sluggish in mind and body to improve their lot. The answer, according to some dead-serious Mexicans, is for government agencies to educate the Indians to eat cheap but nutritious flowers. Argued a flower gourmet last week, after reading a government bulletin deploring the Indians' dietary plight: "Like spices and herbs, flowers pep up the diet and satisfy the appetite." And the maguey worms, though they have also become popular as fried cocktail tidbits in fashionable Mexico City bars, are still cheap.

*   Take one dozen acacia flowers, sprinkle lightly with egg batter, fry in deep fat until brown. In separate pan, fry two dozen maguey worms until crisp. Beat four eggs, season with salt and pepper to taste. Melt one tablespoon lard in large frying pan, pour eggs into hot pan. As soon as omelet is firm enough, add flowers and worms. Fold over. Fry on both sides until well done. Serves six — at least.

Time Magazine, February 27, 1956

To Preserve Whole Roses, Gillyflowers, Marigolds, Etc. Tip a rose that is neither in the bud, nor overblowne in a sirup, consisting of sugar, double refined, and Rose-water boiled to his full height, then open the leaves one by one with a fine smooth bodkin either of bone or wood; and presently if it be a hot sunny day, and whilest the sunne is in some good height, lay them on papers in the sunne, or else dry them with some gentle heat in a close roome, heating the room before you set them in, or in an oven upon papers, in pewter dishes, and then put them up in glasses; and keepe them in dry cupboards neere the fire; you must take out the seeds, if you meane to eat them. You may proove this preserving with sugar-candy instead of sugar if you please.

Sir Hugh Platt, Delights for Ladies, 1594

OYLE OF ROSES. Take of oyle eighteen ounces, the buds of Roses (the white ends of them cut away) three ounces, lay the Roses abroad in the shadow four and twenty houres, then put them in a glasse to the oyle, and stop the glass close; and set it in the sunne at least forty dayes.

> John Partridge, The Treasurie of Hidden Secrets
> and Commodious Conceits, 1586

Roses

OIL COMMONLY CALLED THE SPIRIT OF ROSES. Take of Damask, or Red Roses, being fresh, as many as you please, infuse them in as much warm water as is sufficient for the space of twenty-four houres; then strain, and press them, and repeat the infusion severall times with pressing, until the liquor become fully impregnated, which then must be distilled in an Alembick with a refrigerator, let the Spirit which swims on the Water be separated and the water kept for a new infusion.

This kind of Spirit may be made by bruising the Roses with Salt, or laying a laye of Roses, and another of Salt, and so keeping them half a year or more, which then must be distilled in as much common water or Rose water as is sufficient.

> John French, the Art of Distillation, 1652

OYLE OF ROSES THREE WAYES. The first way is, take a pound of red Rose buds, beat them in a marble morter with a woodden pestle, then put them into an earthen pot, and poure upon them foure pound of oyle of olives, letting them infuse the space of a moneth in the Sunne, or in the chimney corner stirring of them sometimes, then heate it, and presse it and straine it, and put it into the same pot or other vessell to keepe.

The second is, take halfe a pound of red Roses, and half a pound of Damaske roses, beate them together in a marble morter, and put them into a pot, and poure upon them foure pound of oyle, and let them infuse the space of twelve houres, then pour them all into a pan and boyle them two or three boylings, and straine them and presse them in a strong towell in the presse and in the meane time put in the pot as many more Roses and poure the oyle upon them and so beate them and presse them and put Roses to the oyle three times and then boyle it until all the humidity bee consumed. The third is to take all Damask roses and no red and make three infusions as before.

> Philbert Guibert, Esquire, The Charitable Physitian
> and Physitian Regent in Paris, 1639

TO PERFUME ANY SORT OF CONFECTIONS. Take musk, the like quantity of Oil of Nutmeg, infuse them in Rose-water, and with it sprinkle your Banqueting preparations and the scent will be as pleasing as the taste.

> Henry Howard, Free Cook of London, England's newest way in all sorts of Cookery, 1710

Roses

TO MAKE ROSSOLY THE ITALIAN WAY. Gather fresh Damask Roses, Orange Flowers, Jessamy Flowers, Cloves and Gillyflowers; pick them clean, set on some water to boil, when it has boiled well let it stand to cool a little; put these clean Flowers into a China Bason, pour the water upon them when it is not hotter than to bear the finger in it; then cover it up, and let it stand Three Hours, gently pour all into a fine Linen Bag, and let the Water run off without squeezing the Flowers to a pint of this Water, add a quart of fine Melasses Spirit, and halfe a Pint of strong cinnamon water: add three teaspoons of Essence of Ambergrease, and stir all well together. This is the true Rossoly.

> Elizabeth Cleland, The Receipt Book, 1759

HONEY OF ROSES. Cut the white heels from Red Roses, take halfe a pound of them and put them into a stone jar, and pour on them three pints of boiling water. Stir well and let them stand twelve hours. Then press of the liquor and when it has settled add to it five pounds of honey. Boil it well, and when it is of the consistence of a thick syrup it is ready to put away.

> Thomas Tryon, A Treatise of Cleanness in Meates, 1692

ROSE WINE. Take a well glazed earthen vessel and put into it three gallons of rose-water drawn with a cold still. Put into that a sufficient quantity of rose leaves cover it close, and set it for an hour in a kettle or copper of hot water, to take out the whole strength and tincture of the roses; and when it be cold press the rose leaves hard into the liquor, and steep fresh ones in it, repeating it till the liquor has got the full strength of the roses. To every gallon of liquor put three pounds of loaf sugar, and stir it well, that it may melt and disperse in every part. Then put it into a cask, or other convenient vessel, to ferment, and put into it a piece of bread toasted hard and covered with yeast. Let it stand about thirty days, when it will be ripe and have a fine flavour, having the whole strength and scent of the roses in it; and you may greatly improve it by adding to it wine and spices. By this method of infusion, wine of carnations, clove gilliflowers, violets, primroses, or any other flower, having a curious scent, may be made. John Farley, Principal Cook at the London Tavern, The London Art of Cookery, 1804

CONSERVE OF ROSES BOILED. Take a quart of red Rose water, a quart of fair water, boil in the water a pound of red rose leaves, the whites cut off, the leaves must be boiled very tender; then take three pounds of sugar, put to it a pound at a time, and let it boil a little between every pound, so put it up in your pots.

Roses

CONSERVE OF ROSES UNBOILED. Take a pound of red rose leaves, the whites cut off, stamp them very fine, take a pound of sugar and beat it with the roses and put it in a pot and cover it with leather and set it in a cool place.

A Queen's Delight, 1695

In the same manner are prepared the conserves of orange peel, rosemary flowers, seawormwood, leaves of wood sorrel, etc.

CONSERVE OF RED ROSES. Doctor Glisson makes his conserve of red roses thus: Boil gently a pound of red Rose-leaves in about a pint and a halfe (or a little more as by discretion you shall find fit, after having done it once, the Doctor's apothcary takes two pints) of Spring water: till the water have drawn out all the Tincture of the Roses in to it self and that the leaves be very tender and looke pale like Linnen; which may be in good halfe hour, or an hour keeping the pot covered while it boileth. Then pour the tincted Liquor from the pale leaves, strain it out, pressing it gently, so that you may have liquor enough to dissolve our sugar, and set it upon the fire by it self to boil, putting into it a pound of pure double-refined sugar in small powder; which as soon as it is dissolved put in a second pound; then a third, lastly a fourth, so that you have four pounds of sugar to every pound of Rose leaves, (the Apothecary useth to put all the four pounds into the Liquor together at once.) Boil these four pounds of sugar with the tincted Liquor till it be a high syrup, very near a candy height (as high as it can be not to flake or candy). Then put the pale rose-leaves into this high syrup as it yet standeth upon the fire, or immediately upon the taking it off the fire. But presently take it off from the fire, and stir them exceeding well together to mix them uniformly; then let them uncovered some days, putting them in the hot sun or stove, there will grow a fine candy upon the top which will preserve the conserve with paper upon it from moulding till you break the candied crust, to take out some of the conserve.

The colour both of the Rose leaves and the syrup about them will be exceeding beautiful and red, and the taste excellent, and the whole very tender and smoothing and easie to digest in the stomack without clogging it as doth the ordinary rough conserve made of raw Roses beaten with sugar, which is very rough in the throat.

Sir Kenelm Digby, The Closet of Sir Kenelm Digby Opened, 1669

Book IV Number 136. Rose Pie, Rose Custard Or Pudding. Patina de Rosis. Take roses fresh from the flower bed, strip off the leaves, remove the white (from the petals and) put them in the mortar; pour over some broth (and) rub fine. Add a glass of broth and strain the juice through the collander. (This done) Take 4 (cooked calf's) brains, skin them and remove the nerves; crush 8 scruples of pepper moistened with the juice and rub (with the brains); thereupon break 8 eggs, add 1 glass of wine, 1 glass of raisin wine and a little oil. Meanwhile grease a pan, place it on the hot ashes (or in the hot bath) in which pour the above mentioned material; when the mixture is cooked in the bain maris sprinkle it with pulverized pepper and serve.

Roses

> Apicius-Cookery and Dining in Imperial Rome—Translation of this ancient book into English by Joseph Dommers Vehling Chicago, 1936

A Prescription For Melancholy. (Infusion of Flowers) Pluck the petals of fresh red roses and dry them in the sun together with fresh violets, borage flowers, and anchusa flowers in equal quantities. When thoroughly dry — which may take several days, bringing the flowers indoors overnight — mix them thoroughly and preserve them in a sealed glass jar. When feeling depressed, put 3 table-spoonsfuls of the dried flowers into a teapot, pour over them 1 cup of boiling water, infuse for 5 minutes in a warm place, then strain, and, sweetened to taste, drink to your heart's content.

Sherbert Of Roses. Boil two pounds of rose petals until the liquid is reduced to one and one-eighth cups. Filter, add two pounds of sugar and thicken the syrup, as for sherbert. Let cool to lukewarm, then add a little citric acid and the juice of one lemon boiled down. Continue as for other sherbets.

Khir Binola. Ingredients: 1 lb of pilau rice, 4 lbs of binola (cotton seeds), 1 lb of sugar, 1 oz each of almonds, pistachio and chirongee nuts, a handful of raisins and sultanas mixed, rose water. *Method*: Soak the rice for 30 minutes before washing. Boil the binola (cotton) seeds for 1 hour and grind to powder, then make a milk of it with four pints of water, place through the strainer, place in a saucepan and add the rice, stirring gently to prevent burning, when it thickens a little remove from the fire and throw in the 1 lb of dry sugar, cook about 10 minutes. Finely cut the almonds and pistachio kernels, in adding chirongee nuts, sultanas after cleaning and raisins after stoning, mix together and leave on a small fire for a little while. Flavour with the rose water before ready to serve.

> S. N. M. Khan, The Finest Indian Muslim Cooking London 1934

In many of the Muslim sweet rice dishes rose water is used.

Rab-Ri. Ingredients: 1 gallon of milk, 1 lb of sugar, essence of rose water. Method: Take a very wide and shallow frying pan, add the milk and let it boil on a good fire, lower the fire but keep it boiling all the time and when a skin forms roll to one side of pan, repeat this until there is only a little milk left and all is a thick mass of skin, now mix both together, adding the dry sugar and keep on a strong fire until the sugar is fully dissolved. Remove to a dish and allow to cool. A very nourishing sweet.

Roses

> S. N. M. Khan, The Finest Indian Muslim Cooking

Crystallized Whole Rose buds. Take 4 cups of whole rose-buds, stemmed, and place in a pan containing 1 cup of hot water and 2 cups of granulated sugar. Simmer and stir with a wooden spoon, being careful not to damage the petals. Cook until the sugar begins to granulate and empty into a colander or paper towels. Cool and pack in attractive little glasses.

The Emperor Aelius Verus would sleep only on a bed of rose-petals, from which every white tip had been removed.

Oil of roses was first mentioned by Homer.

Rose Butter. Put into a ceramic jar $\frac{1}{4}$ pound of butter, cover entirely with rose petals above and below, and leave overnight in a cool place with the lid on. This butter can be used for spreading on very thin bread.

Arnaud de Villeneuve, a French alchemist and doctor liked his fowl and birds flavored with rose water and wine.

Dr. Arberry translates a manuscript found in the Aya Sofya mosque at Istanbul, written in 623/1226, thirty-three years before the sack of Baghdad by the Mongols. Baghdad was burned February 28, 1258. The manuscript contains every variety of dish used in the times of the Abbasids.

Weights and Measures
  1 ratl equals 12 uqiya equals 16 ounces equals 1 pint
  1 uqiya equals 10 dirham
  1 dirham equals 6 danaq

The author of this 13th century cookbook is one "Muhammad ibn al-Hasan ibn Muhammad ibn al-Karim al Katib al Baghdadi". He writes, "For my own part, I subscribe to the doctrine of the pre-excellence of the pleasure of eating above all other pleasures."

The Baghdad cook liked colored salt, very partial to it. After milling the salt, colour it by placing it for a day and a night in water in which saffron has been dissolved: then dry and mill again. It may also be coloured with sumach-juice or vermilion. If desired, it may be dyed green with beet-juice.

Roses

Saffron mixed with rose-water was a favorite with Baghdad cooks.

Use crystallized roses with chicken curry.

JUDHAB AL-RUTAB. Take a tinned copper dish, and spray with a little rose-water. Spread a thin cake therein, and cover with newly-gathered Khastaui dates. Sprinkle with fine-ground pistachios and almonds, and toasted poppies, to form a layer. Add another layers of dates, and so continue until the dish is half-filled, making the top layer of almonds and pistachios. Pour on half a ratl of syrup, and an uqiya of rose-water which has been coloured with half a dirham of saffron: cover with a thin cake. Hang over it a fat chicken stuffed with sugar, almonds, and pistachios kneaded with scented rose-water, and smeared with saffron inside and out. When thoroughly cooked, remove.

The method of suspending the chicken over judhab is as follows. Hang it up in the oven, and watch: then, when the fat is about to run, place the judhab under it.

Dr. Arberry, A Baghdad Cookery Book

NARSIRK. (This is a Persian word meaning "pomegranate and vinegar". "Nar" means pomegranate and "sirka" means vinegar.) Cut fat meat into middling pieces, then put into the saucepan and cover with water, adding a little salt. Boil, and remove the scum. When almost cooked, throw in coriander, cummin, pepper, cinnamon and mastic: bray all separately from the cinnamon, leaving this last in its bark. Cut up onions, wash, and put into the pot, with a few sprigs of mint. Add cabobs of red meat minced with seasonings. Take pomegranate seeds, grind up fine, mix with wine-vinegar, strain, and pour into the sauce pan. Peel walnuts, grind them fine, soak in hot water, and add, flavouring the mixture to taste, and putting in sufficient walnuts to give it a consistency. Then throw on top a few pieces of whole walnut, and rub in sprigs of dry mint. Spray with rose-water: wipe the sides with a clean rag, and leave over the fire to settle. Then remove.

Ibidem

Roses

KAMAKH RIJAL. First take a large, dry pumpkin-shell from which all the pith and seeds have been removed: soak in water for two hours, then dry thoroughly. Put in 5 ratls of sour milk, 10 ratls of fresh milk, and 1½ ratls of fine-brayed salt, and stir. Cover and leave for some days in the hot sun. This is first made in June at the beginning of mid-summer. Each morning add 3 ratls of fresh milk, and stir morning and evening. Add milk as the liquid lessens, until the beginning of August. Now take mint leaves, shuniz — which is an aromatic herb called nigelle in Greek or fennel-flower — and quarters of peeled garlic, throw in, and stir, adding fresh milk to make up as usual, until the middle of September. Cover until the beginning of October: then remove from the sun until set, and serve. The dried petals of red roses are very often also used.

Ibidem

There are three original species of roses, the China Rose or Rosa Chinensis, the Rose de Provins or Rosa Gallica, and the Damask Rose or Rosa Damascena.

Puddings, fruit drinks, custards, flan, fruit salads, flavored with rose syrup offer new delights to the epicure.

ROSE CUSTARD. Take six ounces of dressed beetroot; pound it in a mortar until perfectly smooth; add enough rose-water to make it pass through a sieve; strain into it the whites of three eggs, beaten, and a pint of thick cream; stir it over the fire until sufficiently thick; then serve in custard-cups or in a glass dish.

Everybody's Pudding Book, London 1866

SABAGLION SAUCE "a la ROSE". (Cataldi.) Have the yolks of 2 eggs and a spoonful of white sugar, well mixed with a wooden spoon, over a gentle fire. In another stewpan have, in a gentle heat, 4 whites of egg, thoroughly well whipped up.

Mix both the yolks and the whites together and colour a delicate rose with cochineal, and flavour with rose water or orange flower water. Beat all well up till quite firm and light, over a gentle fire or in a bain-marie. Whip on till you put the sauce into the sauce boat; or you can smother the pudding in it.

The Cookery Book of Lady Clark of Tillypronie, Edited by Catherine Frances Frere, London 1909

In Paris, during the last century, it was the vogue to give dinners in color. Among the choicest were the rose dinners. Everything was rose colored — including food, centerpiece, candles, menus written in rose ink, wines, and linen. And of course the dining-room was profusely decorated with roses.

Roses

Try iced rose tea.

ROSE PETAL JELLY. Use an apple jelly base. In the bottom of each glass place a rose petal or two, pour in the hot juice, then place a petal on top before sealing with parafin. Mint Jelly mixed with rose petals is very good too.

ROSE
Take flour of ryse, as whyte as sylke,
And hit welle, with almond mylke;
Boyl hit tyl hit be chargyd, penne
Take braune of capone or elle of henne;
Loke pon grynd hit wondur smalle
And sithen pou charge hit withalle;
Coloure with alkenet, sawnder, or ellys with blode,
Fors hit with clowes or macys gode;
Pis is a rose, as kokes telle me.

> *Liber Cure Cocorum—a curious poem on Cookery, written in a Northern dialect of the XVth Century. The author was probably a native of North-West Lancashire. Philological Society of* VRFB— *Richard Morris, Editor. The poem has archaeological as well as philological value.*

A ROSE COCKTAIL. Make as a martini, using gin, dry vermouth and rose brandy. If you like a bit of sweet serve with a candied rose petal floating on top.

FROZEN FLOWER PETALS. Use candied or fresh petals. First freeze tray half filled with water, then center up the flowers, fill tray and freeze. Colored water enhances the petals.

ROSE COLLINS. Make as a gin collins, using gin, grenadine, Creme de Rose and club soda. Serve with ice cubes in a tall glass.

ANOTHER ROSE COCKTAIL. Brandy, Creme de Rose, lemon juice, grenadine, and heavy cream. (A sort of Rose Alexander). Shake with ice and serve in cocktail glasses.

Roses

MEI KWEI TAO. (Pickled Peaches in Red Rose Petals).
50 peaches
 2 lbs sugar
 1 cup water
 1 pint vinegar
 1 tablespoon salt
red roses
cloves

Boil sugar, vinegar, water and salt for 20 minutes. Dip peaches in hot water for three minutes, then rub off fur with a towel. Place on the stem part of each peach a red rose. Stick four cloves through rose on to the peach. Cook rosed peaches in syrup until soft.

> Nellie C. Wong, Chinese Dishes for Foreign Homes
> Shanghai, 1932

Cloves, as you probably know, are flower buds too.

CXXVJ. REDE ROSE — Take ye same, saue a-lye it with ye yolkys of eyroun, & for her — more as vyolet.

> Two 15th Century Cookery Books (about 1430)
> Edited by Thomas Austin for The Early English
> Text Society, 1888

A SALLET OF ROSEBUDS AND CLOVE GILLYFLOWERS. Pickle Rose-buds, and put them into an earthen pipkin, with white wine vinegar and Sugar: so may you use Cowslips, Violets, or Rose-mary flowers.

> John Murrell, Two Bookes of Cookerie and Carving
> London, 1631

ROJAPOOVU MITTAYEE (Rose Tablet). Boil two pounds of sugar and three ounces of ghee in a pound of water to crackling height.

Have ready two pounds of milk reduced to a fourth of its bulk by boiling. Remove the sugar from the fire, and stir in the milk along with some essence of roses or attar of roses and a little carmine colour. Stir till all is thick and creamy, pour into oiled shapes or into a dish an inch deep, and when nearly cold cut into lengths about an inch broad.

> Robert H. Christie, Banquets of the Nations
> Edinburgh, 1911

When making cake or puddings use rose butter.

ROSE ICE-CREAM (For a wedding party).

4 cups light cream	1 to 2 teaspoons rose extract
3 cups heavy cream	¼ teaspoon salt
1 cup milk	Pink vegetable coloring
1 cup sugar	

Mix all the ingredients together thoroughly and freeze without cooking.

Flora Rose, The New Butterick Cookbook, 1924

Roses

The Turk has a bottle of rose water on his dining room table to season his rich dishes.

HOLY WATER. This was a favorite with mediaeval cooks, which they served with fowl. It was made with rose water, honey, marjoram and ginger. .

Cure d'Ars, among other inhibitions, refused to allow himself to smell a rose.

*—In your world, said the little prince, men cultivate five
thousand roses in one garden . . . and still they do not find
what they seek. . . .
—That is true, I said.
—And yet what they are seeking may be found in a single rose
or drop of water.
—So it can, I answered.
And the little prince went on:
—But the eyes are blind: one must seek with the heart.*

Antoine de Saint-Exupery, Le Petit Prince

ROSA MYSTICA

*'The Rose is a mystery' — where is it found?
Is it anything true? Does it grow upon ground?
It was made of earth's mould, but it went from men's eyes,
And its place is a secret, and shut in the skies,
    In the Gardens of God, in the daylight divine
Find me a place by thee, Mother of mine.*

Gerard Manley Hopkins

HE WOULD KISS THE ROSE—

Roses

> *"Fair sir," quoth I, "one great desire*
> *Consumes my soul, like ardent fire;*
> *'Tis this, that of the Rose, whose scent*
> *With all the air like balm is blent,*
> *You would permit me one soft kiss,*
> *Bathing my heart in perfect bliss."*

> *Romance of the Rose—13th Century, Englished*
> *by F. S. Ellis*

Rose conserve is good with popovers.

Try rose petals on junket.

King Minos of Knossos in Crete had roses in his palace frescoes.

Charlemagne put roses at the head of his list in the capitulary of 812 when he was building his palaces at Aix-la-Chapelle and Ingelheim.

The walls of the room had once been painted crimson, but with time the color had faded into a richness of hues, like a glassful of dying red roses.

Some potpourri was being burned on the tall stove, on the sides of which Neptune, with a trident, steered his team of horses through high waves. But the dried rose-petals dated from summers of long ago. Only a very faint fragrance now spread from their funeral pile, a little rank, like the bouquet of fine claret kept too long. . . . They say, thought Miss Fanny, sniffing, that your body is changed completely within the course of seven years. How I have changed, and how I have forgotten! But my nose must be the same. My nose I have still kept and it remembers all.

> *Baronesse Karen Blixen Finecke, (Isak Dinesen),*
> *"The Supper at Elsinore", Seven Gothic Tales*

The Rhodians, the word Rhodes, is derived from the Greek word for rose-Rhodon, used the rose as an emblem on their coins for many centuries.

The Rose Garden of Wurms was encircled by a silken thread instead of a wall, a party of giants who tried to enter were defeated by the Knights, who were rewarded by Princess Chrymhilde with a chaplet of roses and a kiss. Ilsan, a monk and one of the warriors demanded a chaplet and a kiss for each of the fifty-two monks in his convent. Chrymhilde acquiesced after Ilsan fought and conquered fifty-two of the giants.

> *Henry von Ofterdingen, German Heldenbuch*
> *(Book of Heroes)*

Like the vase in which roses have once been distilled,
You may break, you may ruin the vase, if you will,
But the scent of the roses will hang round it still.
Moore

Roses

ROSE FONDANT. Tint a pale rose pink, add a bit of attar of roses or some strong rose water.

ROSE MARZIPAN. Flavor with kirsch and rose geranium, blend into it crystallized rose petals and decorate with same.

FLOWER JELLY. In the same way as the Fruit, only use instead violets, rose petals, primroses or any kind of flower that is not poisonous. Flowers may be used singly or in bunches. There is great scope for taste and ingenuity in this jelly; it can be made to look really lovely, and is not generally known.
(This is made by building up in a mold, pouring in some jelly, then placing the flowers, letting it jell, then more flowers, different colors of jelly, until it suits your fancy.)
Mrs. Grace Johnson, Anglo-Indian and Oriental Cookery
1891

"Doctor Bacon useth to make a pleasant Julip of this Conserve of Roses, by putting a good spoonful of it into a large drinking glass or cup; upon which squeeze the juyce made of a lemon, and slip in unto it a little of the yellow rinde of the lemon; work these well together with the back of a spoon, putting water to it by little and little, till you have filled up the glass with Spring water: so drink it. He sometimes passeth it through an Hypocras bag and then it is a beautiful and pleasant Liquor."
Sir Kenelm Digby

ROSE ICECREAM (Hand freezer).

4 cups light cream or evaporated milk
3 cups heavy cream, unwhipped
1 cup fresh milk
1 cup granulated sugar
1¾ teaspoons rose extract
¼ generous teaspoon salt
1 or two drops red vegetable coloring

Mix all the ingredients thoroughly and freeze in hand freezer, using 3 parts ice and 1 part rock salt. Pack or mold in 4 parts ice and 1 part rock salt for 2 hours to ripen and mellow.

COUPE DE ROSE. Use well-chilled champagne glasses and in each glass put 3 tablespoons fresh or frozen raspberries and 1 tablespoon crushed macaroons. Top with a generous scoop of rose ice-cream and cover with two tablespoons crushed pineapple. Garnish with whipped cream.

Roses

ROSE BEADS. 1 pound rose petals
                      Cloves, allspice, 1 oz. each

Pound in a mortar and work in ½ pound dried salt. Make into pellets. For beads string on straws or otherwise make holes through center for string. They harden with age. It is said rose beads perfume the surrounding air, this perfume being enhanced by the warmth of the body.

Godey's Lady's Book

To MAKE ROSE BEADS. Take about a quart of red rose petals and grind in meat-grinder. One old recipe advises using a rusty, iron pot as it will help to make the beads black. But I don't believe many of us have such an object around so we will have to compromise and use a modern metal saucepan. Cover the ground petals with water and simmer for several hours, until it becomes pulpy. It can be sampled by taking a bit in a spoon and rolling it around to see if it adheres together. Let cool until you can comfortably handle it and then press into desired size and shape. (For the uninitiated something like a baroque pearl would do.) Then it is advised to stick a hatpin through the center and dry. Since we don't have many hatpins around these days, I suppose a thin toothpick would do. In order to save time you could thread them on a coarse thread, though this is for leisure time and cannot be a hurry-up job. Drying time takes about a week, after which time a soft cloth with a little vaseline on it will give them a nice luster. When forming beads remember that they shrink to half the original size when dried. Indentations can be made if desired.

ROSE SUGAR BISCUITS. Mix two whites of eggs with fine sifted sugar and a teaspoonful of essence of roses, in a stiff paste; make it in round balls about the size of a marble; put them on paper, and bake in a cool oven; wet the paper at the back to get them off.

John Conrade Cooke, Cookery and Confectionary, London, 1824

❧ Mr. Cooke's table of cooking sugar:
Small blow—making a bubble in the skimmer when blowing it through
Strong blow—when it has boiled five more minutes
Feather—four more minutes—blows out long from the skimmer
Crack—five more minutes. Ascertained by dipping a small piece of round wood
    in water, then in the sugar, then in water again, sugar which adhers
    will slip off and crack between the fingers

Roses

Caromel—one more minute
    If it is boiled enough, the sugar will not stick to the teeth when put
    between them

DOGROSE. "The fruit when it is ripe maketh the most pleasante meats and banketting dishes as tartes and such-like," the making whereof he commends "to the cunning cooke and teethe to eate them in the riche man's mouth."
    Gerard

LONDON ROSES
"Rowses, rowses! Penny a bunch!" they tell you,
Ruddy blooms of corruption, see you and smell you,
Born of stale earth, fallowed with squalor and tears—
North shire, south shire, none are like these, I tell you,
Roses of London perfumed with a thousand years.

IN ROSE TIME
Oh, this is the joy of the rose:
    That it blows,
    And goes.
    Willa Cather, April Twilights and Other Poems, 1923

KUA LO OP—PEKIN DUCK. Duck is rubbed with honey mixed with hot water, then allowed to dry. About ten hours. Then one teaspoon of fried salt is mixed with two teaspoons of rose wine and put inside of duck. Roast for one hour, slice and serve.
    Armitage, Fit for a King

ROSE FRITTERS. Dip candied rose petals in rather thick batter, fry in hot fat until delicate brown, sprinkle with confectioner's sugar if desired.

Rose Fritters. Make a rich pancake batter and sweeten with a tablespoon of rose sugar. Boil this batter until it sets, pour into a shallow pan and allow to cool, then cut into strips and fry in deep fat until brown. If desired can be rolled in corn meal before serving with rose petal syrup.

Roses

To your hedge-row rose (dog-rose) hip jam cover the pulp with red wine and let it set for six weeks, as the wine is absorbed keep adding more and see that the fruit is completely covered.

"PASSIONATE SHEPHERD TO HIS LOVE"
And I will make thee beds of roses,
And then a thousand fragrant posies,
A cap of flowers, and a kirtle,
Embroidered all with leaves of myrtle.

Christopher Marlowe

Claret Of Roses. Boil a handful of Red Rose petals in a pint of claret for an hour.

Syllabub Of Roses. Beat white of an egg until it stands in peaks, fold into it rose-petal jam, them stir in thoroughly desired amount of rose wine.

Rose petals are a very good heart tonic.

The Red Rose became red because the tears of Venus, when she lost Adonis, fell on the White Rose and turned it red.

"Conserve of Roses comforteth the stomach, the heart and the bowels, it mollifieth and softeneth, and it is good against black cholera and melancholy."
Treasurie of Hidden Secrets, London, 1637

Vijayanagar, India, was begun in 1336. One of its first European visitors was the Italian, Nicolo Conti. The Sultan at Delhi was curious too, and he sent an ambassador, who reported, "The city of Vijayanagar is such that the pupil of the eye has never seen a place like it, and the ear of intelligence has never been informed that there existed anything equal to it in the world. Roses are sold everywhere. These people could not live without roses, and they look upon them as quite as necessary as food."

History of India as Told by Its Own Historians,
London, 1867

The ancient Greeks dedicated the rose to the goddess of dawn as an emblem of beauty, to the goddess of the dawn an an emblem of youth and to Harpocrates the god of Silence.

Some historians regard the White Rose as the emblem of silence, it was either painted or carved on the ceilings of banqueting halls and dining-rooms as a reminder to guests that conversations held under the host's roof were private and not to be repeated. The custom lingered on through the Middle Ages and even today we speak of secrets as "sub rosa", under the rose.

Roses

I will heere adde a common Countrey Custome that is used to be done with the Rose. When the pleasaunt and merry companions doe friendly meete together to make good cheere, as soon as their Feast or Banket is ended, they give faithful promise mutually one to another, that whatsoever hath been merrily spoken by any in that assembly, should be wrapped up in silence, and not to be carried out of the Doores. For the Assurance and Performance whereof, the tearme which they use is that all things there said must be taken as spoken under the Rose. Whereupon they use in their Parlours and Dining-Roomes to hang Roses over their Tables, to put the company in memory of Secrecie, and not rashly or indiscreetly to clatter or blab out what they heare. Likewise, if they chance to shew any Tricks of Wanton, unshamefast, immodest or irreverent behavior either by word or deed, they protesting that all was spoken under the Rose, do give a straight charge and pass a Covenant of Silence and Secrecie with the hearers, that the same shall not be blowne abroad, nor tattled in the Streetes among any others.

Newton's Herball to the Bible, 1587

Most famous of all monastic gardens is the rose garden of St. Francis at Assisi.

Spartan soldiers after the battle of Cirrha refused the wine offered them because it was not perfumed with roses.

The ancient Romans surrounded their bowls of wine with roses and put roses in their wine to add to the fragrance.

The Provence Rose is the hundred leaved rose described by Theophrastus and Pliny and the "provincial" rose of Shakespeare.

When Milton became blind he counted the loss of the sight of summer roses as one of his greatest losses.

> *"With the year*
> *Seasons return, but not to me returns*
> *Day, or the sweet approach of ev'n or morn,*
> *Or sight of vernal bloom, or summer's rose."*

Roses

The rose, it should be crowned with pearls of Arabia and Lydian gold. Better and sweeter are these flowers than all other plants, and rightly called the flower of flowers. Yes, roses and lilies, the one for virginity with no sordid toil, no warmth of love, but the glow of their own sweet scent. Therefore roses and lilies for our church, one for the martyr's blood, the other for the symbol in his hand. Pluck them O maiden, roses for war and lilies for peace, and think of that Flower of the stem of Jesse. Lilies His words were, and the hallowed acts of His pleasant life, but his death re-dyed the roses.
  Walafred Strabo, The Little Garden, 9th Century

For Dante the rose was purity which had blossomed into a flame of heavenly love. The vast army of saints in Heaven, he compares to a white rose,
  "In a circle spread so far
  That the circumference were too loose a zone
  To girdle in the sun."
He symbolized the Blessed Virgin as "the rose wherein the Word divine was made incarnate."

There was the pouting rose both red and white.
  Leigh Hunt

Rose water was known and written about as early as 140 B. C., first mentioned by Nicander.

Some historians say that attar of roses was discovered by the Mogul Emperor, Jehangir, as he and Nur Mahal were walking in the royal gardens. The canals had been filled with roses to celebrate their wedding, they noticed an oily film, ordered that it be bottled, and after that it was known in India as the scent of Emperors.

Theophrastus' herbal is the first to mention Roses.

The rare oil of Dioscorides was olive oil mixed with ground rose petals.

The liqueur Parfait d'Amour, has roses for its main ingredient.

The Moss Rose shielded the angel of the flowers from the sun and was given a cloak of moss as a reward.

Old garden rose trees hedged it in,
Bedroft with roses waxen white,
Well satisfied with dew and light,
And careless to be seen.
  Elizabeth Barrett Browning

Roses

To Make A Sirop Of Roses Or Violets. Take of violets or roses a pounde, steepe them in three pints of warme water, put it in an earthen pot with a narrow mouth the space of seven hours or more. AFTER straine it and warme the water againe and put in again so many Ross or Violets, and likewise let them lye in steepe eight houres, and thus do at the least five times, the oftener the better, in especiall the roses, and after take to every pint a pounde of sugar and steep them together, till the sugar be molten, then seethe them together with a soft sweet fire to the height of a Sirrup; if you have more Roses or Violets, or fewer and let so much be the proportion of the water, according to the proportion before.

The Good Housewife's Handmaid, 1585

A Singular Manner Of Making The Sirup Of Roses. Fill a silver bason three quarters full of rain water or Rose water, put therein a convenient proportion of Rose leaves; cover the Bason and set it upon a pot of hot water in three quarters of an houre, or one whole hours at the most, you shall purchase the whole strength and tincture of the Roses; then take out those leaves wringing out all their liquor gently, and steepe more fresh leaves in the same water: continue this iteration seven times, and then make it up in a sirup; and this sirup worketh more kindely than that which is made meerly of the juyce of the Rose. You may make sundry other sirups in this manner.

Sir Hugh Platt, Delights for Ladies, 1594

A BOUQUET FROM A FELLOW ROSEMAN
Oh, what does the roseman answer
  On receiving a gift bouquet
Of raddled and blowsy roses
  From the garden across the way,
    From a fellow roseman?

If the roseman is a roseman is a roseman,
  And nothing other at all,
He flings that bouquet of roses
  Clear over his garden wall,

    Like a proper roseman.
  But, if only a week-end roseman,
  He does what he has to do:
'What beautiful blooms,' he answers,
  'How exceedingly kind of you!'
    To the flattered roseman.
      Robert Graves, 5 Pens in Hand

To Make Conserve Of Red Roses. Let your Roses be gathered before they are quite blown, pound them in a stone mortar, and add to them twice their weight in double-refined sugar and put them into a glass stopt close up but do not fill it full. Let them stand three months before you use them, remembering to stir them once a day.

Roses

John Nott, Cook to the Duke of Bolton, Receipt Book, 1723

Our mothers used rose water in their pound cakes.

Better than the distilled for culinary purposes. Attar of rose, twelve drops; rub into a half ounce of white sugar and two drachms carbonate magnesia; then add gradually one quart of water and two ounces of pure alcohol, then filter through paper.

The Whitehouse Cookbook

Rose Almond Jumbles. Three cupfuls of sugar, two of flour, half a cupful of butter, one teacupful of loppered milk, five eggs well beaten, two tablespoonfuls of rose water, three quarters of a pound of almonds, blanched and chopped very fine, one teaspoonful of soda dissolved in boiling water.

Cream butter and sugar; stir in the beaten yolks the milk, flour, rose-water, almonds, and lastly the beaten whites very lightly and quickly; drop in rings on buttered paper and bake at once.

The Whitehouse Cookbook

Flower Cheeses. The English particularly, are very fond of flower-scented cheeses. Many different flowers are used. Marigold cheese, of course, is famous, but there are others: cowslip, rose, violet, etc.

FLORENTINUS MAKES MELLONS OF THE FRAGRANT SMELL OF ROSES after this manner: by taking Mellon-seeds, and laying up amongst dry Roses, and so planting them one amongst another. I have procured Mellons to smell like Musk, by opening that part whereby the seed sprouts and steeping them in Rose-water, wherein the same Musk was distilled also, and so planting them after two dayes steeping.

John Baptist Porta, Naturall Magick in XX Bookes, 1658

Sugar Of Roses. Suger Roset is made thus. Take newe gadered roses and stampe them right small with sugar, than put it in a glasse vessel and XXX days let it stande in the sonne and styre it wel and medle it well togyder & so it may be kepte III yere in his virtue. The quantitye of sugar & of the roses should be thus: In IIII pounds of sugar a pound of Roses.

Ascham's Herbal, 1550

Roses

ROSE CORDIAL. (Warranted to "wash the mulligrubs out of a moody brain.") Put a pound of fresh rose leaves into a bason, with a quart of lukewarm water. Cover the vessel and let them infuse for twenty-four hours. Then squeeze them through a linen bag till all the liquor is passed out. Put a fresh pound of rose leaves into the bason, pour the liquid back into it, and let it infuse again for two days. You may repeat this till you obtain a very strong infusion. Then to a pint of the infusion add half a pound of loaf-sugar, half a pint of white brandy, an ounce of broken cinnamon, and an ounce of coriander seeds. Put it into a glass jar, cover it well, and let it stand for two weeks. Then filter it through a fine muslin pinned on the bottom of a sieve, and bottle it for use.

Miss Leslie, Directions for Cookery, 1845.

ROSES AND PINEAPPLE. Half a dozen full blooming red roses
    2 quarts cold water
    1/4 cup lemon juice
    1 can (14 ozs.) crushed pineapple

Pick petals from roses and put in large jar and cover with water. Let stand several hours in a cool place, then strain and to the water add lemon juice and sugar. Stir and add pineapple. Serve cold with rose petal floating on top.

ROSE PETAL WATER ICE. Take a quart of water, 2 cups sugar, 2 teaspoonsful lemon rind, and half a cup lemon juice, mix and add 2 tablespoons rose petal jam. Boil, cool, and freeze.

For a different treat flavor rice pudding with rose water and garnish with crystallized roses.

Place candied rose petals in each glass of iced tea.

Arrange orange sections with rose petals at base of glassware.

Rose syrup is excellent for sour drinks, summer drinks, sherbets and punches.

A simple summer drink is half cup water in a tall glass, flavor with rose syrup and fill with ice cubes.

ROSE SUGAR. Pound white granulated sugar with double its weight of rose petals and put in tightly covered jar.

Rose Petal Punch. Start with required amount (according to amount of punch) red rose petals and cover with a cup of sugar; mix soda water with lemon juice and chill for several hours. Strain, add wine and enjoy.

Roses

Rose Trifle. Cover bottom of cut-glass dish with lady-fingers and soak in rose wine, cover with custard. Add slivered almonds, whipped cream, and crystallized rose petals.

Rose Conserve Balmoral. (Particularly esteemed by Queen Victoria). Use any good rose hip conserve receipe and flavor with lemon juice, ginger and cinnamon to taste. Use as a filling for pastry tarts.

Rose Wine Adds Zip To Fried Chicken. Use rose wine to make extra flavorful fried chicken. Add about ½ cup Rose wine to rich pan drippings left after chicken is browned. Cover and continue cooking on top of stove, or in oven, until chicken is tender.

Joseph R. Anderson, Librarian—New York Public Library

SAFFRON

Pare saffron plot
Forget him not;
His dwelling made trim
* look shortly for him.*
When harvest is gone
* then saffron comes on;*
A little of ground
* brings saffron a pound.*

Tusser, *Five Hundred Points of Good Husbandry, 1580*

Saffron Sauce For Asparagus. Cook asparagus, tops upright, until tender. Butter toast and dot edges with a bit of saffron. Put asparagus on toast and pour over a white sauce.

Saffron is the flavor of sunlight, use it to dust potato chips.

SAFFRON SUGAR. Pound 1 lb. of loaf sugar in a mortar, add 2 oz. of powdered Saffron, mix, and sift through a silk sieve, and keep the sugar in a dry place.

Jules Gouffe, The Royal Book of Pastry and
Confectionery, London, 1874

Saffron

SAFFRON TOAST. (Muzaffer.) Put six thick slices of bread toasted very crisp into a pan, and pour over half a pound of melted butter. In another vessel boil for fifteen minutes three glasses of milk, half a pound of sugar, a quarter pound of ground almonds, and half a teaspoonful of saffron. Pour this into the first vessel, and boil the whole for a few minutes till it gets to a thick porridge. Pour it into a dish, and when cold serve with cream.

Robert H. Christie, Banquets of the Nations
Edinburgh, 1911

Saffron has been used for hundreds of years in soups, meats, eggs, and fish dishes, also desserts.

SAFFRON SAUCE FOR CHICKEN-CORNBREAD SANDWICHES. Make a sauce of chicken stock, celery stalks, a sliced carrot, a teaspoon of saffron, salt, a pint of light cream, worcestershire sauce, pepper, curry powder, alspice, sherry and a bit of sugar. Heat and thicken with three tablespoons of Wondra flour. Place chicken on corn muffins or cornbread squares and pour on sauce.

Saffron is the Karcom of the Hebrews (Song of Solomon, IV-14).

MISHMISHIYA. (In the chapter of fried and dry dishes.) Dissolve the tail and throw out the sediment. Cut fat meat small, then leave in the dissolved tail, stirring until browned. Cover with water, and add a little salt and cinnamon-bark. Then take red meat, chop fine, and make into cabobs the shape of apricots, placing in the middle of each a peeled sweet almond. When the meat has boiled in the water, and the scum has been skimmed off, drop in these cabobs, adding dry coriander, cummin, mastic, cinnamon and ginger all ground fine. When the liquid has all evaporated and only the oils remain, sprinkle with a trifle of vinegar to form a little broth. Then grind sweet almonds fine, mix with water, colour with saffron and add to the saucepan: wipe the sides with a clean rag. Leave over the fire an hour to settle: then remove.

Dr. A. J. Arberry, A Baghdad Cookery Book
(Islamic Culture, Vol. XIII, No. 2, April, 1939)

(In this 12th Century Cookbook there are many recipes which use saffron and rosewater.)

Saffron

SAFFRON CORDIAL. Fill a large still with marigold flowers, adding to them of nutmegs, mace, and English Saffron, of each an ounce; then take three pints of muscadine, or Malaga sack, and with a sprig of rosemary dash it on the flowers; then distill if off with a slow fire, and let it drop on white sugar-candy, draw it off till it begins to be sour; save a pint of the first running to mix with the other waters on an extraordinary occasion, mix the rest together to drink it by itself.

E. Smith, The Compleat Housewife, 1736

"We applied ourselves wholeheartedly to this dessert and our joviality was suddenly revived by a fresh diversion, for at the slightest pressure all the cakes and fruits would squirt a saffron sauce upon us, and even spurted unpleasantly in our faces."

The Satyricon ofPetronius Arbiter

Saffron symbolizes Marriage.

> *They shall wear*
> *The Bridal Saffron; all their locks shall bloom*
> *With garlands; and their blazing nuptial torches,*
> *And hymeneal songs, prepare the way.*
> *Henry Hart Milman*

SYRUP OF SAFFRON. Take a pint of the best canary, as much balm-water, and two ounces of English saffron; open and pull the saffron very well, and put it into the liquor to infuse, let it stand close cover'd (so as to be hot but not boil) twelve hours; then strain it out as hot as you can, and add to it two pounds of double refined sugar, boil it till it is well incorporated, and when it is cold bottle it, and take one spoonful in a little sack or small cordial, as occasion serves.

E. Smith, The Compleat Housewife

Saffron and honey balls were very popular in the 18th Century.

"What made the English people sprightly was the liberal use of saffron in their broths and sweetmeats."
Francis Bacon

King Soloman's garden had a saffron plot. It was used in Rome to strew the streets and baths, powdered scent. The odor of saffron was the only thing that could make crocodiles weep.

COKYNTRYCE. Take a capoun, and skald hym, and draw hem clene and smite hem in the waste across; take a Pigge, and skald hym and draw hym in the same manner, and smyte hem also in the waste; take a nedyl and a threde, and sewe the fore party of the Capoun to the After parti of the Pygge; and the fore partye of the Pigge to the hynder party of the Capoun, & than stuffe hem as thou stuffest a Pigge; putet hem on a spete, and Roste hym; and whan he is y-now, gild hem with yolkes of Eyroun, and pouder Gyngere and Safroun, thenne wyth the Jus of Percely withowte; and than serve it forth for a ryal mete.

Saffron

SMAL COFYNS. Take fayre Floure, Safroun, Sugre & Salt, & make ther-of a past; than make smal cofyns; then take yolkys of Eyron & separate hem fro the whyte & lat the yolkes be al hole, & not to-broke, & lay iii or iv in a cofyn; and than take marow of boyne, ii or iii gobettys, and cowche in the cofynn; than take pouder Gyngere, Sugre, Pasonys, & caste a-bove; & than cover the cofyn with the same past, & bake hem, & frye hem in fayre grece, & serve forth.

Early English Recipes, Selected from
the Harl. Ms. 279, circa 1430

SAFFRON SAUCE. Make a strong infusion of saffron in a breakfast-cupful of milk; stir it over the fire with two ounces of butter rubbed in flour, one ounce of blanched sweet-almonds slightly chopped, a little cinnamon, and two ounces of white sugar. When well thickened, serve it.

Everybody's Pudding Book

SAFFRON SAUCE FOR FISH. Take a can of tomatoes, 2 medium-size onions, and two cloves of garlic, all chopped fine. Cook in half a cup of olive oil, after about 10 minutes add half cup white wine and half cup of water. Season with salt and coarsely ground black pepper and add 2 teaspoons saffron. Simmer for ten or fifteen minutes and it can be served hot or cold.

In early cookery books it was directed that "Saffron should be put into all Lenten sauces, soups, and other such dishes; also without Saffron we cannot have well-cooked peas."

The Irish frequently used Saffron to dye their bed linen.

The cottagers of Cornwall and Devon used Saffron often in making their bread and cakes. Use your yeast recipe for plain buns, but add cinnamon, saffron and lemon peel. It was used also for Simnel Cakes for Mothering Sunday.

Saffron Tea. A pinch of saffron in a cup of hot water.

Apicius gives a recipe for a saffron sauce to be served with wild boar.

In the 18th Century saffron was made up into balls and then sprinkled over salads. No less an authority than John Evelyn considered it a must.

Saffron

A Saffron Confection. Soak a half pound of saffron and a half pound of zedoary (a fragrant East Indian drug, of a bitter, aromatic taste) in six cups of water. Strain and add 2 ounces of cinnamon, 2 ounces of nutmeg, 1 ounce of cloves, and ½ ounce of cardamon seeds. Add two pounds of sugar and cook until it forms a soft ball. Pour into a shallow pan and cut into 1-inch squares.

In Roman times yellow colored foods were considered luxury eating, even though it was just as costly then as it is now, fifty dollars a pound.

According to Rasis (Latinized name of Muhammed Ibn Zaka riya al Rasi), an Arabic medical writer of the 10th Century—when saffron is infused in wine it is a tonic to the stomach and relieves shortness of breath, and produces a most satisfactory elevation of spirits.
Mensa Philosophica

SAGE

"How can a man die who has sage in his garden?"
Arabian Proverb

Sage who by many virtues gains't renown
Sage whose deserts all happy mortals own
Since thou, dear Sage, preserv'st the memory
I cannot sure forgetful prove of thee.
Abraham Cowley

Sage Cream. Boil a quart of cream, pound red sage in a mortar, put into the cream a quarter of a pint of canary, and a quarter of a pint of Rose-water with half a pound of sugar. After the same manner you may do by any sort of good herbs.
The Receipt Book of Joseph Cooper, Cook to Charles I, 1654

Vinegar Of The Four Thieves. Take of the tops of sea and Roman Wormwood, Rosemary, Sage, Mint, and Rue, of each an ounce and a half; Lavender Flowers two ounces, Calamus Aromaticus, Cinnamon, Cloves, Nutmeg, and Garlic, of each a quarter of an ounce; Camphire, half an ounce; Red Wine Vinegar, a gallon. Choose all the foregoing ingredients dry, except the Garlic and Camphire; beat them into grose powder, and cut the Garlic into thin slices; put the whole into a matrass; pour the Vinegar on them, and digest the mixture in the sun, or in a gentle sand-heat, for three weeks to a month. Then strain off the Vinegar by expression, filter it through paper, and add the Camphire dissolved in a little rectified Spirit of Wine. Keep it for use in a bottle, tightly corked.

Sage

Toilet of Flora

Sage Water. Take sage flowers, sprinkle them with white wine, or water. Let them stand awhile. Then distil them.

Joseph Cooper, Receipt Book, 1654

Conserve Of Sage. Take new flowers of Sage one pound, Sugar one pound; so beat them together very small in a Marble Mortar, put them in a vessel well glased and steeped, set them in the Sun, stir them dayly; it will last one year.

The Queen's Closet Opened, By W. N., Cook to Queen Henrietta Maria, 1655

When distilled it has a muscat scent and is used as an ingredient for perfumes and to flavor German wines. Tournefort said, "In England, they take the leaves with beaten Eggs, Cream and some Flower, and fry them in a Frying-Pan, and bring them to Table as a second Course, which they Commend exceedingly for Weakness in the Back."

The aromatic odor is entirely in the bracts of the flower.

In Mexico *s. fulgens* has a bright scarlet color, *s. splendens* also comes from Mexico. It is not pollinated by insects but by tiny birds entranced by its color.

Ruskin did not like these flowers, "The velvety violent blue of the one and the scarlet of the other, seem to have no gradation and no shade. There's no color that gives me such an idea of violence—a sort of rough, angry scream—as that shade of blue ungradated. In the gentian it is touched with green, in the cornflower with red . . . but in the salvia it is simply blue cloth."

Sage

How To Dish Up A Dish Of Fruits With Preserved Flowers. Take a large Dish, cover it with another of the same bigness, and place the uppermost over with Paste of Almonds, inlaid with red, white, blew, green Marmalade in the Figure of Flowers and Banks; then take the branches of candied Flowers, and fix them upright in order, and upon little Bushes erected and covered with Paste. Fix your preserved and candied Cherries, Plumbs, Pease, Apples, Gooseberries, Currans and the like, each in their proper Place; and for Leaves you may use colored Paste or Wax, Parchmant or Horn; and this especially in Winter will be very proper.

> Henry Howard, England's Newest Way in All Sorts of Cookery,
> London, 1717 (Cook to His Grace the Duke of Ormond,
> and since to the Earl of Salisbury, and Earl of Winchelsea)

"This herb yf left to putrify with the blood of a serpent or a bird like a oysell, if it be touched on ye brest of a man he shall lose his sence or felynge the space of fifteen dayes or more. And yf the foersaid serpent be burnd and the ashes of it put in ye fyre, anone shall there be a rayne bowe with an horible thunder. And yf ye aforesaide ashes be put in a lampe, and be kindled, it shal appeare that all the house is full of serpints and this hath been proved of men of late tyme."
The Boke of the Secrets of Albertus Magnus, 1560

Sage Wine. Take 15 pounds of raisins and chop or grind, a peck of sage chopped. Boil $2\frac{1}{2}$ gallons of water, cool until it is lukewarm, add the sage and raisins and let it stand five or six days, stirring two or three times a day. Then strain and press out the liquid and put it into a cask, let stand for six months, then draw off into another vessel and let stand for two days, bottle and let it set for a year before drinking.

Sage Tea. A pint of boiling water on one ounce of sage. For the sake of variety it can be flavored with orange juice or lemon and sugar.

Sage Cheese. At one time very popular, "Marbled with Sage, the hardening cheese she pressed." Mix it with cottage cheese for a refreshing flavor.

Decorate tomato salad with sage blossoms.

SNAPDRAGON

"I took leave of my first College, Trinity, which was so dear to me. Trinity had never been unkind to me. There used to be much Snapdragon growing on the walls opposite my freshman's rooms there, and I had for years taken it as the emblem of my own perpetual residence, even unto death, in my university. On the morning of the 23rd I left the observatory. I have never seen Oxford since, excepting the spires, as they are seen from the railway."

Cardinal Newman

Antirrhinum, more modest, takes the style
Of Lion's Mouth, sometimes of calf-snout vile;
By us Snap-Dragon call'd, to make amends,
But say what this 'Chimera'-name intends?
Thou well deserv'st it, if, as old wives say,
Thou driv'st nocturnal ghosts and sprights away.

Abraham Cowley

SNAPDRAGONS IN APPLESAUCE. Soak a cup of large raisins in Cognac until they are plump. A jar of applesauce from the supermarket (unspiced) is then mixed with the raisins. A nice surprise for the unwary.

SNAPDRAGONS. I have read several versions of this ancient game, how it came by its name I don't know, but it is a popular Christmas game. Place raisins in a silver dish, casserole, or a chafing dish and pour over them a cup of warmed brandy. Clear the table and invite the guests to gather round. Turn out the lights and light the brandy. The guests help themselves to a raisin at a time, and seemingly swallow whole, while still flaming.

This is also a good game for All Hallow's Eve.

SQUASH BLOSSOM

A Flower Song

Where thou walkest, O singer, bring forth the flowery drum,
let it stand amid beauteous feathers, let it be placed in
the midst of golden flowers;
Let us be glad, dear friends, let us rejoice while we walk
here on this flowery earth; may the end never come of our
flowers and songs, but may they continue in the mansion of
the Giver of Life.
Scattering flowers I rejoice you with my drum, awaiting what
comes to our minds.

—Ancient Nahuatl Poems by D. G. Brinton (1887)

Squash Blossom

ɛ⚇ *Quetzalcoatl, whose full name was Topiltzin Ce Acatl Quetzalcoatl was supposed to be a reincarnation of the goddess of flowers, Xochiquetzal (Flowery Plume). She lived in a heavenly garden and was the wife of Tlaloc, the rain-god. Her male counterpart was Xochipilli (Flower Prince), god of joy and pleasure. He is also the patron of painters, weavers, and artists. Later, so the Codex Telleriano-Remensis tells us, they transgressed by picking roses and branches from the sacred trees of Tamoanchan, the Western paradise, and were banished into the world of men. Xochiquetzal was the Venus of Mexican mythology, and is frequently called the "Mexican Eve."*

ɛ⚇ There are many ways of preparing the squash blossom.

SCRAMBLED EGGS de NATIVIDAD. 6 eggs
        1 cup minced squash blossoms
        ½ teaspoon onion seasoning
        Pinch sweet basil
        1 diced green pepper

ɛ⚇ Saute green pepper in butter. Beat eggs lightly and blend with other ingredients. Add to green pepper and scramble as usual.

CHAPALA CHEER. 10 or 12 squash blossoms
      2 eggs, beaten
      2 or 3 tablespoons water
     flour
     salt and pepper
      1 cup cooking oil

ɛ⚇ Wash blossoms and remove stems. Let them drain dry on a paper towel. Mix other ingredients and make a smooth batter. Dip in hot oil and fry until brown. Serve hot.

VIVA GUADLAJARA. 2 tablespoons fat
      1 sliced tomato, 2 if small
      Quarter pound thinly sliced pork
      2 crushed cloves garlic
      Salt
      About 2 dozen squash blossoms

ɛ⚇ Heat fat and brown garlic; add tomato and cook about 5 minutes. Add pork and cook for 15 minutes, then about ½ cup water. Lastly add squash blossoms and season with salt. (Be sure that stems and calyxes have been removed from blossoms.)

Mercado de Chapala (Enchiladas). Fry required number of tortillas in hot oil and spread with minced onion and grated cheese. Serve with a sauce made of green tomatoes, green peppers, onion, salt and a pinch of sugar. Just before serving add squash flowers.

Squash Blossom Omelette. Take kitchen scizzors and cut blossoms only into rather large pieces, then fry in butter and mix with eggs which have been seasoned with salt, pepper, and parsley. Serve with tomato sauce.

Squash Blossom

*Out of the place of flowers, I, Xochopilli, come
Priest of the Sunset, Lord of the Twilight.*

*Out of the land of the rain and the mist,
I, Xochiquetzal, come.*

Flower Duck. Place duck in sufficient water to nearly cover. Cook slowly two and a half to three hours. At the end of half an hour add several squash blossoms, scattering them over the duck. When done remove duck and slice; make a paste of soy sauce and flour to thicken the broth. Cook two minutes, pour over sliced duck and garnish with fresh squash blossoms.

Quesadillas Of Squash Blossoms. On each tortilla place a mixture of powdered cheese, chopped squash blossoms and peppers (the hot is better), then fold tortillas, fasten with toothpick and fry in salad oil.

Another variation is to fry onions, 4 leaves of epazote (American wormwood) and blossoms, and then proceed. Also in place of the powdered cheese a thin slice of fresh cheese may be placed on each tortilla before frying.

Chimoie. Take about a pound of pork, or beef, and cook in salted water until tender. Then cut in small pieces—about an inch, or inch-and-a-half square. Take seeded, and veined peppers and onion and two or three tomatoes and grind together. Fry these ingredients in hot fat and add meat and 2 cups of stock. After 30 minutes add ½ cup string beans, ½ cup fresh corn, and 3 or 4 squash blossoms cut up. Season with a leaf of epazote, salt, and pepper, cover and cook for another hour.

Stuffed Squash Blossoms. Use two flowers for each person and stuff with sweet corn, green chillis, squashes, onion, eggs. Stuff, add a bit of cheese and butter, dip in flour and beaten eggs. Serve hot on a platter garnished with radishes, and lettuce.

St. John's-Wort ~~~~~~~~~~~~~~~~~~~

Hypericum all bloom, so thick a swarm of flowers, like flies, clothing its slender rods that scarce a leaf appears.

This plant has many legends associated with it, the flowers when rubbed together make a red juice which was believed to be the blood of St. John the Baptist. In the Isle of Man it is believed that whoever treads on it at night will ride a fairy horse and not be allowed to rest until the sun rises.

Symbol: Animosity and superstition.

Some Notes Upon The Use Of Herbs In Norwegian Households By Sigrid Undset. I should like to give the recipe for a herb tonic, which is not so much used in Norway as in Denmark, where the rural population believes in it as a cure-all: "Perkom-Brandy." Gather the flowers and fullblown buds of St. John'swort (Hypericum perforatum) and dry on a tray in the sun. As it shrinks in drying you will need a lot, so pick a basketful every day on your morning walk. Fill dried flowers into bottles but do not press, and pour over Aquavit (or gin or vodka, I believe would do it). It is quite exciting to see how the fluid immediately turns a delicate pink. Cork and store for three months, and strain off the brandy which has now taken on a deep garnet color. Brandy may be filled on to the flowers a second time, but this brew will not turn out quite as strong as the first. As the liquor is very bitter it may be diluted like one does with Angostura. My maternal grandfather in Denmark, who otherwise never touched wine or hard liquor save twice a year, on his birthday and New Year's day, started every day of his adult life with a dram of Perkom bitter before breakfast. As he lived to be 93 years old and enjoyed splendid health at least till he was 87, it probably did him good. I wonder if Perkom bitter might not be introduced with advantage in some kinds of cocktail?

The Herbarist (1945)

Sir Kenelm Digby recommends many flowers in his recipes for mead and metheglin . . . gillyflowers, cowslips, yellow wallflowers, avens, borage, bugloss, elder, hops, St. John'swort, marigold, marshmallow, melilot, primrose, roses and violets.

St. John's-Wort

THE DIVINE CORDIAL. To make this, take, in the beginning of the month of March, two ounces of the Roots of the true Acorus, Betony, Florentine Orriceroots, Cyprus, Gentian, and sweet Scabious; an ounce of Cinnamon, and as much Yellow Sanders: two drachms of Mace; an ounce of Juniper-berries; and six drachms of Coriander-seeds; beat these ingredients, in a mortar, to a coarse powder, and add thereto the outer Peel of six fine China Oranges; put them all into a large vessel, with a gallon and a half of Spirit of Wine; shake them well, and then cork the vessel tight till the season for Flowers. When these are in full vigour, add half a handful of the following; viz. Violets, Hyacinths, Jonquils, Wall Flowers, Red, Damask, White and Musk Roses, Cove-July-Flowers, Orange-Flowers, Jasmine, Tuberoses, Rosemary, Sage, Thyme, Lavender, Sweet Marjoram, Broom, Elder, St. John'swort, Marigold, Chamomile, Lilies of the Valley, Narcissuses, Honeysuckle, Borage, and Bugloss.

Three seasons are required to procure all these Flowers in perfection; Spring, Summer, and Autumn. Every time you gather any of these Flowers, add them immediately to the infusion, mixing them thoroughly with the other ingredients; and three days after you have put in the last Flowers, put the whole into a glass cucurbit, lute on the head carefully, place it in a water bath over a slow fire, keep the receiver cocked, and draw off five quarts of Spirit, which will prove of rare Quality.

—*The Toilet of Flora*

Some names for St. John's wort: Amber, balm of warrior's wounds, cammock, devil's scourge, herb John, penny John, Grace of God, the Lord God's wonder plant, rosin rose, touch and heal, perfoliate St. John'swort, hundred holes, sol terrestris, fuga daemonum, witch's herb.

BOTANISTS AT DINNER

"*Another incident in the experience of the senior author illustrates the prejudice against not too attractive or conventional foods. Planning for a meeting of botanists in his study, he set to work on the menu to follow the business meeting: puree of dried Fairy-ring mushrooms, escalloped canned Purslane, salad of cooked blanched Pokeweed seeds was decided upon. Proceeding in January to the border of a frozen truck-farm, a peck of seeds with husks and other fragments was quickly gathered. Winnowed by pouring back and forth from containers out-of-doors, so that the lighter husks and debris blew away, a yield of a full quart of the black and drab fruits was left. When supper was served, Mrs. Fernald brought in the soup which found favor, with thin biscuits of Jack-in-the-Pulpit flour, then the Purslane and salad, with a plate of intensely black muffins. I explained that,* *having no cook, I had volunteered to make the muffins. The plate went around the table, regularly to receive a polite, "No, I thank you", until it reached the late Emile Williams, half-French and with more than usual Yankee consideration for others.* Everyone else having declined my black muffins, Williams took one, put on his eyeglasses and inspected it, then sniffed at it. "Ah, Chenopodium album" was his immediate diagnosis. Asked how he guessed, he replied: "I've just been reading Napoleon's Memoirs. Napoleon at times had to live on it." The plate was promptly cleared and returned to the kitchen for more, to nibble with the Beach-Plum preserve."*

St. John's-Wort

> *Edible Wild Plants of Eastern North America*
> *by Merritt Lyndon Fernald and Alfred Charles*
> *Kinsey (Harper & Row)*

*In a preceding paragraph Dr. Fernald had explained that they are highly nutritious, tasting somewhat like buckwheat but with a characteristic "mousey" flavor.

SUNFLOWER

Ah, Sun-flower! weary of time,
Who countest the steps of the sun,
Seeking after that sweet golden clime
Where the traveller's journey is done.
> *Blake*

SUNFLOWER CORDIAL. Simmer two ounces of sunflower seeds and a piece of ginger in a quart of water for an hour. Add two tablespoons honey, strain and add two ounces of brandy.

Boil sunflower buds and eat with butter like artichokes. Pepper and vinegar may also be added.

Ere it comes to expand and show its golden face (the sunflower) being dress'd as the artichouk, is eaten as a daintie.

John Evelyn, 1699

PRAYER FOR A PROFUSION OF SUNFLOWERS

Send sunflowers!
With my turkey-bone whistle
I am calling the birds
To sing upon the sunflowers.
For when the clouds hear them singing
They will come quickly,
And rain will fall upon our fields.
Send sunflowers!

Sunflower

> *Amy Lowell, Ballads for Sale*

The buds before they be flowered, boyled and eaten with butter, vinegar and pepper, are exceeding pleasant meat or they may be broiled upon a gridiron and eaten with oil and vinegar.

> Gerarde, Herball

Sunflower (helianthus) — Your devout adorer.
> *Lofty and true thoughts.*

The Sun-flower turns to her God when he sets
The same look which she turned when he rose.
> *Moore*

SUNFLOWER GIN. Boil 2 ounces of the seeds in a quart of water till it is reduced to a pint. Strain and add six ounces of any good gin and sugar to taste.

Long before the coming of the white man and the exploitation of **Sunflower-oil**, the American Indians were using the seeds of the larger species of **Sunflowers** as important sources of food . . . they serve in making bread, cakes and rich soups. Explorers state that the roasted seeds were used in preparing a drink "tasting just like coffee."

The Jerusalem artichoke is a member of the sunflower family and the name is probably a corruption of girasol, an old name for sunflower.

There are many excellent sunflower seed flour recipes in Stella Standard's book "Whole Grain Cookery."

TANSY ⟿⟿⟿⟿⟿⟿⟿⟿⟿⟿⟿⟿⟿

"Every night after supper Dave changed his shirt and went down the track to court Susanna and before he started he rolled over and over in the tansy bed to make himself smell sweet."

Willa Cather

TANSY PUDDING. Soak half cup of bread crumbs in half a cup of milk. Meanwhile beat an egg with a teaspoon of sugar and a teaspoon of finely chopped young tansy leaves. Mix with soaked crumbs to which has been added a tablespoon of melted butter. Put into individual custard dishes, or a small casserole and bake in a moderate oven until set. This should be eaten cold with thick cream and honey.

TANSY TEA. Take dried tansy leaves and flowers. To one heaping tablespoonful of the tansy mixture add one pint of boiling water.

TO MAKE A TANSY IN LENT. Take all maner of hearbes and the spawn of a Pike or of any other fish and blanched almond and a few crums of bread and a little faire water and a pinte of Rose-water and mingle altogether and make it not too thin and frie it in oyl and so serve it in.

The Good Housewife's Handmaid, 1588

HOW TO MAKE A TANSY. Take a little tansy, featherfew, parsley and violets, and stampe them altogether and straine them with the yolkes of eight or tenne eggs, and herte or foure whites, and some vinegar and put thereto sugar or salt and frie it.

Ibidem

TANSY PUDDING. Blanch and pound a quarter of a pound of Jordon almonds, put them into a stew pan, add a gill of a syrup of Roses, the crumb of a French roll, some grated nutmeg, half a glass of brandy, two tablespoonfuls of tansy juice, three ounces of fresh butter and some slices of citron. Pour over it a pint and a half of boiling cream or milk; sweeten and when cold mix it, add the juice of a lemon and eight eggs beaten. It may be either boyled or baked.

Ibidem

Jupiter ordered Mercury to give Gannymede tansy in the cup that would make him immortal and cup-bearer to the gods.

Tansy symbolizes 'I declare against you', and in Italy its presentation is regarded as an insult.

Tansy

And, golden rods, and tansy running high
That o'er the pale top smiled on passers by.
John Clare, peasant poet of England

TANSY AMBER CAKES. Blanch a pound of Almonds, steep them in a pint of cream, pound them in a mortar, add to them the yolks of twelve and whites of six eggs, put in half a pint of juice of spinage and a quarter of a pint of juice of Tansy, add to it grated Bread; sweeten it with sugar to your palate fry it in sweet Butter and keep it stirring in the Pan till it is of a good thickness strew sugar over it and serve it up.
John Nott (Cook to the Duke of Bolton),
Receipt Book, 1723

TANSY PANCAKES. Put four spoonfuls of flour into an earthen pan, and mix it with a half a pint of cream to a smooth batter, beat four eggs well and put in, with two ounces of powdered sugar, and beat all well together for a quarter of an hour; then put in two spoonsful of the juice of spinich and one of tansy, a little grated nutmeg, mix all well together, and fry them in fresh butter; garnish them with Seville oranges cut in quarters, and strew powdered sugar over them.
Richard Briggs, The New Art of Cooking, 1788
(For many years Cook at the Globe Tavern, Fleet Street,
the White Hart Tavern, Holborn, and at
the Temple Coffee House.)

"Made a pretty dinner for some guests, to wit: 'A brace of stewed carps, six roasted chickens and a jowl of salmon, hot, for the first course; a Tansy and two neat's tongues, and cheese, the second.'"
Samuel Pepys

Dr. Fernald states that in Maine occasionally tansy-cheese is made by steeping the herb and pouring the extract into the milk before the curds are made.

The Irish also like tansy and use it to flavor *drisheens*, a popular dish in County Cork.

TANSY FRITTERS. Take the crumbs of a small loaf of bread, pour on it half a pint of boiling milk; let it stand an hour, then put in as much juice of tansy as will give it a flavour, but not to make it bitter, then make it a pretty green with spinach juice, put to it a spoonful of ratafia water, or brandy. Sweeten it to taste, grate over it the rind of half a lemon, beat the yolks of four eggs, mix them all together, put them in a tossing-pan, with four ounces of butter, stir it over a slow fire till it is thick, take it off and let it stand two or three hours, then cut into fritters and drop them into a pan of boiling lard; a spoonful is enough for a fritter. Serve them up surrounded by slices of orange, grate sugar over them, and serve a wine sauce separately.

Tansy

Elizabeth Raffald, 1825

MINNOW TANSY. Minnows should be washed well in salt, and their heads and tails cut off, and their guts taken out and not washed after. They make excellent minnow tansies; that is being fried in yolks of eggs, the flowers of cowslips and of primroses and a little tansy: thus used they make a dainty dish of meat.

Izaak Walton

THISTLES 〰〰〰〰〰〰〰〰〰〰〰〰〰〰〰

...the seeded thistle, when a parle,
It holds with Zephyr, ere it sendeth fair,
Its light balloons into the summer air.
John Keats

The thistle is the emblem of Scotland and symbolizes austerity, and independence.

THISTLE SALAD. Chardoons are a wild thistle that grow in every ditch or hedge. You must cut them about two inches, string them, tie them up twenty in a Bundle, and boil them like asparagus; or you may cut them in small bits and boil them as pease, and toss them up with pepper, salt, and melted butter.

Adam's Luxury and Eve's Cookery (1744)

(They may also be soaked in wine vinegar for thirty minutes, chilled and served with a dressing of salt, pepper and olive oil.)

CHARDOONS WITH CHEESE. Cut them in bits an inch long, after they are string'd. Then stewe them in Gravy till tender, season them with pepper and salt, and squeeze in an orange; thicken it with butter brown'd with flour. Put it in your dish and cover it all over with grated Parmesan or Cheshire Cheese, and then brown it all over with a hot cheese iron and serve it up.

Ibidem

Thistles

TO RAGOUT CHARDOONS. Take the inside of the cardoons wash them well, boil them in salt and water, put them in a tossing-pan, with a little veal gravy, a teaspoonful of lemon pickle, a large spoonful of mushroom catsup, pepper and salt; thicken it with flour and butter, boil it a little and serve up on a soup plate.

—R. Huish, The Female's Friend, London, 1837

There are several kinds of thistles: the Milk Thistle, Marsh Thistle, Woolyheaded Thistle, the Scotch Thistle, Dwarf Thistle, Star Thistle and Carline Thistle. Mexico has a very beautiful scarlet thistle (Erythrolena conspicua). The Sow Thistle is not a real thistle.

Milk is coagulated by an extract of thistle or cardoon flowers in two to six hours, and after several weeks forms a very fine cheese.

The haughty thistle o'er all danger towers
In every place the very wasp of flowers.
    —John Clare

COEUR DE CARDON AUX FINES HERBES. Having cooked the heart of the cardoon, trim it all round so as to give it a cylindrical shape, and cut it laterally into roundels one-third inch thick. Roll these roundels in some pale, thin, buttered meat glaze combined with chopped herbs. Prepared in this way, the heart of a cardoon constitutes an excellent garnish for Tournedos and sauted chickens.

A. Escoffier, A Guide to Modern Cookery (1920)

And what do we find in South America? "In the Pampas of Buenos Ayres the cardoon, although only naturalized there during the nineteenth century has grown wild and spread with such abundance as to obstruct travel and traffic in some parts."

Law's Grocer's Manual

Thistles

✍ Cardoon, a thistle-like plant . . . is used in salads, stews and soups, and as a separate vegetable.

Artemus Ward, The Encyclopedia of Food

THISTLE PUNCH. In a cut-glass or silver bowl slice a lemon, add a few tarragon leaves, and several cloves. Add a cup of vermouth and three cups of whisky. While these flavors are melding boil several thistle heads in a quart of water for a few minutes. Pour the water and thistle heads into the bowl and decorate with fresh thistles. May be served hot or cold.

CHARDON FLOWER HEADS. Chardons are usually blanched and stewed like celery, but my brother boils the heads of his, which are very sweet and in flavour like artichokes; the chief objection is that they are very small and afford little substance in their bottoms. The heads of chardons are sold in the markets and are thought to be delicate morsels. Chardons are strong, vigorous plants, grow six and seven feet high, and have strong sharp prickles like thistles.

Journals of Gilbert White, July 11th, 1791

THYME

✍ I was utterly alone with the sun and the earth. Lying down on the grass, I spoke in my soul to the earth; the sun, the air, and the distant sea far beyond sight. I thought of the earth's firmness — I felt it bear me up; through the grassy couch there came an influence as if I could feel the great earth speaking to me. I thought of the wandering air — its pureness, which is its beauty; the air touched me and gave me something of itself. I spoke to the seas though so far, in my mind I saw it, green at the rim of the earth and blue in deeper ocean . . . I turned to the blue heaven over, gazing into its depth, inhaling its exquisite colour and sweetness. The rich blue of the unattainable flower of the sky drew my soul towards it, and there it rested, for pure colour is rest of heart. By all these I prayed . . . Then returning, I prayed by the sweet thyme, whose little flowers I touched with my hand; by the slender grass; by the crumble of earth, the blade of grass, the thyme flower, breathing the earth-encircling air, thinking of the sea and the sky, holding out my hand for the sunbeams to touch it, prone on the sward in token of deep reverence, thus I prayed. . . .

—*Richard Jefferies, The Story of My Heart*

Symbolizes — Courage and Energy

HONEY OF HYMETTUS. Collected by bees from the wild thyme of Attica.

Aristotle said that honey was "Dew distilled from the stars and the rainbow."

For a real treat try Feta cheese and Hymettus honey on an unsalted cracker.

Thyme

THYME VINEGAR. Take a pound of thyme flowers and mix with two quarts of good malt vinegar. Let stand for 40 days in the sun and strain.

"Mrs. Todd was an ardent lover of herbs, both wild and tame, and the sea-breeze blew into the low end-window of the house laden not only with sweet-brier and sweet-mary, but balm and sage, borage and mint, wormwood, and southern-wood. If Mrs. Todd had occasion to step into the far corner of her herb plot, she trod heavily upon thyme and made its fragrant presence known with all the rest.

At one side of the herb plot were other growths of a rustic pharmacopoeia. Strange and pungent odors that roused a dim sense and remembering of something in the forgotten past.

Some of these might have belonged to sacred and mystic rites and have had some occult knowledge handed with them down the centuries; but now they pertained only to humble compounds brewed at intervals with molasses, vinegar or spirits in a small cauldron on Mrs. Todd's kitchen stove. It sometimes seemed as if love and hate and jealousy and adverse winds at sea might also find their proper remedies among the curious wild-looking plants in Mrs. Todd's garden."

—Sara Orne Jewett, Country of the Pointed Firs

THYME CORDIAL. Dr. Fernie highly recommends this. Make in the usual way by infusing flower tops in brandy.

There are many varieties of thyme—Basil Lemon, Wild, Cat thyme (comes from Spain) Corsican (Mentha requiene) and not really a thyme, Garden, Caraway (Thymus baronne), Orange, Silver and Variegated Thyme.

It is used extensively in cooking, though the Persians nibbled on fresh flowerets. Kipling was so fond of it he said it was like "the perfume of the dawn of Paradise."

Some of its uses: to flavor salads, cottage cheese, vegetable soup, oyster stew, clam chowder, gumbos, borscht and seafood. Also for poultry stuffings, egg dishes, beef stew and hash, meat loaf, lamb, veal and pork dishes.

TUBEROSE ～～～～～～～～～～～～～～～

"The mistress of the night, the Polyanthes tuberosa, was in profusion in the garden. It is used in Poonja; the natives call it Gol-shub-boo — meaning night scented.
    Parkes, Wanderings of a Pilgrim, 1850

Many people have observed that the tuberose gives out flames and sparks of light after a thundershower.

It symbolizes dangerous pleasures.

TUBEROSA-FLOWER WATER. The leaves of these Flowers are to be taken likewise, without the Yellow and the Stalks, and infus'd from the Evening till the next Morning, or for the space of half a Day; with a sufficient quantity of Sugar. Otherwise, if it be requisite to prepare it sooner, the Liquor may be beat up, as before, by pouring it out of one Pot into another, till it be well impregnated with the Tuberosa-flower: Then it must be strained thro' a Sieve, or a Linnen-cloth, and well iced.
    Francois Massialot, The Court and Country Book, London, 1702

TUBEROSE CANDY. Make a fondant and flavor with the essence of tuberose, a bit of orange-flower water; color it a very pale yellow. Decorate if you wish with a bit of candied tuberose flower or for contrast, a crystallized violet.

TULIPS ～～～～～～～～～～～～～～～～

You are a tulip seen to-day
But, dearest of so short a stay
That where you grew scarce man can say.
    Robert Herrick

In mythology the Tulip was a Dalmatian nymph.

"I do verily thinke that these are the Lillies of the field mentioned by our Saviour for He saith that Solomon in all his royaltee was not arrayed like one of these. The reasons that induce me to thinke thus are these: First their shape, for their flowers resemble Lillies, and in these places whereas our Saviour was conversant

they grow wilde in the fields. Secondly, the infinite varietie of colour, which is to be founde more than in any other sorte of flowre: and thirdly the wondrous beautie and mixtures of these flowres.

This is my opinion, which any may either approve or gainsay as he shall thinke goode."

John Gerard, Herball, 1597

Tulip bulbs preserved in sugar are recommended by the old writers.

Tulips

Remove pistils of tulips. Wash. Stuff with chicken salad.

In the Speech of Flowers by Thomas Fuller, written about 1640, he causes the rose to complain about the popularity of the tulip: "There is lately a flower — shal I call it so? — in courtesie I will tearme it so, though it deserve not the appellation, a Toolip, which hath engrafted the love and affections of most people unto it; and what is this Toolip? An ill favour wrapt up in pleasant colours; as for the use thereof in Physic no Physitian hath honoured it yet with the mention, nor with a Greek or Latin name."

"Some fair tulip by a storm oppressed,
Shrinks up, and folds its silken arms to rest."
Dryden

PEAS OF THE SEEDY BUDS OF TULIPS. In the Spring the flowry leaves of Tulips do fall away, and there remains within them the end of the stalk, which in time will turn to seed. Take that seedy end and pick from it the little excresscencies about it, and cut it into short pieces, and boil them as you would do Pease; and they will taste like Pease, and be very savoury.

Sir Kenelm Digby

Mrs. Hollingsworth says she found them to taste more like asparagus than peas.

From time immemorial the young Persian uses the tulip as his declaration of love, by this flower he conveys to his sweetheart that like this flower his countenance is on fire, and his heart reduced to coal....The Turks have a Feast of Tulips, celebrated annually in the Grand Seignor's Seraglio....Toward the middle of the seventeenth century the rage for flowers and particularly for Tulips, was carried to such an excess both in Holland and in France, as to produce bankruptcy and ruin to many families. It was called TULIPOMANIA.

Henry Phillips, Flora Historica, 1824

In flower language tulip means a declaration of love, also beautiful eyes.

NAMES OF FLOWERS

> *Gertrude*
> *The peace of Europe.*
> *The Princess of Monaco.*
> *Victory.*
> *Tulips.*
> *I murmur to my servant. Don't ring the bell. I also say.*
>   *Don't attack me.*
> *By being unkind I please brothers.*
> *Brother brother go away and stay.*
>
> Gertrude Stein, Short Poems, 1914-1925

Tulips

"Some of the Ancients, and likewise divers of the Modern writers, that have laboured in Naturale Magick, have noted a Sympathy, between the Sun, Moon and some Principal Starres; And certain Herbs and Plants. And so they have denominated some Herbs Solar and some Lunar; and such like Toyes put into great Words. It is manifest that there are some Flowers, that have respect to the Sunne in two kinds, the one by opening and shutting, the other by Bowing and Inclining the Head. For Mary-golds, Tulippes, Pimpernell, and indeed most Flowers, doe open or spread their leaves abroad, when the Sunne shineth serene and fair; And again, (in some part) close them or gather them inward, either toward Night or when the Skie is overcast. Of this there needeth no such Solemn Reason to be assigned, As to say that they rejoyce at the presence of the Sunne; And mourn the absence thereof." Francis Bacon, Sylva Sylvarum

Tulips and asphodels were used as salads in Hesiod's time.

At a poet's supper party, Ezra Pound ate all the table decorations of red tulips.

VEGETABLE MARROWS

Then said Judes triumphantly: I would suggest lamb, roast chicken, and pimented rice; I would suggest sausages, stuffed vegetable marrow, stuffed mutton, stuffed ribs, a kenafa with almonds, bees' honey mixed with sugar, pistachio fritters perfumed with amber, and almond cakes.

> *From the Tale of Juder or the Enchanted Bag*
> *Translated by E. Powys Mathers from the Book of the*
> *Thousand Nights and One Night of Dr. J. C. Mardrus*
> *(476th Night)*

STUFFED COURGES (VEGETABLE MARROW FLOWERS). Take about 15 perfect flowers, trim the pistils and wipe. (The flowers should be of the same size.) Meanwhile prepare a stuffing of lamb, suet, cooked rice, pepper, salt and choppd parsley.

🕮 Fill flowers and close. Place on a bed of bacon in a casserole and chopped vegetables. Cover with several slices of bacon and moisten with broth and a little tomato ketchup. Cook for 30 minutes to one hour and serve on a hot plate. Make a sauce of the drippings and pour over the flowers.

Vegetable Marrows

CRYSTALLISED MARROW. Pare and slice a small marrow. Mix 2 pounds sugar, ½ pint water, cloves and crushed ginger. Stir until dissolved. Add cochineal (red food coloring) and the marrows, boil till tender, pour over syrup till it thickens. Arrange on a glass dish and garnish with almonds and whipped cream.

MARROWS ON TOAST. Marrows are fit for use when about the size of a turkey's egg. After being washed clean, it is put on in boiling water, with a little salt, and when tender, it is drained from the water, cut into half, and served on toasted bread, over which some melted butter has been poured. Or, after being boiled in milk and water, they may be fricasseed as Jerusalem artichokes, or stewed like cucumbers.

Mrs. Dalgairns—The Practice of Cookery, Edinburgh, 1830

MARROW JAM.   1 lb. marrows
                1 lb. sugar
                ¼ cup orange-flower water
                ¼ cup blanched almonds

🕮 Peel marrows and thinly slice. Make a syrup of orange-flower water and sugar; add marrows. When done add nuts and store in small glasses. Makes a very good Christmas gift.

MARROWS STUFFED WITH EGGPLANT. Take small eggplants tenderize in water to which a bit of salad oil has been added. (Do not peel the eggplants.) At the same time cook unpeeled marrows with fresh or canned tomatoes. When cool, remove eggplant centers and also marrow meat and mix with hamburger, rice, salt and pepper. Season with salt, pepper and the juice of half a lemon. Stuff the marrows and the eggplant. Put into a casserole with a bit of water and cook until it is piping hot and then serve.

STUFFED MARROWS AND APRICOTS. Stuff marrows with usual stuffing of ground meat, rice, parsley, salt and pepper. Place in a casserole and cover with dried apricots and ¼ cup of lemon juice. Cover and cook in a slow oven for three or four hours.

VERBENA ～～～～～～～～～～～～～～～～～～～

A leaf of Vervain heralds wear,
Amongst our garlands named....
                    Drayton

Symbollizes: Enchantment and is under the dominion of Venus.

⚬ Verbena has many legends attached to it and was used extensively in magic and sacrifices. Some of its common names are Holy Herb, Herb of Grace, and Enchanter's plant.

⚬ Flower flavored salt is frequently used in Turkish cooking and one of the most popular is verbena.

VERBENA WINE. Carefully pick one gallon of verbena flowers (free of stems and leaves). Boil one gallon of water with three pounds of sugar. Cool, and add two lemons (sliced thin) and the flowers. Ferment with yeast spread on a slice of toast, allowing one tablespoonful of yeast to three gallons of liquor.

⚬ Books on wine making, in the English language, are not numerous and there is a tendency to repeat old recipes, many dating back to the time when principles of wine fermentation were not properly understood. Various fruits or their juices, such as lemons, oranges, raisins, apples and sometimes cereals are added to blossoms because they do not contain enough organic matter to ensure adequate fermentation.

FRUIT CUP. Sweeten strawberries, raspberries and currants and mix with lemon juice to taste. Moisten with white wine and decorate with verbena flowers.

One should not take the life of flowers just for a whim.

Violets ∿∿∿∿∿∿∿∿∿∿∿∿∿∿∿∿∿∿

To gild refined gold, to paint the lily,
To throw a perfume on the violet,
To smooth the ice, or add another hue
Unto the rainbow, or with taper light
To seek the beauteous eye of Heaven to garnish,
Is wasteful and ridiculous excess.
                              Shakespeare

Venus and Violets. The goddess of bloom and beauty, the protectress of gardens and its most modest inhabitant.

VIOLET ICE. Take the heads of some violets, crush them in a glass bowl with some sugar, adding a little finely-powdered orris-root. Chill. Serve the ice in glasses, top with crystallized violets.

The paper covers used to cover flower jellies should be steeped in brandy.

Cooking is an art, but the artistry lies as much in the eating as in the preparing of food.

THE DUCHESS OF KENT, the mother of Queen Victoria, especially liked a Violet Tea made with a teaspoon of dried violets in a cup of boiling water. Steep for five minutes and sweeten with honey.

QUEEN VICTORIA LIKED A VIOLET SYRUP made of half a pound of dried violets, a pound of sugar, an ounce of gum arabic and a bit of powdered orris root, mixed with half cup of water. Make syrup in usual way. Bottle when cold.

VIOLET JAM. Take a pound of stemmed violets, put three-fourths of them in a bowl and cover with 2 pints of boiling water and let steep for 12 to 15 hours. Strain and put into a saucepan, add three pounds of sugar, boil and add the balance of the violets. Boil until it sets.

VIOLET JELLY. Take a cup of stemmed violets, add to a pint of boiling syrup, cover and simmer 30 minutes. Strain, add 2 tablespoons frozen orange juice concentrate and an envelope of unflavored gelatin. Chill and serve.

224

Violets were the favorite flowers of Mahomet.

The violet is the state flower of Illinois, New Jersey, Rhode Island and Wisconsin.

In the Middle Ages a broth was made of violets, fennel and savory.

Violets

"There was a great bunch of double violets on the table, the lovely dark variety (Viola odoratissima flore pleno) with their short stems, freshly plucked from the garden, and the room was scented by their delicious breath.

A bowl of broad-leaved Batavian Endive, blanched to a nicety and alluring as a siren's smile, was placed upon the table. I almost fancied it was smiling at the violets. A blue-violet salad, by all means! there are violets and to spare.

On a separate dish there was a little minced celery, parsley and chives. Four heaped salad-spoonfuls of olive oil were poured upon the herbs, with a dessert-spoonful of white wine vinegar, and the necessary salt and white pepper, and a tablespoonful of Bordeaux. The petals of two dozen violets were detached from their stems, and two-thirds of them were incorporated with the dressing. The dressing being thoroughly mixed with the endive, the remaining flower petals were sprinkled over the salad and a half-dozen whole violets placed in the center.

The lovely blue sapphires glowed upon the white bosom of endive.

A white-labelled bottle, capsuled Yquem, and the cork branded 'Lur Saluces', was served with the salad. You note the subtle aroma of pineapple and fragrance of flower ottos with the denotation of the cork — the grand vintages of Yquem have a pronounced Ananassa flavor and bouquet that steeps the palate with its richness and scents the surrounding atmosphere."

George H. Ellwanger, *Pleasures of the Table*

VIOLET AND SALMON SALAD. Cook salmon and arrange with cucumber slices, fennel and violet leaves. Garnish with a few violets and serve with mayonnaise sauce.

In the 15th Century violets were often used in soups and sauces.

SALLETS OF FLOWERS preserved in Vinegar and Sugar as either Violets, broome flowers, or gillyflowers of all kindes.

G. Markham, The English Husbandman, 1615

DR. FERNIE'S VIOLET SYRUP. Pick a pound of violet flowers and put into two and a half pints of boiling water. Place in a china vessel and let stand for twenty-four hours. Then strain through a muslin cloth. Add double the quantity of sugar but do not boil.

Violets

VIOLET BLOSSOM JELLY. Pick sufficient scented blossoms to get 10 ounces of the petals, put them into a basin, pour over 1 quart of nearly boiling Clarified Syrup registering 30 degrees, cover the basin, and let the flowers steep thus for two hours;

✎ Strain the violet syrup through a jelly bag, mix it with 2¼ ozs. of clarified gelatin, add a tablespoonful of Kirschenwasser and a little prepared cochineal, to give the jelly a bright pink tinge, and pur it into a mould set in the ice;

✎ When the jelly is set cover the mould with a baking sheet with some ice on the top, and, after two hours, turn the jelly out of the mould and serve. OBSERVATION. For this, like all coloured jellies, untinned-copper utensils and silver spoons should alone be used for the preparation of both syrup and gelatine, or the colour and limpidity of the jellies would be spoiled, and their pleasing appearance destroyed.

Jules Gouffe', Royal Book of Pastry and Confectionery

"March Violets of the Garden have a great prerogative above others, not onely because the minde conceiveth a certaine pleasure and recreation by smelling and handling of those most odoriferous Flowers, but also for that very many by these Violets receive ornament and comely grace: for there bee made of them Garlands for the head, Nosegaies and poesies, which are delightful to look on, and pleasant to smell to, speaking nothing of their appropriate vertues; yea Gardens themselves receive by these the greatest ornament of all, chiefest beautie and most gallant grace; and the recreation of the minde which is taken hereby, cannot be but very good and honest: for they admonish and stir up a man to that which is comely and honest; for floures through their beautie, variety of colour, and exquisite forme, doe bring to a liberall and gentlemanly minde, the remembrance of honestie, comelinesse and all kinds of vertues."
Gerard

Violet and camomile flowers mixed make a delicious tea.

VIOLET MOUSSE. 1 teaspoon gelatine, 3 tablespoons boiling water, 2 cups milk, whites of three eggs, 1 cup whipping cream, 2 tablespoons sugar, ½ teaspoon violet extract, candied violets.

✎ Put gelatine into a saucepan, add water and milk, stir over fire till hot, then add sugar and stiffly beaten whites of eggs. Stir till thick, allow to cool, add the whipped cream and extract. Pour into a mould. Pack in ice and salt until thoroughly frozen. Garnish with violets and serve.

Cox Gelatine Cookery, Edinburgh 1909

Violets

VIOLET SOUP. Make a chicken soup and add a handful of violets and a few grains of rice. Simmer a few minutes and serve.

VIOLET VINEGAR. Take three handsful of fresh, well scented violets, pull off the stems, put them in a bottle, cover with wine vinegar, cork and let it stand for a fortnight in the sun or warm place. Strain through a cloth, cork up well, and it is ready for use. A tablespoonful sweetened in a glass of ice water makes a soothing drink.

Lia Rand, The Philosophy of Cooking, 1894

VIOLET TEA. A utensil should be reserved for the purpose of flower infusions. As a general rule no infusion should extend over one hour and should not be too strong. Flowers should be picked and dried in the shade, and when perfectly dry put into tins or paper bags.

VIOLET JELLY. Make apple jelly, putting enough violets in to flavor it. Before pouring into jelly jars it should be strained.

"The History of Gastronomy is that of manners, if not of morals; and the learned are aware that its literature is both instructive and amusing; for its is replete with curious traits of character and comparative views of society at different periods, as well as with striking anecdotes of remarkable men and women whose destinies have been strangely influenced by their epicurean tastes and habits."

Abraham Hayward

"Your name pronounced brings to my heart
A feeling like the violet's breath...."

Coventry Patmore

Pliny saith that Violets are as well used in Garlands as smelt unto; and are good against heavinesse of the head.

John Gerard, The Herball, 1597

An eighteenth century book suggests a *"salette of salmon, cut long waies with slices of onion laid upon it and upon that is cast violets, oyle, and vinegar."*

CONSERVE OF VIOLETS IN THE ITALIAN MANNER. Take the leaves of blue violets separated from their stalks and green, beat them very well in a stone mortar, mix them with double their weight of sugar, and reserve them for your use in a glass vessel. It will keep one year.

The Queen's Delight, 1671

Violets

CRYSTALLIZED VIOLETS. Take some large violets. Pick off the petals and nip off the bit where they join the stalks, and crystallize as follows: Clarify and boil some sugar to the blow. (240-445 F.) Put the violets into it and let the sugar again boil to the blow. Take the pan from the fire and rub the sugar against the sides of the pan until it turns white. Stir all together until the sugar separates from the violets. Then sift and put them into a cool oven to dry.

Maitre Escoffier in his "Guide to Modern Cookery" uses the juice of three lemons in his *violet ice* recipe. Just violets, sugar syrup and lemon juice.

"Violet is a lytyll herbe in substaunce and is better fresshe and newe than whan it is olde.... Also floures of spryngynge tyme spryngeth fyrste and sheweth some. The lytylnes thereof in substaunce is nobly rewarded in gretnesse of sauour and of vertue."
Bartholomaeus Anglicus, De Proprietatibus Rerum

"The Violet is of two kindes: white and purpled. His best goodnesse is in a sweete kinde of smel, and especially that Violet which groweth in Cirena. Some say that there is a kinde of Violet like Honie. Looke howe much the more effectuous or good in working this his flowre is: So much the more it is saide to holde down his head, and to bow and bende his bodie downward, to the earth.
J. Maplet, A Greene Forest, 1567

The violet is better that is gathered in the morninge whose vertue nether the heat of the sun hath melted away nether ye rayne hath wasted and driuen away.
William Turner, Herball, 1568

CANDY OF VIOLETS—CANDI DE VIOLETTES. Take half a pound of picked violets; have a pound of sugar at the *fort perle*; when it is half cold, put in the flowers, and set the pan upon hot cinders for two hours, that the flower may give all its colour; put it through a search; rub the flowers in sifted sugar to dry them; put them into the stove till next day; then search them to take out the superfluous sugar; put the candy into moulds, and cover the surface with flowers, without making them too thick in pressing them in with a fork, that the flowers may attach to the sugar, and that they should be well covered; put the moulds into the stove for five hours without heating it too much; drain them to take off the syrup: when cold, take them out of the moulds, put a sheet of paper upon the table, and turn them quickly over as with a stroke, to make the candy fall. Beauvilliers, Art of French Cookery

VIOLET CAKE. When mixing cake batter add two tablespoons of violet syrup and a fourth cup of crystallized violets to the mixture. When cold make almond or lemon icing and decorate with candied violets.

Violets

OYLE OF VYOLETTES. Sette vyolettes in oyle and streyne it. It will be oyle of vyolettes.

Peter Treveris, The Grete Herball, 1526

The flowers and leaves of Violets are cold and moist.

Bullein's Bulwarke of Defence, 1562

HONEY OF VIOLETS. Take of the Flowers of Vyolets 1 parte, of good Honey III partes, seeth them with a softe fier.

John Gerard, The Herball, 1597

HONEY OF VIOLETS. The Honey of Violets is made like the Honey of Roses, making three infusions, and the first infusion being strained, boyle as much honey with it, and at the last scumme it.

Philbert Guibert, The Charitable Physitian, 1639

Mademoiselle Clairon, famous French actress was given a nosegay of violets by one of her admirers every morning for thirty years, and every afternoon she stripped off the flower petals and used them for her violet tea.

The violet is the symbol of Athens.

Two thousand years ago Italian gardeners planted garlic and onions in their violet beds thinking that it would improve the perfume.

Napoleon always gave a bouquet of violets to Josephine on their wedding anniversaries.

"I shall be more able for the future, by a meritorious and learned Indolence, to make amends for the unnecessary Labours of my past Life: for such is the Unhappiness of Man, that he is forc'd to think, to find out that he ought not to think.

And now, O my worthy Partners in Tranquility, since it costs me no new Pains, ye also are welcome to enjoy the Fruits of my Labours. Learn from hence to loll with a becoming assuredness in your easy Chairs, on your soft Couches, and your downy Beds; learn in Winter to wrap your selves well up in furr'd Gowns, and in Summer to stretch your Limbs on Violets and Roses beneath some shady Tree; and when you move, for Man alas! must sometimes move, that it may be with the least Inconvenience possible, remember to have Springs to your Coaches, and long Poles to your Chairs; nor be disturbed at the Reflexions of restless Mortals,

who overlook the sweet Repose of Life and absurdly imagine that Happiness, i. e. Ease, is to be found among the busy Scenes of Scholars, Heroes, and Patriots."
Benjamin Stillingfleet, London 1738

The golden violet was the high prize in the floral games of Athens.

Violets   VIOLET BUTTER. If you make your own butter just add some violets to the churn. Otherwise, in a stone crock or pyrex dish, alternate layers of butter and violets, cover and let it stand for twenty-four hours.

VIOLET ICE. Combine 1½ cups sugar, ½ cup water, ½ cup grape juice, the washed petals from 3 violet nosegays. Boil slowly 10 minutes: cool. Strain: add the juice of 3 lemons and blend well. Freeze in ice-cube tray about 6 hours, or until firmly frozen. Serve garnished with fresh violets and leaves. Serves 6.

Use violet vinegar for salads or cooking.

For something different add violet petals to pancakes, custards, and puddings.

VIOLET LUNCHEON. A luncheon for six people that I had the pleasure of attending recently was an exceedingly dainty affair. The table was luxuriantly decorated with violets; the china service was all, more or less, hand-painted with the violet as the chief color. The menu was as follows:

> *Bierre de Malaga*
> *Toast with anchovy paste*
> *Oysters a la John Chamberlin*
> *Egg en casserole*
> *Quail, chafing-dish style*
> *Creme Yvette sorbet a la Waldorf*

Three silver chafing-dishes stood ready on the side-table, one being placed in front of the host for each course. The servant passed him the materials for making each dish just as they were wanted, everything being temptingly placed on the side-table close at hand. The first was simply an imported appetizer. Directions for the three following courses can be found by consulting the index. The quail was cooked as the recipe is given for spring chicken. The last, a violet sorbet, especially delighted the women; the recipe I obtained from the Hotel Waldorf, as follows: One gallon orange and lemon ice, one-half bottle Creme Yvette, and two teaspoonfuls of vegetable violet color.
Deshler Welch, The Bachelor and the Chafing Dish

ARABIAN PROVERB. The excellence of the violet is as the excellence of El Islam above all other religions.

In mediaeval symbolism the violet signifies the humility of Our Lord and as such Botticelli used it in his Adorations.

Violets

VIOLET MARZIPAN. Flavor with orange-flower water and essence of violets, blend into it small pieces of crystallized violets, dip into pale Parma violet coloured fondant and decorate with crystallized violets on top.

FRANCIS BACON'S RECIPE. Take violets and infuse a good pugil in a quart of vinegar, let them stand three quarters of an hour and take them forth and repeat the infusion with like quantity of violets seven times and it will make a vinegar so fresh of flower, as if a twelve months after it brought you in a saucer, you shall smell it before it comes to you.
Note: It smelleth more perfectly of the flower a good while after than at first.

VIOLET SHERBET. Add 1/4 cup Creme de Violette to two cups sugar syrup, cool and add 2 cups of grape juice and 2 tablespoons lime or lemon juice. Freeze, and when it has reached the mushy stage add the white of an egg and 2 tablespoons powdered sugar which have been well beaten together. Serve in sherbet glasses garnished with violet blossoms.

VIOLET COCKTAIL. Add to gin half as much cognac and Creme de Violette. Shake with cracked ice and serve immediately.

VIOLET FIZZ. Make the same way as the famous New Orleans Ramos Gin Fizz, but instead of orange-flower water add Creme de Violette. Serve in the same way, though the flavor could be enhanced with just a small drop of violet essence.

VIOLET PUNCH. Two pints of claret mixed with a cup of sour cherry juice. Buy sour cherries at the supermarket and drain. Add sugar to taste and a teaspoon vanilla. Add 1 cup of rich dark rum, a bottle of charged water and a half cup of pitted cherries. Garnish with fresh violet petals.

The violet is the emblem of the Bonaparte family.

Napoleon was often spoken of "Caporal la Violette" or "Papa la Violette", signifying that he would return from Elba in the spring. When the violets bloomed

Napoleon returned. Violets were everywhere. Ladies assembled to meet him wore violet-colored gowns and carried bouquets of violets, and as he mounted the steps of the palace they were showered upon him. He walked on carpets of violets. Pictures of violets were sold everywhere. Marie Louis retired to the Duchy of Parma where the sweet double violets that Napoleon loved grow in abundance.

Violets *When Eugenie became Empress her wedding wreath was violets.*

The pall of the coffin of Napoleon III was made of violets.

That which above all others yields the sweetest smell in the air, is the violet especially the white double violet, which comes twice a year, about the middle of April, and about Bartholomew tide — Next to that is the musk rose and then the strawberry leaves drying with a most excellent cordial smell.

Francis Bacon

The Romans liked violet wine.

CANDIED VIOLETS. Brush fresh blossoms with egg white and sprinkle well with granulated sugar. Dry carefully and store in covered containers.

Use chopped violet leaves in omelets.

VIOLET SOUFFLE. Make a roux of 2 tablespoons butter and two tablespoons flour. Add a cup of hot milk and cook until mixture coats spoon. Cool. Mix 1 tablespoon cherry brandy with 2 tablespoons sugar and the yolks of three eggs. Add stiffly beaten whites to the mixture plus a half cup of chopped crystallized violet petals. Pour into souffle dish and bake until a light brown. Decorate with more candied violets.

COUPE DE PARMA. Soak fresh pineapple pieces in brandy, place in a large glass and place a scoop of orange sherbet on top. If desired whipped cream topped with crystallized violets.

ANOTHER VIOLET SOUFFLE. This souffle is made with Creme de Violet. Make the souffle mixture as in the other souffle recipe. Now add 5 egg yolks which have been sweetened with 4 tablespoons sugar (brown sugar may be used for a different taste) and a quarter cup of the Creme de Violet. Next fold in the stiffly beaten egg whites. Butter a souffle dish and dust with confectioner's sugar. Place half of the mixture in the dish, then a layer of glazed fruits; next, a layer of chopped nuts. Cover with the balance of the mix and brown in a hot oven (about ten minutes) reduce heat and cook another twenty minutes. This may be garnished with crystallized violets and serve with a sauce flavored with the Creme de Violet or a couple of drops of violet essence.

A Salad Of Violets. Take endive, finely curled celery, a sprinkling of chopped parsley, a single olive and the petals of two or three dozen blue violets; mix these with the purest olive oil, a seasoning of salt and pepper, a dash of Bordeaux and a soupcon of white wine vinegar.

> Charles Cooper, English Table in History and
> Literature, London 1929

Violets

To Pickle Violets For Sallets. Cut your stalks very close put them in a glass strew some Sugar on ym mingled with a little Salt so do till all be in then pour on your vinegar a pint of vinegar to half a pound of sugar and press them down till the flowers sinke which they will in 4 or 5 days.

> H. W. Lewer, A Book of Simples

The violet symbolises constancy:
"Violet is for faithfulnesse
Which in me shall abide."

The sixth century bishop-poet Fortunatus sent Queen Radegonde violets, and wrote: "He who offers violets must in love be held to bring roses. Among the odorous herbs which I send these purple violets have a nobleness of their own. They shine tinted with purple which is regal and unite in their petals both perfume and beauty. What they represent may you exemplify, that by association a transient gift may gain lasting worth."

In "Twelfth Night" the Duke likens the odor of violets to fairy music,
"It came o'er my ear like the sweet sound,
That breathes upon a bank of violets,
Stealing and giving odour."

Violet Butter. A kind of butter is made of almonds with sugar and rose water, which being eaten with violets, is very wholesome and commodious for students, for it rejoiceth the heart and comforteth the liver.

> Nicholas Culpepper

Violet Tea. Pour half a pint of boiling water on to one teaspoonful of dried violets; leave it for five minutes. Strain it, and sweeten with honey.

In the Middle Ages violet fritters were a popular dish.

Make fondant and mix with crystallized violets.

Charles II (1660-1685) was very fond of violet lozenges or plates. This was sometimes known as Violet Sugar.

.Cxxv. Vyolette.—Take Flourys of Vyolet, boyle hem, presse hem, bray hem smal, temper hem with Almaunde mylke, or gode Cowe Mylke, a-lye it with Amydoun or Flowre of Rys; take Sugre y-now, an putte her-to, or hony in defaute; coloure it with ye same but flowrys be on y-peyntid a-boue.

Two 15th Century Cookery Books (about 1430) Edited by
Thomas Austin for the Early English Text Society, 1888

Violets

Two hundred years later: "Violets are the Spring's chiefe flowers for beauty smell and use."

John Parkinson, Paradisus, 1629

The violet was the favorite flower of Queen Alexandra.

Violet Marmalade. Take about a half pound of violets, separated from their stalks, pound in a mortar, some of the old writers recommend alabaster, make a syrup of a pound and a half of sugar and a half cup of water. When it is boiling add the flowers, cook on a slow fire until it is of the proper constituency. Some cooks recommend adding apple marmalade.

John Evelyn suggests that young violet leaves be fried and eaten with orange or lemon juice and sugar.

Sliced oranges decorated with violets.

Special Bouquets. Take fresh violets; tie them in bunches of ten or twelve flowers.

Boil some sugar until it pearls or bubbles. Try a little in a spoon and blow hard upon it. The bubbles should leave the spoon and float in the air like soap bubbles. Then let the sugar cool. Dip into it the bunches of flowers; drain them and put them on a wire rack. When dry surround with decorative paper circlets and serve cold.

In the 14th century violets were among the ingredients for stuffing a roast hare.

Violet Cakes. Take the juice of one lemon, and put it into a silver porringer, and add to it some sweet Violets; then let it stand a night, and put to it some more Violets, and so stand until it be as deep coloured as you wish: then take a spoonful of fine-powdered sugar, and wet it with the juice; then hold your spoon over a chafing dish of coles, stirring it; smoak, but not boil; take it off, and drop it into cakes (lozenges).

Dr. Fernie, Meals Medicinal

234

For great elegance violet paste was often gilded.

SANDWICH: Slice pumpernickel, spread with chicken salad, sprinkle with poultry seasoning and layer with violets.

Violets TO MAKE VIOLET CAKES. Wet double refined sugar and boil it, till it is almost come to sugar again, then put into it Juice of Violets; put in Juice of Lemons, this will make them look red; if you put in Juice and Water, it will make them look green. If you will have them all blue, put in the Juice of Violets without the Lemon.

John Middleton, Receipt Book, 1734

CONSERVE OF VIOLETS. Conserve Moelleuse a la Violette. Take some violets and pick them, taking nothing but the leaves of the flower; a handful will make three quarters of a pound of conserve: beat them well in a marble mortar, to obtain the juice; clarify three quarters or a pound of sugar, which must be brought to the first *souffle'*; take it off the fire, and let it cool; add the juice with a few drops of lemon, that the colour may be as bright as possible; work it well together with a silver spoon till it begins to whiten and dry; put it immediately into cases of any size, but the conserve must be only the sixth part of an inch thick; when cold, mark it lightly with a knife the size it is to be of; handle it tenderly in the moulds.

A. B. Beauvilliers, The Art of French Cookery

VIOLET SNOWBALL. As my favorite dessert at The Stork is a coconut snow ball, I envisioned the following dessert: Use a portion of Italian biscuit tortoni, about the size of a ping pong ball. Roll in crystallized violets and pour over 2 tablespoons Creme de Violette.

Royalty has always liked violets and here is a ROYAL POTATO SALAD. Mix diced, cold potatoes with a cup of diced apples (unpeeled). Add a dressing of olive oil and lemon juice, together with salt and coarse ground pepper. Decorate with green pepper or very small pieces of finely chopped hard-boiled eggs. For added color and taste garnish with a few de-stemmed violets.

In the days of the Troubadors a golden violet was awarded to the composer of the best poem. Tennyson's "Becket" in Eleanor of Aquitaine says, "You know I won the violet at Toulouse."

A MESSAGE FROM BRAZIL. Make a gelatin of 2 cups of strong clear, black coffee (Yuban would be good), an envelope of Knox gelatine, ⅓ cup sugar and ¼ cup of water. When the jelly is at the setting stage, beat until it becomes a light tan. Then add a teaspoon of vanilla. Make a coffee frosting of ½ cup of strong coffee and 1 cup of sugar. When it has reached the soft ball stage, add the well-beaten whites of two eggs, and a teaspoon of vanilla. Fold stiffly whipped cream into it, place on gelatin and garnish with candied violets.

Violets

Try to gain a new insight, when it comes within our grasp, reach for it and try to draw them into expression. Some people might think that a Violet is a weed.

With your next shrimp curry try crystallized violets.

VIOLATUM. "Put" says Apicius, "some violet leaves into a clean linen cloth; sew it up, and leave it seven days in the wine; take out the violets, and put in fresh ones; repeat the operation three times, and then strain the wine. Add some honey at the time of drinking. The violets must be fresh, and free from dew."

Pantropheon, or History of Food and Its Preparation by A. Soyer (1853)

For a different taste treat sprinkle chicken breasts lightly with cinnamon and garnish with crystallized violets.

WISTERIA ∾∾∾∾∾∾∾∾∾∾∾∾∾∾∾∾∾∾∾∾∾∾∾

Wistaria pours at last its waves of bloom
Along the lintel of my door . . .
Planted long since for joy when one should come
Who comes no more.

—*The Manyoshyu*

WISTERIA FLOWER FRITTERS. Make up a thin batter and dip the flowers first in the batter then in hot fat. Dust with sugar and serve.

Dr. Fernald also suggests that the fresh flowers, properly dressed, make a good salad.

Wisteria

WISTERIA SQUARES. Take a pound of blanched almonds and put them in a tightly covered jar with a handful of wisteria blossoms, let these stand for ten days, open and add more flowers daily for the next ten days, stirring after each addition. When well perfumed, discard flowers and keep tightly covered. Then add pounded almonds with half-pound sugar. Reserve ⅓ of the moisture, add remaining two-thirds to ⅔ cup hot water and cook until it spins a thread. Knead the candy and form into a ball. Press out flat onto a cookie sheet and sprinkle with remaining sugar and almond mixture. This should be 1 inch thick. Let it set awhile and later cut into cubes.

WISTERIA PRESERVES. Take about a pound of fresh wistaria blossoms and 1 pound of sugar. Add two cups water to blossoms and boil for a couple of minutes. Make a syrup of the sugar and 1 cup of water. Add a half teaspoonful crushed cardamons and a cup of chopped almonds and boil about five minutes then add petals and mix well. Pour into small jars.

WISTERIA WINE. Use any of other flower wine recipes. Make some wisteria honey and use in place of sugar.

WOODRUFF ~~~~~~~~~~~~~~~~~~~~~~~

Lenten is come with love to toune
With all blosmen and with briddes roune,
*   That all this blisse bryngeth.*
Dayes-eyes in this dales,
Notes suete of nyhtegales;
*   Uch fowl song singeth.*
The threstelcoc him threteth oo;
Away is here wynter woo
*   When woderove springeth.*
*   Song of the late 13th Century*

The Romans introduced the Feast of Flowers into Britain. But long before the foundation of Rome, Flora was venerated among the Phoenicians and the Sabines. The early Greeks worshipped her under the name of Chloris. Beginning with the time of Romulus there was a Roman festival in honor of Flora. The Floralia began 516 years after the foundation of Rome, and after consulting the Sybil books it was ordained that the feast should be commemorated annually on the 28th day of April, four days before the calends of May. Flora is an original Roman goddess.

MAI-BOWLE or MAI-TRANK. This famous cool tankard is made by pouring a bottle of Moselle or cider on a little bunch of woodruff. Stand it on ice, closely covered over, for 30 minutes. Then melt 2 oz. of sugar in ¼ pint of water, and mix with the wine, removing the woodruff and adding an orange, carefully peeled and cut into slices. It is important that a tankard should not be too sweet and should be quite cold.

Woodruff

✌ For fruit "bowles" or tankards allow ½ lb. fresh fruit to 2 bottles of wine or cider, and use only real Seltzer water as chemically prepared Seltzer ruins the flavour of the wine. Add any Seltzer used just before serving.

Ella Oswald, German Cookery for the English Kitchen, 1906

Champagne can also be used, with a soupcon of Benedictine or cognac, and strawberries are the traditional fruit.

Sweet woodruff may be used in soups, salads and sauces, although it is usually associated with the mai-bowle. The fresh flowers give a wonderful fragrance to wines and liqueurs.

WOODRUFF TEA. Pour a pint of boiling water on a handful of the leaves and flowers.

Woodruff symbolizes modest worth, though it engenders cordiality.

WOODRUFF CAKES. Boil sugar and add woodruff flowers, boil until the proper consistency, pour and cut into squares.

In Germany it is known as *Waldmeister*, or "master of the woods" as it grows abundantly along the banks of the Rhine. It has a sweet smell of hay, though one author says it resembles "*a pungent combination of vanilla, cinnamon bark and tarragon.*"

In the 15th Century "wodrove" garlands were hung up in churches, floors were strewn with it, beds were stuffed with it, and it was placed in the linen chests.

Try candied woodruff tips as a nibble at teatime.

WOODRUFF SAUCE. 10 egg yolks
½ cup sugar
1 bottle May Wine

✌ Blend ingredients in top of double boiler. Cook over hot water and stir constantly until it coats spoon. This can be served as a custard or a sauce for pudding or cake.

CHICKEN BREASTS A LA WOODRUFF. 4 breasts of chicken
Salt, pepper, and paprika
½ pound butter
1 tablespoon flour
1 cup light cream
½ bottle May Wine

Woodruff

႖ Season chicken with salt, pepper, and paprika. Saute in butter until golden brown. Remove chicken. Add flour to butter and lightly brown. Add cream and wine; bring to a boil; return chicken to pan and simmer for 15 minutes, or more if necessary.

WOODRUFF WINE. 1 quart woodruff blossoms
2 lemons
2 gallons water
6 pounds sugar
2 packages yeast

႖ Add half of the flowers and sliced lemons to water and boil for about twenty minutes. Strain into wine vessel (crock or barrel) and dissolve sugar into it and add remainder of the blossoms. Dissolve yeast and add. Cover and let stand for two weeks, then strain into bottles or jars. It should stand for a year before drinking.

YARROW ～～～～～～～～～～～～～～～～

"I rose early in the morning yesterday.
I plucked yarrow for the horoscope of thy tale
In the hope that I might see the desire of my heart
Ochone there was seen her back towards me."
  —An old "Raum" sung in the Hebrides

႖ The old song quoted above refers to the story of a certain bard who fell in love with a girl in Stornaway, who married another. He was always conjuring up her image, and every Wednesday he composed a song to her till he pined away and became so small that his father had to carry him in a creel on his back. Yarrow from time immemorial has been used in incantations and by witches, and in the seventeenth century a witch was tried for using it.

Yarrow

YARROW TEA. On a large handful of leaves and flowers of yarrow pour one pint of boiling water. This has a very pleasant smell.

Some of the common names for yarrow are: Arrowroot, Green arrow, Bloodwort, Camil, Cammock, Carpenter grass, Devil's nettle, Eerie, Garwe, Hundred leaved grass, Nosebleed, Old man's pepper, Sneezewort and Yarroway.

The botanical name for yarrow is Achillea millefolium, so named because it is said that Achilles used it very often, having learned about it from his friend, Chiron the Centaur.

YUCCA

"Our Soldiers of the Desert (yucca elata) delight to take possession of the bahadas, the mountain canyons, especially the lower table lands or mesas, sometimes climbing up to an altitude of five thousand feet, then again covering the foothills in one vast forest of solid ivory, or mustering an army of golden armor as far as eye can see; occasionally we find a solitary sentinel high up on the mountain top, his golden helmet gleaming in the bright sun of noon."
—*Sage of the Desert by Frances Bonker and John James Thornber*

YUCCA FLOWER SOUP. ½ pound of yucca petals (be sure that none of the heart of the flower is included as it is very bitter) boiled in salted water for about ten minutes. Mash to a pulp and add to a quart of milk, ⅛ pound butter and a pinch of nutmeg. Add salt and pepper. Stir and add a tablespoonful of flour. Serve on toast.

Yucca Salad. These blossoms which are cool, crisp and aromatic combined with a vinegar and oil dressing make for a delightful experience in both texture and flavor. (Some gourmets like the golden centers shredded over them.)

Yucca

In Peru they make a delicious doughnut of yucca.

The stalk is also cooked and eaten as a vegetable.

The physical and structural design of the Yucca is quite complicated in the extreme. There are 1,500 to 2,000 blossoms in each cluster of its panicle-like infloresence, they are 2½ to 3 inches long and tinged with green. The Yucca whipplei are of a lovely golden hue glowing like lighted candles and are known as "God's Candlesticks."

The Spanish Bayonet has a fleshy fruit when ripe which resembles a banana in size and shape. They are much used by the Southwestern Indians as a breakfast or supper dish.

Yucca Flower Soup. Take two cups of yucca blossoms and cook with medium-sized tomato, onion, garlic, green pepper, peas (canned or frozen) and season with salt, pepper and a bit of sugar. Cook slowly for thirty or forty minutes. Tortillas are good with this.

" . . . the weird cactus plant life of the Southwestern desert—strange and marvellous growths which we call the Fantastic Clan . . . "

Bonker and Thornber

James Forbest in his "Journal of a Horticultural Tour" (1835) catalogued over 600 species of cacteae in the Gardens of Woburn Abbey.

Cacti are indigenous to the Western Hemisphere and there are more than 1,000 specie.

In the words of Sir Kenelm Digby "I think it unhandsome, if not injurious, by the trouble of any further discourse, to detain thee any longer from falling to: Fall to therefore, and much good may it do thee."

MISCELLANEOUS ∞∞∞∞∞∞∞∞∞∞∞∞∞∞∞∞∞

On the island of Corfu a yellow flower is enjoyed—called asphaka.

Periwinkles sprinkled on salads and soups are delightful to the sight, smell and taste.

In Japan, camelia rice cakes called Tsubaki-Mochi, are frequently served. They also make a delicious tea.

Horehound can be used to flavor beef stews, sauces and hot drinks. In cookies or cakes it can be either dried or fresh. And of course, all of us remember the horehound candy, so highly prized when we were children. In England, in early days, it was cultivated for use in ale, beer, and tea, but is a little too strong for modern tastes. Bees like it and horehound honey is much sought after.

The gentian, russet or yellow colored, not the blue makes a very unusual liqueur. The blue gentian is the main ingredient of angostura bitters.

SYRUP OF THE JUYCE OF ANCHUSA — In size pound of the juyce of buglosse, boyle a pound of the flowers, then strain them and clarifie them; boyle with the decoction four pound of sugar, and the Syrup commeth to twopence the ounce. — The Charitable Physitian, by Philbert Guibert, Physitian, Regent in Paris, 1639.

Blue tea is made from the dried flowers of the large anchusa.

Buds of a pale gold thistle are relished in southern Italy.

Locust flowers, dipped first in brandy, and then in batter—fry and powder with sugar.

Jamaica—a popular Mexican drink—is made from the red tropical flower of the same name. Use twenty flowers to one quart of water.

Quiotes, the yellow flower of the maguey plant (grows from the center) are good when fried. And in Yucatan they make a liquor of xtabentum flowers.

Cook rhubarb flower buds with sugar, makes a delicate, refreshing sauce.

Larch blossoms are served as an hors-d'oeuvres in China.

Goldenrod makes a delicious tea . . . also a beautiful, golden wine.

Meadowsweet was Queen Elizabeth's favorite strewing herb.

Fried apple blossoms dusted with sugar is one of the desserts at the Four Seasons restaurant, New York City.

Atoles, a popular drink in Mexico, made from masa, is often flavored with flowers.

Miscellaneous

A cheese made from the prickly pear (called tuna in Mexico) is chocolate-colored and sharp. It is frequently enriched with nuts and flowers. Pita (Mexico) is a red flower which makes delicious fritters.

Huanzontle (Mexico) are tiny close-clustered flowers, which when cooked with egg batter and dressed with tomato sauce are delicious and delicate.

Flowering ends of Cat-Tail, very. tender in the spring and are eaten raw, or when boiled in water make a good soup. The root is eaten as a salad "The Cossacks of the Don peel off the outer cuticle of the stalk and eat raw the tender white part of the stem extending about 18 inches from the root. It has a somewhat insipid, but pleasant and cooling taste." —The Book of Camping and Woodcraft,
Horace Kephart, New York, 1906

The Indians of Northern Panama depend upon the piva palm as one of their food supplies. The flower buds are excellent and taste like corn meal and honey.

In many parts of South America the tepijilote palms are cultivated for their edible flower-buds.

The flower buds of the wild plantain are sweet and popular with Indian children.

The Cuckoo flower (cardamine pratensis)—a common meadow plant flowering in May—both young leaves and flowers may be eaten raw like watercress.

Dissolve 2 scruples (1/24 of an ounce) of flowers of Benjamin in a quart of good rum and it will give the flavor of the finest Arrack.

William Kitchiner, The Cook's Oracle, 1818

A good brown sugar can be made from the flowers of the common milkweed.

MARJORAM COOLER. 3 pounds of sugar
2 egg whites, whipped
1 pint wine vinegar
Handful marjoram flowers

Mix first three ingredients in saucepan and boil for one minute, skim and add marjoram flowers tied in a nylon net bag. Cool, strain and bottle.

Fennel is mentioned in the old Anglo-Saxon herbals as one of the "nine sacred herbs" which acts as a charm against evil influences.

Miscellaneous

KATURAY SALAD. 6 cups katuray flowers, stamens removed
(flowers of the Katuray tree called Sesbania)
$\frac{1}{3}$ cup sliced onion
2 tsps. ginger
$\frac{1}{3}$ cup vinegar
3 tbsps. sugar
1 tsp. salt
1 tsp. garlic

Saute the garlic in lard until brown. Add the onions and ginger. Stir and cook for 3 minutes. Add the vinegar, sugar and salt. Let boil, add the katuray flowers and stir. Cook for ten minutes. Serve with pork.

Recipes of the Philippines by Enriqueta David-Jones
Capitol Publishing House, Philippines, 1953

In the Pacific islands the tamarind flower is used with pork and beef dishes to give a sour flavor.

SOME NUTRITIVE VALUES:

Katuray: .5 protein, .6 calcium,. 9.5 iron. 5.3 vitamin C
Kalabasa: .9 protein; 1.0 calcium; 2.9 iron; 9.8 vitamin A;
2.5 bone; 1.6 vitamin E; .9 riboflavin; 1.4 niacin
Banana Bud: .7 protein; 1.1 calcium; 5.8 iron

Centaurea (C. cyanus) also called the cornflower and blue-bottle was abundant in Britain during the late Glacial period. It was used in beer and also was the favorite flower of the late Emperor of Germany. Other uses: painters prepared a blue color from its petals; also used to color sugar and gelatine; butter-fly collectors used it to attract butterflies. It is said that the plant was discovered by Chison the Centaur who was healed by it, his method was to boil it in wine and drink while warm.

In Ceylon the MOON FLOWER (piomoea Bona-nox) is much relished as a curry vegetable. Also in Ceylon the Rivea Ornata, which produces fleshy flowers are used, though they are not cultivated.

The flowers of the Sesbania Grandiflora are boiled or fried.

The Abutilon esculentum flowers are commonly used as a vegetable in Brazil.

Miscellaneous

The CHALTAH resembles a large tulip. It consists of eighteen petals, six green ones above; six other, some red, some green, some greyish yellow; and six white. In the midst of the flower, as in the flower called Hameshah Bahar, there are nearly two hundred little yellow leaves, with a red globule in the center. The flower will remain quite fresh for five or six days after having been plucked. It smells like the violet. When withered, the flower is cooked and eaten. The tree resembles the pomegranate tree; and its leaves look like those of the orange tree. It blooms in seven years.

> Volume I of the Ain i Akbari (Akbar, one of the most enlightened Moguls, reigned in India during the 16th Century.

The KARIL has three small petals. It flowers luxuriantly, and looks very well. The flower is boiled and eaten; they also make pickles of it.
The Lahi has a stem one and a half yards high. The branches, before the flowers appear, are made into a dish which is eaten with bread. When camels feed on this plant, they get fat and unruly.

> Ibidem

JAMBOS: (rose-apple or pomarossa-Eugenia Jambos) is called Rosejaman or gulab jaman in India. You can see the trees in my garden from this veranda. The small ones have been planted two years and in four they will yield plenty of good fruit and several times in the year. The shape of the tree, like that of the fruit is oval with fruit the size of a plum. The flower is red and very sweet, with a taste like sorrel. The leaf is like the point of a lance, large and of a very pleasant green colour. The roots of this tree strike far into the ground to uphold the tree, when it is loaded with fruit, which is the case many times in the year. Conserves are made both of the fruit and the flower.

> Colloquies on the Simples and Drugs of India by Garcia da Orta (1490?-1570?) tr. by Sir Clements Markham (1913). This is part of the 28th colloquy.

RED COTTON TREE — (Bombax malabaricum). In Burma the calyces of the large red flowers are gathered as they drop and are relished as a curry vegetable.

In Northern India the flowers of the Phogalli (calligonum polygonoides) are made into bread and cooked with butter.

The MOHWA or INDIAN BUTTER TREE. (Bassia Latifolia or Madhuca Indica). The tree was named in honor of Fernando Bassia, at one time the curator of the Botanical Gardens at Bologna. The tree is much cultivated in the Central Indian dry, rocky hill regions, which it prefers, and is one of the most important trees in India.

Miscellaneous   The gathering of these flowers from February to April is important to the country people. The ground beneath the tree is cleared and swept clean and at dawn (the tree blooms at night) the flowers are swept up. The average yearly yield per tree is two and a half maunds (the maund is a greatly varying weight in India, but the government maund is 100 pounds), and about 25,000 tons are gathered every year. The flowers are very tasty, resemble pressed figs, and are made into puddings and sweet-meats. And of course, strong drink, something like gin.

Other inhabitants of Central India, who first have to get past the vigilant night guards are the deer and bears, also the peafowl and many other birds and animals love these flowers and will travel for miles for a feast.

OSWEGO TEA. The Indians were very fond of Oswego Tea (Monarda didyma), made from the dried flower heads. A modernization of it is make it half and half with China tea. Make the regular way — 1 regular teabag with another muslin bag with a bit of dried tops. The Indians drank many teas: Sweet Gale, Sweet Goldenrod, Sassafras, Clover and Basswood.

The ancient Egyptians made a jam of lotus blossoms, also, when freshly plucked were nibbled as a fruit.

SYRUP OF MAIDENHAIR. Take half a pound of maidenhair, and half a pound of liquorice-stick; peel off the skin, and slice it down; take an ounce of tiffilago; put them all into a pot of cold water; set it on the fire, and let it boil for seven or eight hours; then strain it through a cloth. To every mutchkin of juice take a pound of white sugar candy; clarify it with the white of an egg; let it boil well; scum it, and when cold bottle it up.

The Practice of Cookery, Pastry, Pickling, and
Preserving by Mrs. Frazer (Edinburgh 1791)

Rue was an antidote for poison, recommended by Dioscorides and others, and Henry VIII especially liked it, mixed with dandelion flowers and yolks of hard-boiled eggs, then used as a sauce for strawberries!

Miscellaneous

Flowers are used extensively in the Persian cuisine. The pussy-willow (musk of willow) is used to make a distilled aromatic water, sweetened and iced; also preserves of quince blossoms and jasmine petals. They also make delicious and delicate halvas and baglava of many kinds of blossoms.

BLUE, GREEN AND GOLD: MY GRANDMOTHER'S OMELETTE

Make an omelette mixture of six large, fresh eggs, salt and pepper, and a heaping tablespoon each of chopped chives and parsley, lastly add eighteen chive blossoms.

In a castiron skillet melt three tablespoons butter, when melted add egg mixture and cook as you would any omelette. With hot biscuits and blackberry jam this makes a delicious supper for three.

"Thus have I ended my booke . . . and yf to some I shall seeme not fullye to have satisfied their desyres herein accordinge to their expectation or not so cunninglye have handled the same as the matter itself offereth and is worthy of, then I referre my self wholye to ye learned correction of the wise, desyrynge theym frendelye to geeve knowledge to the printer, or to me, and beinge detected of my fault, will wyllyngelye correct and amend the same: for well I wotte that no treatise can alwaies so workmanly be handeled but that somewhat sometimes may fall out amisse contrary both to the minde of the wryter and contrary to the expectation of the reader. Wherefore my petition to the gentle reader is to accept these my trevails with that minde I do offer them to thee and to take gentelye that I geeve gladly, in so doinge I shal thinke my paynes well bestowed and shal be encouraged hereafter to trust more, unto thy curtesye. And therefore I cravve at thy handes the thankefull acceptance of these rude labours of myne. The favour of God bee with thee alwayes."

Thomas Hill, The Proffitable Arte of Gardening, 1568

BIBLIOGRAPHY

Abu al Fadhl, Ain I Akbari (tr. by Blochmann-1873) Vol. 1-3 Calcutta Asiatic Society of Bengal, 1873-94

Adair, A.H. Dinners, Long and Short, Knopf New York, 1929

Adams, Henry Gardner. Flowers, their moral, language, and poetry London: H. G. Clarke & Co. 1845

Adam's Luxury and Eve's Cookery, London, 1744

Ainsworth-Davis, James Richard. Cooking Through the Centuries, London: J.M. Dent & Sons Ltd. 1931

Allhusen, Dorothy. A Book of Scents and Dishes, London: William & Norgate Ltd. 1926

Andrews, Julia C. Breakfast, Dinner and Tea viewed classically, poetically, and practically, Appleton 1869

Apicius: Cookery and Dining in Imperial Rome Translated into English by Joseph Dommers Vehling. Chicago: W.M. Hill, 1936

Arberry, A.J. A Baghdad Cookery Book — Islamic Culture, Hyderabad 1937 Vol. 13

Armfield, Anne Constance. The Flower Book, London: Chatto & Windus, 1910

Armitage, Merle. Fit for a King, Longmans, Green & Co. 1939

Askari, Hussani Muhammad. The Food of Kings London: C. Stembridge & Co. 1936

Athenaeus: The Deipnosophists: or banquet of the learned. Translated by C.D. Yunge. 3 vols. 1854

Austin, Thomas. Two 15th Century Cookery Books—Early English Text Society (Original Series) 91

Avery, Susanna. A Plain Plantain, 1688

Bacon, Francis. Moral and Historical works. Sylva Sylvarum London 1852.

Beals, Katharine McMillan. Flower Lore and Legend, N.Y. H. Holt & Co. 1917

Beauvilliers, Antoine. The Art of French Cookery London: Longman, Hurist, Rees, Orme, Brown, and Green, 1827

Beeton, Isabella Mary. Dictionary of Every Day Cookery London: S.O. Beeton, 1865

Berjane, J. Comtesse de. French Dishes for English Households London:F. Warne & Co. 1931

Berman, Louis. Food and Character, N.Y. Houghton Mifflin, 1932

Berners, Juliana. The Boke of St. Albans (1486) facsimile London: E. Stock, 1881

Black, Rene. Cookbook: Cuisine versus Cooking N.Y. Holt 1955

Blencowe, Ann W. The Receipt Book of Mrs. Ann Blencowe, A.D. 1694

Blixen Finecke, Karen Baronesse (Isak Dinesen). Seven Gothic Tales, N.Y. H. Smith & R. Haas, 1934

Boas, Franz. Ethnology of the Kwakiutl, American Ethnology Bureau, Washington, 1921

Boehme, Jakob. The Works of Jacob Behmen (Rev. William Law-4 vols.) London: M. Richardson 1764-81

A Book of Cookrye: very necessary for all such as delight therein, Edward Allde, London: 1587

A Book of Fruits and Flowers, London, 1653

Boorde, Dr. Andrew. Dyetary of Helthe, London, R. Wyer, 1542

Borella, M. The Court and Country Confectioner (1770) By head Confectioner to Spanish Ambassador in England. London, G. Ripley and A. Cooke

Boulestin, Xavier Marcel. Simple French Cooking, 1923, London. W. Heinemann, Ltd.

Boumphrey, Goeffrey M. Cunning Cookery, 1938. London: T. Nelson & Sons

Bradley, Martha. The British Housewife, 1770. London: S. Crowder & H. Woodgate

Brinton, Daniel Garrison. Ancient Nahuatl Poetry, Philadelphia, D. G. Brinton, 1887

The British Jewell, or complete housewife's best companion. London: J. Miller, 1782

Brook, Richard. A New Family Herbal. London: 1871

Brooke, Jocelyn. Mine of Serpents. London: The Bodley Head, 1949

Bullein's Bulwarke of Defense, 1562 — Imprinted at London by Ihan Kyngston

Bunyard, Edward A. The Anatomy of Dessert. Dulau & Co. Ltd. London: 1929
    Epicure's Companion. J.M. Dent & Sons Ltd. London (1937)

Bynner, Witter. Take Away the Darkness, John Day & Co. The Jade Mountain, Knopf, 1929 — Lin Yu-hei, tr. by W. B.

Carey, Mabel C. Flower Legends London: C.A. Pearson Ltd, 1929

Carruthers. Flower Lore, Teachings of Flowers, Historical, Legendary, etc. McCaw, Stevenson & Orr. Belfast; 1879

Carter, Charles. The Complete Practical Book (1730) London: W. Meadows. The Complete City and Country Book, London: A. Bettesworth & C. Hitch, 1732

Carter, Susannah. The Frugal Housewife (1796) of Clerkenwell, London. Published by James Carey, 83 N. Second Street, Philadelphia, 1796

Cary, Elizabeth Luther. Books and My Food, N.Y. Rohde & Haskins, 1904

Chandler, Josephine C. Romance of the Rose, Boston: C. T. Branford Co. 1949

Chao, Pu-wei (Yang). How to Cook and Eat in Chinese. John Day, 1945

Cheng, Shao-Ching. Chinese Cookery Book, London: The Shanghai Restaurant, 1936

Christie, Robert H. Banquets of the Nations, Edinburgh, 1911

Clark, Lady Charlotte Coltman. The Cookery Book of Lady Clark of Tillypronie. Ed. by Catherine Frere, London: Constable & Co., 1909

Clarkson, Rosetta. Green Enchantment, 1940. Herbs, their Culture and Uses, 1942. Magic Gardens, 1939, MacMillan, N.Y.

Cleland, Elizabeth. A New and Easy Method of Cooking (1755). Edinburgh: W. Gordon, 1755

Clermont, B. The Professed Cook, London: W. Davis 1776

Coates, Austin. Invitation to an Eastern Feast, London: Hutchinson, 1953

Cockayne, Thomas Oswald. Great Britain Public Record Office. Chronicles and Memorials of Great Britain and Ireland during the Middle Ages. No. 35. 3 vols. Leechdoms, Wortcunning, and Starcraft of Early England (1864-1865)

Cole, Mary. The Lady's Complete Guide (cook to Earl Drobega) London: G. Kearsley, 1791

Coleridge, Samuel T. The Table Talk and Omniana, London: G. Routledge & Sons, 1884

Colonial Everyday Cookery—Auckland, New Zealand, 1918. Whitcomb & Tombs, Ltd.

Conil, Jean. Haute Cuisine, London: Faber & Faber, 1953

Conrad, Jessie George (Mrs. Joseph) Homecookery, London: Jarrolds Ltd, 1936

Cooke, John Conrade. Cookery and Confectionary, London: W. Simkin & R. Marshall, 1924

Cooper, Charles. English Table in History and Literature, London: Low, Marston, 1929

Cooper, Joseph. The Art of Cookery (cook to Charles I)

Core, Mary K. The Khaki Kook Book, N.Y. Abingdon Press, 1917

Craies, Euterpe. Receipes from East and West, London: G. Routledge & Sons, 1912

Crane, Walter, Flora's Feast, a masque of flowers. Cassell & Co. Ltd. London, 1892

Crocker, Ernest C. Flavor, N.Y. McGraw-Hill, 1945

Crommelin, May Henrietta. Poets in the Garden, Published by A. C. Armstrong and Son — New York (1887)

Culpeper, Nicholas. Complete Herbal. W. Foulsham, London, 1952. English Physician, London, 1812

Cunynghame, Francis. Reminiscences of an Epicure, London: P. Owen, 1955

Darwin, Erasmus. The Botanic Garden, London: Jones & Co. 1824

David-Perez, Enriqueta. Receipes of the Philippines. Capitol Pub. House, Manila, 1953

Dawson, Thomas. The Good Housewife's Jewel, London. Imprinted by John Wolfe for Edward White, 1587

De la Mare, Walter John. Pleasures and Speculation, London, Faber & Faber, 1940

Department of Agriculture and Natural Resources, Bureau of Science, Manila, Philippine Islands. January, 1932

De Salis, Mrs. Ann Harriett. Art of Cookery, London: Hutchinson & Co., 1898

Digby, Sir Kenelm. The Closet of the Eminently Learned Sir K. Digby, London: 1669. The Queen's Closet Opened

Doubleday, Nellie Blanchan. Nature's Garden, Doubleday Page, N.Y. 1900. Wild Flowers Worth Knowing, Doubleday Page, N.Y. 1917

Drake, Lucy. The Original and Only Miss Drake's Home Cookery. Melbourne, Australia: "Truth" & "Sportsman" Ltd. 1944

Dubois, Urbain. (Cook to King and Queen of Prussia). Artistic Cookery, Longmans, Green — London 1870

Dumas, Alexandre, the elder. Grand Dictionnaire de Cuisine. (Translated by Louis Colman — Simon & Schuster, 1958)

Eales, Mary. The Compleat Confectioner. (Confectioner for Queen Anne) London: R. Montague, 1742

Earle, Mrs. Alice Morse. Sundials and Roses of Yesterday, N.Y. Macmillan, 1902.

Earle, Maria Theresa. Pot-pourri from a Surrey Garden, London: Smith, Elder & Co. 1898

Ellwanger, George H. Pleasures of the Table. N.Y. Doubleday, Page 1902

Emerson, Lucy R. New England Cookery. Montpelier, Vt. Printed for J. Parks, 1808

Esling, Catherine Harbeson. Flora's Lexicon, Philadelphia: Hooker & Claxton, 1839

Estienne, Charles. Maison Rustique, London, 1606

Evelyn, John. Acetaria; A Discourse of Sallets, London: 1699

Fairfax, Arabella. The Family's Best Friend. London, 1753

Farley, John. The London Art of Cookery (1783)

Farrer, Reginald John. Garden of Asia, London: Methuen & Co. 1904. In a Yorkshire Garden. E. Arnold, London: 1909

Fernald, Merritt L. and Alfred Charles Kinsey. Edible Wild Plants of Eastern North America (Harper & Brothers 1958)

Fernie, Dr. W.T. Meals Medicinal. Bristol: John Wright & Co. 1905

Fisher, Mary Frances K. Serve It Forth, Harper & Bros. 1937

Fleming, Atherton. Gourmet's Book of Food and Drink. London: John Lane, 1933

Flora's Bouquet: A Collection of Elegant Flower Plates and Floral Poems, Belfast: Brackett & Co. 1881

The Flowers of Anecdote; wit, humor, gaiety, and genius. London: A. K. Newman & Co. 1837

Flowers, Language, Poetry and Sentiment. Porter & Coates—Philadelphia, 1870

Fox, F.W. Some Bantu Recipes from the Eastern Cape Province. Bantu Studies—Johannesburg, 1939

Frazer, Mrs. The Practice of Cookery. Edinburgh, 1791

Frere, C.F. (Ed.) Proper, A, newe booke of cokerye. Cambridge: W. Heffer & Sons, 1913

Friend, Hilderic (Rev.). Flowers and Flower Lore, Nims & Knight, Troy, N.Y. 1889

Gaskell, Mary M. A. Yorkshire Cookery Book. Wakefield: Sanderson & Clayton, 1916

Gayre, George Robert. Wassail! In Mazers of Mead. London: Phillimore & Co, 1948

Gerard, John. Gerard's Herball or Generall Historie of Plantes, London, 1597

Glasse, Hannah. The Art of Cookery Made Plain and Easy, London, 1774. The Complete Confectioner

The Good Housewife; or, Cookery Reformed, London, 1756

Gordon, Jean. Pageant of the Rose. Studio Publications, Inc. in association with Thomas Y. Crowell Company, New York, 1953

Gouffe, Jules. The Book of Preserves, London: S. Low, Son, and Marston, 1871 Royal Book of Pastry and Confectionery, London, 1874

Gourley, James E. Eating Round the World, New York, 1937

Grieve, Maud. Culinary Herbs and Condiments, London: W. Heinemann, 1933

Griswold, Rufus Wilmot, Poetry of Flowers, Philadelphia: U. Huint & Son, 1846

Haig, Elizabeth. Floral Symbolism of the Great Masters. K. Paul, Trench, Trubner & Co. Ltd. 1913

Haines, Jennie Day. Ye Gardeyne Boke. San Francisco and N.Y., P. Elder & Co., 1906

Hale, Sarah Josepha. Flora's Interpreter. Boston: Marsh, Capen & Lyon, 1835

Hall, T. The Queen's Royal Cookery. London: C. Bates, 1709

Hampton, Frank Anthony. The Scent of Flowers and Leaves. London: Dulau & Co. 1925

Harcum, Cornelia G. Roman Cooks. Baltimore: J.H. Furst Co, 1914

Harrison, Sarah. The House-Keeper's Pocket Book, Dublin: E. Exshaw, 1738

Hartley, Olga and Leyel, Hilda. Lucullus, the Food of the Future, London: K. Paul, Trench, Trubner & Co. Ltd. 1926

Hayward, Abraham. Art of Dining. London: J. Murray, 1852

Hazlitt, William Carew. Old Cookery Books and Ancient Cuisine. London: E. Stock, 1902

Heartman, Charles Fred. Aphrodisiac Culinary Manual (Cuisine de l'Amour) Gourmet Co., New Orleans, 1942

Henry, Teuira. Ancient Tahiti, Bishop Museum Bulletin No. 48, Honolulu, 1928

Hill, Jason. The Curious Gardener, London: Faber & Faber, 1932

Hodous, Lewis. Folkways in China, London: A. Probsthain, 1929

Hollingsworth, Buckner. Flower Chronicles. Rutgers University Press, New Brunswick, New Jersey, 1958

(The) House Keeper's Pocket Book and Complete Family Cook, London: 1785

Howard, Henry. Englands Newest Way in All Sorts of Cookery, Pastry, etc. London: C. Coningsby, 1708

Humphreys, Henry Noel. The Gallery of Exotic Flowers, London: O. Jones 18—?

Hunter, Alexander. Culina Famulatrix Medicinae, York: T. Wilson & R. Spence, 1804

Hurt, Eric Francis. Sunflowers for Food. London: Faber & Faber, 1946

Indian Cookery as Practiced and Described by Natives. Oriental Translation Fund (Miscellaneous Translations, Vol. 1) London, 1831

Indian Domestic Economy and Receipt Book. Christian Knowledge Society Press Madras: 1853

Irwin, Florence. Irish Country Recipes, Belfast: The Northern Whig Ltd. 1937

Jank, Joseph K. Spices; botanical origin. St. Louis: C.P. Curran Prtg. Co. 1915

Jekyll, Lady Agnes. Kitchen Essays, London: T. Nelson & Sons, Ltd. 1922

Jenks, James. The Complete Cook, London: E & C Dilly, 1768

Jewett, Sarah O. Country of the Pointed Firs, Houghton Mifflin, 1896

Johnson, Mrs. Grace. Anglo-Indian and Oriental Cooking, London: W.H. Allen & Co, 189-?

Johnstone, Christian Isabella (Meg Dods). The Cook and Housewife's Manual, Edinburgh: Oliver & Boyd, 1828

Judson, Helena. The New Butterick Cookbook. N.Y. Butterick Pub. Co. 1924

Keen, Adelaide. With a Saucepan Over the Sea. Boston: Little, Brown Co. 1902

Kent, (Countess of Kent) Elizabeth Grey. A Choice Manuall, or Rare and Select Secrets, London, 1653

Khan, S.N.M. Finest Indian Muslim Cooking, London: G. Routledge & Sons, 1934

King, William. The Art of Cookery, in Imitation of Horace's Art of Poetry, London, B. Lintott, 1709

Kitchiner, William. Apicius Redivivus; or The Cook's Oracle, London: A. Constable & Co. 1822

Koehn, Alfred. Fragrance from a Chinese Garden, the Lotus Court, Peking, 1936

La Chapelle, Vincent. The Modern Cook. London, 1744 (3rd Edition) T. Osborne

Lacy, John. Wyl Bucke, his Testament, Imprinted at London, by Wyllyem Copland (16th Cen.)

Lady's (The) Book of Flowers and Poetry — botanical introduction— Floral Dictionary. Ed. by Lucy Hooper, N.Y. J.C. Riker, 1842

Lamb, Corrinne. The Chinese Festive Board, Peiping: H. Vetch, 1935

Lamb, Patrick. Royal Cookery; or The Complete Court Book, London: A. Roper, 1710

Lamprey, Louise. The Story of Cookery, N.Y.: Frederick A. Stoker, 1940

Language of the Flowers with Illustrative Poetry — Calendar of Flowers. Revised by the editor of Forget-Me-Not. Philadelphia: Lea & Blanchan, 1839

Laubreaux, Alin. The Happy Glutton. I. Nicholson & Watson, 1931

LaVarenne, Francois P. The French Cook. Englished by I.D.G. London, Printed for Charles Adams, 1654

Leipoldt, Christian L. The Belly Book. London: Williams & Norgate Ltd. 1936

Lewer, H.W. A Book of Simples. London: Low Marston & Co. 1908

Leyel, Hilda. Elixirs of Life, Faber & Faber Ltd. London, 1948. Hearts-Ease, Faber & Faber Ltd. London, 1949; Green Medicine, Faber & Faber Ltd. London, 1942

Liber Cure Cocorum—Copied and edited from Sloane ms. 1896 by Richard Morris, Philological Society, London 1862-64. The Philological Society, Early English, Vol. 1

Livings, A. Twelve White Flowers, London: Hamilton, Adams & Co. 1888

Lorris, W. and J. Clopinel. Romance of the Rose, London: 1900. (Englished by F.S. Ellis)

Lowinsky, Ruth. Russian Food for Pleasure. London: The Nonesuch Press, 1935.

Lovely Food, London: The Nonesuch Press, 1931.

Macdougall, Allen Ross. Almanac, N.Y. Covice-Friede, 1930 and The Greeks, N.Y. Near East Foundation, 1947

Maeterlinck, Maurice. Chrysanthemums and Other Essays, N.Y. Dodd, Mead & Co., 1907. Intelligence of the Flowers, N.Y. Dodd, Mead & Co., 1907. Life and Flowers London: G. Allen, 1907. Old Fashioned Flowers, N.Y. Dodd, Mead & Co., 1905.

Maggs Brothers, Ltd. Food and Drink Through the Ages, 2500 B.C.—1937 A.D. London: 1937

Mantegazza, Paolo. The Legends of Flowers (Leggende de flori). London: T.W. Laurie, 1930

Markevitch, Marie Alexander. The Epicure in Imperial Russia. Colt Press, San Francisco, 1941

Markham, Gervase. Countrey Contentments, London: R. Jackson, 1615. Farewell to Husbandry, London: Printed by John Beale for Roger Jackson, 1620. The Pleasures of Princes, London: 1635

Massialot, Francois. The Court and Country Cook. London: 1702

Matthew, of Westminster. The Flowers of History. c. 1310 tr. by C.D. Yonge, London: H.G. Bohn, 1853

Mauduit, George. The Vicomte in the Kitchen. London: S. Nott, 1934

May, Robert. The Accomplist Cook. London, 1685.

Mayerne, Theodore Turquet de. Archimagirus Anglo-Gallicus, tr. by Edward Grimeston, London: 1612

McCollum, Alma Frances. Flower Legends and Other Poems, Toronto: W. Briggs, 1902

McDonald (D.) Sweet Scented Flowers and Fragrant Leaves, Scribner's N.Y.
     1895

McNeil, Blanche and E.V. First Foods of America. N.Y.: Sutton House Ltd. 1936

Mead, William Edward. The English Medieval Feast. G. Allen & Unwin Ltd.
     1931

Meade, Julian. Bouquets and Bitters. N.Y.: Longmans, Green & Co. 1940

Mensa Philosophica. The Science of Dining by W. B., Esquire (1614) London:
     Printed by T. C. for Leonard Beckett

Meredith, Louisa A. Flora's Gems, London: C. Tilt, 1837

Moncrieff, R.W. The Chemical Senses. London: L. Hill, 1944

Montagu, Lady Mary. Letters and Works. 2 vols. London: G. Bell & Sons, 1887

Moore, Alice. Chinese Recipes. N.Y. Doubleday, Page & Co. 1923

Moore, Hanah Hudson. Flower Fables and Fancies. N.Y. Frederick A. Stokes & Co.
     1904

Morgan, Harry Titterton. Chinese Symbols and Superstitions. South Pasadena,
     Calif. P.D. and Ione Perkins, 1942

Moss, Maria J. A Poetical Cookbook, Philadelphia: C. Sherman, Son & Co.
     1864

Moxon, Elizabeth. English Housewifry. LEEDES: Printed by Griffith Wright for
     George Copperthwaite, Bookseller in Leedes, and sold by Mr. B. Dod, Book-
     seeller in Ave-Mary-Lane; Mrs. Richardson, in Paternoster-Row; and Mr.
     Johnson, opposite the Monument, London, 1764

Murrell, John. Two Bookes of Cookerie and Carving. Printed by M.F. for John
     Marriot, 1631

Nash, Elizabeth Todd. One Hundred and One Legends of Flowers. Boston: The
     Christopher Pub. House, 1927

Neale, Frederick Arthur. Narrative of a residence at the Capital of Siam. London:
     1852.

Newman, Isidora. Fairy Flowers. N.Y. H. Holt & Co. 1926

New York State College of Agriculture at Cornell. Ithaca, N.Y. 1917

Noble Boke of Cookry, (A) for a Prynce Houssolde or eny other estately Houssolde
     London: E. Stock, 1882

Nott, John. The Recipe Book. London: 1723. (Cook to the Duke of Bolton)

Old Master Cookery Book: Recipes of Various Kinds, Collected and Improved
     by an Amateur of the First Distinction. London: H. Jenkins Ltd. 1927

Orta, Garcia de. Colloquies on the Simples and Drugs of India. Tr. by Sir
     Clements Markham (1913). Lisbon: 1895 and London: H. Sotheran & Co.
     1913. Venetia: 1597

Osgood, Irene. Garden Anthology, London: J. Richmond 1914

Oswald, Ella. German Cookery for the American Home, N.Y. The Baker & Taylor
     Co. 1907

Parkinson, John. Paradisi in Sole Paradisus Terrestris, London: 1629, Theatricum
     Botanicum, London: 1640

Partridge, John. Treasurie of Hidden Secrets, London: Richard Johns 1573

Passe, Crispijn van de. Hortus Floridus, London 1615

Pearless, Anne P. Flowers and Their Associations, London: C. Knight & Co. 1846

Pegge (S). The Forme of Cury, a Roll of Ancient English Cooking A.D. 1390 By Master-cooks of Richard II. Afterwards Presented to Queen Elizabeth

Pellegrini, Angelo M. The Unprejudiced Palate, N.Y. Macmillan Co. 1948

Pennell, Elizabeth Robins. Feasts of Autolycus (1896 Edition), N.Y., The Merriam Co.

Perez, Presentacion T. Everyday Foods in the Philippines, Banawe Pub. Co., Quezon 1953

Peter II (Prince-Bishop of Montenegro, P. P. Nyegosh), Tr. by Anica Savic—Rebac Harvard Slavic Studies V. 3, 1957, The Rays of the Microcosm; The Mountain Wreath, Tr. by James W. Wiles, Allen & Unwin Ltd., 1930

Peto, Pauline Q. Recipes Rare from Everywhere, London: Simpkin Marshall Ltd. 1934

Phillips, Henry. Flora Historica, 2 vols. London: 1824

Plat, Sir Hugh. Delights for Ladies, London: 1594

Poole, Joshua. English Parnassus, London: 1677

Porter, Rose. Flower Songs for Flower Lovers, N.Y., A.D.F. Randolph & Co. 1880

Prentice, Ezra Parmalee. Progress: An Episode in the History of Hunger, N. Y., Privately printed 1947

Prescott, William Hickling. Conquest of Mexico. Lippincott, 1863

Raffald, Elizabeth. The Experienced English Housekeeper, London 1794

Rand, Lia (pseud.). The Philosophy of Cooking, By the author, 1894

Redgrove, Herbert Stanley. Spices and Condiments, London: Sir I. Pitman & Sons Ltd. 1933

Rohde, Eleanour S. Garden of Herbs London, P. L. Warner, 1920, The Scented Garden, London: Medici Soc. 1931; Rose Recipes, London: Routledge, 1939

Russell, Nellie Naomi. Gleanings from Chinese Folklore, N.Y., F. H. Revell Co., 1915

Ruskin, John. Deucalion 2 vols. Wiley & Sons 1886, Prosperina—Studies of Wayside Flowers, 2 vols. Orpington, Kent: G. Allen, 1875-86

Rutter, Joan. Here's Flowers London: Golden Cockerel Press, 1937

Ryan, Marah Ellis. Pagan Prayers, Chicago: A.C. McClurg & Co., 1913

Safford, William E. Useful Plants of Guam, Vol. IX, Government Printing Office, Washington 1905

Sala, George Augustus Henry. The Thorough Good Cook, N.Y., Brentano's 1896

Salmon, William. The Family Dictionary, London: 1792

Searle, Townley. Strange News from China, London: A. Ouseley, Ltd., 1932

Selby, Charles (pseud. Tabitha Tickletooth). The Dinner Question, London: Routlege, Warne, and Routledge, 1860

Senn, Charles Hernan. Ye Art of Cookery in Ye Olden Time, Universal Cookery and Food Association (1896), 329 Vauxhill Bridge Road; Century Cookery Book, London: Ward, Lock & Co. Ltd., 1923

Sinclair, Upton Beall. The Fasting Cure, Pasadena, Calif., 1911 (By the author)

Sitwell, Edith. A Book of Flowers, Macmillan & Co. Ltd., London: 1952

Skinner, Charles Montgomery. Myths and Legends Beyond Our Borders, Philadelphia: Lippincott & Co., 1899, Myths and Legends of Flowers, 1925

Smith, Herman. Kitchens Near and Far, Barrows: New York 1944, Stina, The Story of a Cook, New York: Barrows, 1942

Society of Antiquaries of London, A Collection of Ordinances and Regulation for the Government of the Royal Household, London, 1790

Society of Gentlemen in New York. Universal Receipt Book, 1814

Sorokin, Pitirim A. The Ways and Power of Love, Boston: Beacon Press, 1954

Soyer, Alexis. Pantropheon—History of Food, London: 1853

Stillingfleet, B. Thoughts Concerning Happiness, London: W. Webb, 1738

Sylvester, James Joseph. Collected Mathematical Papers 4 vols., Cambridge: University Press, 1904-1912

Thomas, Edith Matilda. Flower from the Ashes, Portland, Me., T. B. Mosher, 1915

Thompson, John Eric. Mexico Before Cortez, N. Y.: C. Scribner's Sons, 1933

Thorndike, Lynn. A Mediaeval Sauce Book, Speculum Vol. IX, 1934

Thornton, Robert John. Temple of Flora, 2 vols., London: T. Bensley (1799-1807)

Thudichum, J. L. W. The Spirit of Cookery, London: F. Warne, 1895

Timbs, John. Hints for the Table, George Routledge & Sons, London: 1866

Times Telescope, or Complete Guide to the Almanack, London: 1827

Tonna, Charlotte E. B. P. Floral Biography, N. Y., J. S. Taylor & Co., 1843. The Flower Garden, N. Y., M. W. Dodd, 1842

Toor, Frances. A Treasury of Mexican Folkways, Francis Toor Studios, 1946

Trovillion, Violet. Tussie Mussie, Trovillion Private Press.

Turner, Cordelia Harris. The Floral Kingdom, Chicago: M. Warren, 1877

Verral, William. The Cook's Paradise, (Complete System of Cookery), London: 1759, Cook to the Duke of Newcastle

Vitale, Guido. Chinese Folklore, Peking: Pei-t'ang Press, 1896

Wainwright, Elizabeth. The Receipt Book of a Lady of the Reign of Queen Anne, Medstead, Hamphire, The Azania Press, 1931

Walker, Thomas. Aristology, Philadelphia: E. L. Cary & A. Hart, 1837

Warner, Reverend Richard. Antiquitates Culinariae; or Curious Tracts Relating to Culinary Affairs of the Old English, London: 1791

Wayman, Dorothy. An Immigrant in Japan, 1926, Boston and N. Y., Houghton Mifflin

Webb, Margaret J. Early English Recipes, selected from Harleian ms. 1430 A. D., Cambridge, England, The University Press, 1937

Welby, Thomas E. The Dinner Knell

Welch, Deshler. The Bachelor and the Chafing Dish, New York: 1896

Whitcombe's Every Day Cookery, New Zealand and Australia, Christchurch: Whitcombe & Tombs Ltd. 1942

White, Florence. Flowers as Food, Jonathan Cape Ltd., London: 1934

Whited, Zillah. Flower Fables, New York, 1946

Wirt, Elizabeth W. G. Flora's Dictionary, Baltimore, F. Lucas, 1830

Woolley, Hannah. The Queen-like Closet, London: 1684, The Gentlewomans Companion: or, A Guide to the Female Sex. London, 1682

INDEX

262

Evening Primrose

Pachylophus hirsutus